EURO-CEMENTS

Impact of ENV 197 on Concrete Construction

BOOKS ON CEMENT AND CONCRETE FROM E & FN SPON

Application of Admixtures in Concrete. *Edited by A.M. Paillere*

Blended Cements in Construction. *Edited by R.N. Swamy*

Calcium Aluminate Cements. *Edited by R.G. Mangabhai*

Cement-based Composites: Materials, Mechanical Properties and Perfomance. *A.M. Brandt*

Concrete 2000: Economic and Durable Construction through Excellence. *Edited by R.K. Dhir and M.R. Jones*

Concrete in Hot Environments. *I. Soroka*

Concrete Mix Design, Quality Control and Specification. *K.W. Day*

Creep and Shrinkage of Concrete. *Edited by Z.P. Bazant and I. Carol*

Durability of Concrete in Cold Climates. *M. Pigeon and R. Pleau*

Energy Efficiency in the Cement Industry. *Edited by J. Sirchis*

Fly Ash in Concrete: Properties and Performance. *Edited by K Wesche*

High Performance Concrete: From Material to Structure. *Edited by Y. Malier*

Hydration and Setting of Cements. *Edited by A. Nonat and J-C. Mutin*

Manual of Ready-Mixed Concrete. *J.D. Dewar and R. Anderson*

Protection of Concrete. *Edited by R.K. Dhir and J.W. Green*

RILEM Technical Recommendations for the Testing and Use of Construction Materials. *RILEM*

Special Concretes: Workability and Mixing. *Edited by P.J.M. Bartos*

Structural Grouts. *Edited by P.L.J. Domone and S.A. Jefferis*

Structural Lightweight Aggregate Concrete. *Edited by J.L. Clarke*

Thermal Cracking in Concrete at Early Ages. *Edited by R. Springenschmid*

For details of these and other titles, contact the Promotions Department, E & FN Spon, 2-6 Boundary Row, London SE1 8HN, Tel: 071-865 0066

EURO-CEMENTS
Impact of ENV 197
on Concrete Construction

Proceedings of the National Seminar
held at the University of Dundee
on 15 September 1994

Edited by

Ravindra K. Dhir
Director, Concrete Technology Unit
University of Dundee

and

M. Roderick Jones
Lecturer in Concrete Technology
University of Dundee

E & FN SPON
An Imprint of Chapman & Hall
London · New York · Tokyo · Melbourne · Madras

**Published by E & FN Spon, an imprint of Chapman & Hall,
2-6 Boundary Row, London SE1 8HN, UK**

Chapman & Hall, 2-6 Boundary Row, London SE1 8HN, UK

Blackie Academic & Professional, Wester Cleddens Road, Bishopbriggs, Glasgow G64 2NZ, UK

Chapman & Hall GmbH, Pappelallee 3, 69469 Weinheim, Germany

Chapman & Hall USA, One Penn Plaza, 41st Floor, New York, NY 10119, USA

Chapman & Hall Japan, ITP-Japan, Kyowa Building, 3F, 2-2-1 Hirakawacho, Chiyoda-ku, Tokyo 102, Japan

Chapman & Hall Australia, Thomas Nelson Australia, 102 Dodds Street, South Melbourne, Victoria 3205, Australia

Chapman & Hall India, R. Seshadri, 32 Second Main Road, CIT East, Madras 600 035, India

First edition 1994

©1994 E & FN Spon, except pages 113-147 and
pages 169-182 ©1994 Crown

Printed in Great Britain by St Edmundsbury Press, Bury St Edmunds, Suffolk

ISBN   0 419 19980 2

A catalogue record for this book is available from the British Library
Library of Congress Cataloging-in-Publication Data available

∞ Printed on permanent acid-free text paper, manufactured in
accordance with ANSI/NISO Z39.48-1992 and ANSI/NISO Z39.48-1984 (Permanence of Paper)

Publisher's Note
This book has been produced from camera ready copy provided by the individual contributors in order to make the book available for the seminar.

PREFACE

Work on drafting the Europe wide specification for cement, was initiated in 1969 by the then EEC. Responsibility was later transferred to the European Committee for Standardisation (CEN) in 1973. The task has not been simple due to the wide regional variability of cement types in Europe and the fact that around seventy different kinds of cement had already been standardised on a national basis within the CEN member countries. In addition, the wide climatic and historical construction differences has meant that even cements with nominally similar titles could be based on different raw materials and have different requirements for performance under the respective climatic conditions.

In view of the large number of different type of cements involved, it has been decided that the emerging standard ENV 197 will be divided into several parts. Although around ten parts have been considered, only few have made sufficient progress with drafts receiving majority acceptance.

The first part, ENV 197-1 deals essentially with those cements that would traditionally be regarded as Portland-based, ie. those which harden principally from the hydration of calcium silicates and which are provided for common construction uses. The second part, ENV 197-2 deals with conformity evaluation. These subjects formed the main theme of this National Seminar.

At the same time, test methods for cements have made more progress towards harmonisation with the EN 196 series all but finished and already called up in ENV 197-1 and the revised British Standards for cements. Details of these methods and their implications were also discussed.

These proceedings of the National Seminar, organised by the Concrete Technology Unit of Dundee University, review the requirements and conformity criteria of the European pre-standard ENV 197-1 and its implications for current cement and concrete specifications, concrete production and site practice. Additionally, the test methods for these cements to ENV 196 are covered. The emergence of the pre-standards for cements with additional special properties and different mechanisms of hardening are also covered.

Dundee
September 1994

Ravindra K Dhir
M Roderick Jones

CONTENTS

CONTRIBUTORS

P. Brookbanks
Quality Controller, Technical Services, Rugby Cement

A. T. Corish
Manager, Product Services and Quality Development, Blue Circle Industries plc

R. K. Dhir
Director, Concrete Technology Unit, University of Dundee

T. A. Harrison
Technical Director, British Ready Mixed Concrete Association

M. R. Jones
Lecturer, Concrete Technology Unit, University of Dundee

P. Livesey
Chief Chemist, Castle Cement Ltd

J. D. Matthews
Head, Silicate Chemistry Section, Building Research Establishment

G. Moir
Chief Chemist, Blue Circle Industries plc

G. J. Osborne
Head, Concrete Durability Section, Building Research Establishment

M. G. Taylor
Standards Manager, British Cement Association

OVERVIEW OF BRITISH AND EUROPEAN STANDARDS FOR CEMENT AND ADDITIONS

T A HARRISON
Technical Director
British Ready Mixed Concrete Association, UK

Abstract
This paper describes the types of European standards and the background to why Europe is developing a set of standards. The relationship between the European Union and the European Committee for Standardisation is explained as are the problems created when there are different objectives for a standard.

The European standards for cements and additions are introduced and their relationship with British Standards is explained.
Keywords: Additions, cements, standardisation, standards.

1 Introduction

For most practising engineers, knowledge of the current work on European standardisation and its impact on British Standards and UK practice is scant. Regretfully, in some cases, the engineer is also ill informed. 'Europe' will not remove the engineers freedom to select materials and concrete properties, even from those working on public works contracts. In fact, in time he is likely to have available a wider choice of materials and options. However, the impact of European standardisation will be profound: during the next decade the British standards for most construction products will be withdrawn and replaced by European standards.

In many cases the basic product will not change, or change significantly, although it will conform to a new standard and may be given a different title. Cement is such a product. There is unlikely to be any change in the product during the transition from the current British standards to European standards because the recent British standards for cements have already adopted the concepts in the European standard. During this seminar, most of the technical comments made about the performance of cements conforming to the European standards will also apply to the equivalent cements in the new set of British standards. Differences in the properties and proportions are best made between the European standards and the pre-1990 British standards for cement. The main technical difference between the current British standards for cement and the European standards

Euro-Cements: Impact of ENV 197 on Concrete Construction. Edited by R.K. Dhir and M.R. Jones. Published in 1994 by E & FN Spon, 2-6 Boundary Row, London SE1 8HN. ISBN: 0 419 19980 2.

will be the introduction of a wider range of cements. The new types of cement will include those containing high-lime fly ash, non-ferrous slags, natural pozzolanas, silica fume and cocktails of three or more main constituents.

In reality, not all of these cements will be available in the UK and, given the fact that our practice of combining materials in the concrete mixer to produce 'equivalent combinations' will continue, no significant change in the market share is anticipated in the next five years.

Before introducing the structure of the European cement standards, the status and background to European standards is described.

2 Types of European Standards

2.1 Voluntary European Standard, ENV
An ENV has similar status to a BSI 'Draft for Development' and exists alongside existing national standards. ENV's have a maximum life of three years before either being upgraded to a full European standard or withdrawn. In practice it has often been possible to extend the life of an ENV for up to a further 2 years.

2.2 European Standard, EN
When a European standard is published, conflicting national standards, or conflicting parts of national standards, have to be withdrawn within 6 months. Every CEN member will publish the European standard with a national foreword, but in this national foreword it cannot change the content of the standard even if it voted against its adoption. This is to ensure that, for example, BS EN 196-1 is the same as DIN EN 196-1. Every 5 years, European standards are reviewed and, if necessary, amended.

2.3 Harmonised European Standard, hEN
A Harmonised European Standard only contains clauses that relate to the essential requirements. What this means, and the difference between an hEN and a EN, is explained in the next section.

You may see documents or references where the EN or ENV is preceded by the letters "pr". This stands for "pre" and it shows that the document is a draft with no official status other than a committee paper.

EN's and ENV's are agreed by a complex majority voting system. No single CEN member has the power to stop a standard being adopted. CEN members, such as the British Standards Institution, can ask CEN to produce a standard for a new product or one that is standardised nationally. In the latter case, it would propose that the European standard is based on the national standard. This is a strong position to be in, but it often means that you have to provide the secretariat for the drafting committee.

Increasingly, standardisation work is being instigated by the European Commission. When the Commission publish a Directive, such as the Construction Products Directive, they then produce Interpretative Documents which identify the need for standardisation work to make the Directive effective. The Commission then ask CEN to undertake this work which will eventually result in an EN

3 Background to European Standardisation

When the European Economic Community (EEC) agreed to create a single market for goods and services, they commissioned a review of barriers to trade. This review identified national standards as the most important technical barrier to trade. Most national standards tend to have a combination of performance and prescriptive requirements. For example, British cement standards have performance requirements for strength and prescriptive requirements for constituents. Harmonisation of standards is extremely difficult when they are based on prescriptive requirements. Therefore the Commission and CEN requires harmonised European standards to be expressed, as far as possible, in terms of product performance.

The Commission's preferred solution to overcome this barrier to trade was for the Community to adopt standards produced by the International Organisation for Standardisation (ISO). However, it was apparent that ISO standards did not cover all the needs of the European Union (EU), the new name for the EEC. (For convenience the term EU will be used even though some of the decisions described were made when the Community was called the EEC). In some cases, the quality of the ISO standards were lower than the Member States national standards. It was therefore decided that if a suitable ISO standard did not exist, the EU would produce its own standards to replace national standards. The EU delegated this task to the European Committee for Standardisation (CEN) whose membership comprises the standardisation bodies of the EU and EFTA countries, Table 1.

This immediately created a potential problem as members of the EU are required to adopt European standards and withdraw conflicting national standards whilst the EFTA countries are not. This could lead to the situation where the EFTA countries were blocking the adoption of a standard required and acceptable to EU members. The solution was a complex voting system where, after failure to agree a positive vote in CEN, the EU members votes would be reassessed and, if this re-count gave a positive vote, the standard would be adopted within the EU.

A more fundamental problem exists between the EU and CEN which is still not fully resolved. CEN and its members have a long tradition of writing standards for users. The scope of these standards contains all the material that users require and this varies from member state to member state. The EU, however, has as its objective the creation of a free market. It recognised that agreement on all product characteristics was not feasible and therefore agreed in the "new approach"[1] to base the free market for products on six essential requirements:

1   mechanical resistance and stability;
2   safety in case of fire;
3   hygiene, health and the environment;
4   safety in use;
5   protection against noise;
6   energy economy and heat retention.

With respect to construction products, these essential requirements relate to the structure. Consequently, it is relatively easy to translate the essential requirements for a precast concrete floor unit into product characteristics, less easy for fresh concrete and difficult for,

Table 1: Membership of CEN

EU MEMBERS	EFTA MEMBERS
BELGIUM Institut Belge de Normalisation/ Belgisch Instituut voor Normalisatie (IBN/BIN)	AUSTRIA * Österreichisches Normunginstitut (ON)
DENMARK Dansk Standard (DS)	FINLAND * Suomen Standardisoimisliitto r.y. (SFS)
FRANCE Association française de normalisation (AFNOR)	ICELAND Technological Institute of Iceland (STRI)
GERMANY Deutsches Institut für Normung e.V. (DIN)	NORWAY * Norges Standardiseringforbund (NSF)
GREECE Ellinikos Organismos Typopoiisis (ELOT)	SWEDEN * Standardiseringskommissionen i Sverige (SIS
IRELAND National Standards Authority of Ireland (NSAI)	SWITZERLAND Schweizerische Normen-Vereinigung (SNV)
ITALY Ente Nazionale Italiano di Unificazione (UNI)	
LUXEMBOURG Inspection du Travail et des Mines (Luxembourg) (ITM)	
NETHERLANDS Nederlands Normalisatie-instituut (NNI)	
PORTUGAL Instituto Português da Qualidade (IPQ)	
SPAIN Asociación Española de Normalización y Certificación (AENOR)	
UNITED KINGDOM British Standards Institution (BSI)	* Have applied to join the EU

say, cement. Since this "new approach", all mandates from the EU for standardisation work have been limited to harmonising these essential requirements. Such a standard is called a "harmonised" European standard. Therefore the EU regards harmonised European standards as a vital means of achieving the free market.

Products satisfying just the six essential requirements have the freedom to be placed on the market anywhere in the EU and they can carry the CE-mark if they have the designated level of attestation of conformity. The level of attestation of conformity will be decided by the EU and not by CEN. The levels range from full third party certification to declaration by the manufacturer. Thus a harmonised European standard, together with its designated level of attestation of conformity, provides the basis for awarding a CE-mark.

The EU has been mandating CEN to produce harmonised European standards, but the Technical Committees writing these standards have continued to write standards for users. These contain more than the six essential requirements and consequently conformity to a standard exceeds the legal requirements necessary for products to have free access to the market and carry the CE-mark. At first, the EU wanted CEN to limit the mandated standards to the six essential requirements, but eventually a compromise was reached whereby CEN could produce standards for users provided the harmonised clauses were identified.

In reality the drafting of the "Interpretive Documents" (one for each of the six essential requirements) to the Construction Products Directive[2] took the EU much longer than anticipated. The final mandates for standardisation work required to implement this Directive have still not been issued and the levels of attestation of conformity for each of the 2000+ construction products have not been decided. In consequence it is not possible to produce a harmonised European standard for any construction product.

To avoid undue delay to the work of standardisation, the EU have agreed with CEN that they should produce standards for users drafted, as far as possible, in performance terms and containing a clause on the evaluation of conformity. Evaluation of conformity is "how" conformity is established whilst attestation of conformity deals with "who" will determine conformity. This change of tactics will allow European standards to be completed and published. At some time in the future, when a related cluster of CEN standards has been published, CEN will identify the clauses that relate to the essential requirements and copy them into a single harmonised European standard. A level of attestation of conformity will be applied to this cluster standard and this harmonised European standard will form a basis for awarding the CE-mark. The details of this scheme have still to be worked out.

The Commission will not be mandating CEN to produce hEN's for every product. They can only mandate products that are placed on the market and traded across national boundaries. Cement is such a product and therefore it is likely to be mandated. Their attitude to fresh concrete is more difficult to predict. Site mixed concrete is never placed on the market and therefore it cannot be mandated. Ready mixed concrete is placed on the market but only a small proportion is traded across borders. Fresh concrete, however, is made to purchasers individual specification and therefore the supply of this concrete does not pose a barrier to trade. At the specification stage, the designer will not know how the concrete is going to be produced and wishes to use a common concrete specification regardless of who is going to produce it. For these reasons, it is the author's view that fresh concrete will not be a priority item to mandate and may never be mandated as an hEN. There is, however, a vital need to produce a common European concrete standard for, for example, to help contractors when they tender for public works contracts in other Member States.

CEN has been given an almost impossible task of standardising thousands of products from conflicting national standards. The willingness of Member States to compromise is not often apparent particularly when commercial interests are at stake. Workload is the biggest problem facing CEN. Not all related standards can be produced at the same time and therefore the concept of hierarchy of packages of standards was developed, Figure 1. At the lowest level, level 1, a package is a product with its associated test methods. For example, EN197-1: Common cements[3] with EN196: Methods of testing cement[4], would form a level 1 package. The next level, level 2, would be concrete and the highest level, level 3, would be the concrete design code. The proposal in the package concept is

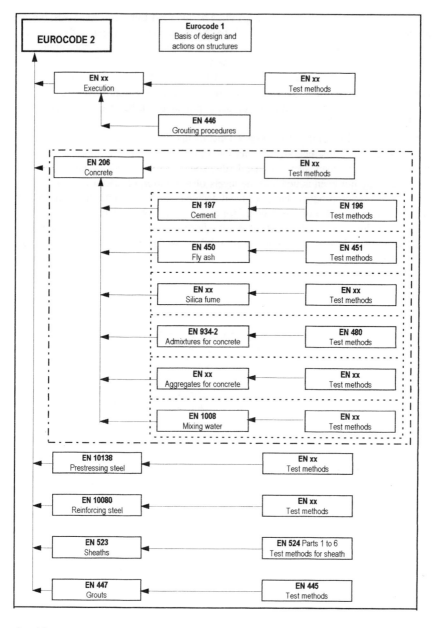

Level 1   - - - - - - - - - - - - - -
Level 2   — · — · — · — · —
Level 3   ───────────

Figure 1. Hierarchy of standards

that Member States need not withdraw conflicting national standards until a package is complete. This would over-ride the concept described earlier in which conflicting national standards have to be withdrawn within six months of the publication of an EN. This concept is helpful to CEN members as it will reduce the need to publish numerous amendments to national standards. However, the downside is that it may delay the national adoption of some European standards, such as the concrete standard, for many years.

A European standard cannot reference a national standard except in approved circumstances, which includes it being acceptable for use in all Member States. This is a highly unlikely situation and if it did occur, the national standard could be turned into a European standard relatively quickly. In the author's view, it would be helpful to the adoption of European standards by Member States if CEN were to modify this rule for products in the process of European standardisation or postponed by CEN and permit in these conditions the use of phrases such as "shall conform to European standards when available". The foreword should also contain a comment of the form 'Where European standards are not yet available, national standards valid in the place of use or equivalent shall be used.' This is the type of wording that is being put into public works contract specifications that are open for tender throughout the EU. The use of this approach would encourage Member States to adopt new European standards rapidly.

4 European standardisation of cements and additions

4.1 Cements
The European standard for cement is prEN 197. The original structure of this standard was

Part 1	Common cements
Part 2	Sulfate resistant cements
Part 3	Low heat cements
Part 4	Low effective alkali cements
Part 5	White cement
Part 6	Leaching resistant cement
Part 7	Natural prompt cement
Part 8	'Danish Block cement'
Part 9	
Part 10	Calcium aluminate cement

With time the structure has evolved, and the current working structure is now:

Part 1	Common cements
Part 2	Conformity evaluation
Part xx	Calcium aluminate cement
Part xx	Sulfate resistant cements
Part xx	Low heat cement

Part1: Common cements, is about to be published as an ENV. Work has also started on upgrading this ENV to an EN. When EN197-1 is published, the cement standards BS12[5], BS146[6], BS4246[7], BS6588[8], BS6610[9] and BS7583[10] will be withdrawn. Part 2: Conformity evaluation, has been agreed as an ENV, but it will be some months before the translations are completed and it is published. Part XX: Calcium aluminate cement, will be sent for CEN enquiry as an ENV in the near future. CEN enquiry is where the CEN members are asked to indicate if they will give the standard a positive vote when formally

asked and if not, the changes they would need before they will give a positive vote. The other parts of prEN 197 are at the discussion or early drafting stages.

Below is the structure of the standard on methods of testing cement. Other papers will give the details of the progress of this standard.

Part 1   Determination of strength
Part 2   Chemical analysis of cement
Part 3   Determination of setting time and soundness
Part 4   Quantitative determination of constituents
Part 5   Pozzolanicity test for pozzolanic cements
Part 6   Determination of fineness
Part 7   Methods of taking and preparing samples of cement
Part 8   Heat of hydration : Solution method
Part 9   Heat of hydration : Semi-adiabatic method
Part 21   Determination of the chloride, carbon dioxide and alkali content of cement
Part xx   Determination of total organic carbon content (TOC)

It should be noted that tests in Part 21 were missing from Part 2 and, at some time in the future, Part 21 may be included within Part 2

4.2 Additions
"Additions" is the collective noun used in the European concrete standard (ENV 206)[11] for materials such as ground granulated blastfurnace slag (ggbs), fly ash and silica fume etc. when they are added as separate powders at the concrete mixer. The materials used as additions are also used as main constituents for cements. The main difference is that, when they are used as part of a cement, the complete cement has to conform to EN 197 and there are, in general, only vague requirements placed on the individual materials. Conformity is assessed against the cement and not the individual components. On the other hand, additions, being separate products, have to comply with a standard including clauses for the evaluation of conformity.

In ENV 206, additions are split into Type 1 additions which are nearly inert and Type 2 additions which are latent hydraulic or pozzolanic. In committee, the French are proposing a new Type 3 addition for limestone flour. This is because ENV 206 does not permit the minimum cement content and the maximum w/c ratio to be modified when Type 1 additions are used.

Table 2 summarises the present position with respect to fly ash.
As will be seen, it is complex. The European standard for fly ash, EN 450, notes that BS 3892: Part 1 fly ash has been used in the UK in a different way to other European states. It is therefore possible for the UK to retain BS 3892: Part 1. Part of the current version of BS 3892: Part 2 conflicts with EN 450-1 and therefore it has to be amended. Within the British Standard committee, two drafts are being prepared, one on the use of pfa in grouts and the other on pfa for use as a Type 1 addition in concrete. The result is that, within the UK, there will be 4 standards on fly ash for concrete all with different rules for their use. How they may be used in concrete is summarised in Table 3

Table 2. Standards related to fly ash for concrete

Reference	Title	Status in June 1994
EN 450	Fly ash for concrete - Definitions, requirements and quality control	Will be published shortly as an EN
EN 451-1	Methods of testing fly ash. Part 1: Determination of free calcium oxide	Will be published shortly as an EN
EN 451-2	Methods of testing fly ash Part 2: Determination of fineness by wet sieving	Will be published shortly as an EN
EN xxx	High lime fly ash for concrete	Request from Spain and Greece to standardise. No decision reached
BS 3892:Part 1:1993	Pulverized-fuel ash Part 1: Specification for pulverized-fuel ash for use with Portland cement	Covers a different use and will remain in force
BS 3892:Part 3	Pulverized-fuel ash Part 3: Specification for pulverized-fuel ash to be used as a Type 1 addition	New standard being drafted

Table 3. Proposed rules for the use of fly ash

	EN 450	EN xxx High lime fly ash*	BS 3892 Part 1	BS3892 Part 3
EN 206 value of k in (C+kA) and w/(C+kA)	0.40	?	In effect 1.0	0
Maximum proportion of fly ash in relation to cement	$\dfrac{A}{C+A} \leq 0.25$	$\dfrac{A}{C+A} \leq ?$	Controlled by equivalence procedure and permitted cements	No limit
Other	Maximum reduction in the minimum cement content of 30kg/m^3	?	(C+A) has to comply with the properties and proportions of the permitted EN 197 cement	None

* The rules for the use of high-lime fly ash have not been discussed in a CEN committee

A European standard for silica fume, which is based on the Norwegian standard, is being prepared and is at the advanced draft stage.

Requests to CEN to standardise limestone flour and high lime fly ash have also been made. No decisions on these requests have been made. These materials are standardised and widely used in one or two CEN member states, but on the European scale they are not familiar materials. Given the current workload of CEN, the committee responsible for these products is examining possible ways in which Member States with national standards for these materials and rules for their use in concrete could continue their local practice, yet claim that the resulting concrete conforms to EN206. If this is possible, it is likely that European standardisation of these materials will be postponed.

There has been no request to standardise ggbs at the European level. Therefore ggbs will be outside the scope of EN 206 and BS 6699: Ground granulated blastfurnace slag for use with Portland cement[12], will continue. The problem is to find a way in which the traditional method of using ggbs in the UK can be clearly recognised as being within the scope of concrete conforming to EN 206. If it is not clearly within its scope, the use of ggbs will be severely disadvantaged in concrete that is specified by reference to EN 206. The UK is working with CEN CS to try to a find suitable solution.

5   References

1   EEC Council Resolution. *New approach to technical harmonisation and standards*, 7 May 1985 (OJ No.C136, 4.6.85,p1)
2   EEC Council Directive. *The Construction Products Directive*, 89/106/EEC.
3   British Standards Institution. *Cement - composition, specifications and conformity criteria. Part 1 : Common cements BS ENV197-1.* To be published in 1994.
4   British Standards Institution. *Methods of testing cement.* (In various parts). BS EN196.
5   British Standards Institution. *Specification for Portland cements.* BS12:1991.
6   British Standards Institution. *Specification for Portland blastfurnace cements.* BS146:1991.
7   British Standards Institution. *Specification for high slag blastfurnace cement.* BS4246:1991.
8   British Standards Institution. *Specification for Portland pulverized-fuel ash cements.* BS6588:1991.
9   British Standards Institution. *Specification for pozzolanic pulverized-fuel ash cement.* BS6610:1991.
10 British Standards Institution. *Specification for Portland limestone cement.* BS7583:1992
11 British Standards Institution. *Concrete - performance, production, placing and compliance criteria.* BS DD ENV206:1992.
12 British Standards Institution. *Specification for ground granulated blastfurnace slag for use with Portland cement.* BS6699:1992.

COMMON CEMENT TYPES AND CLASSES (ENV 197-1: 1992)

A T CORISH
Manager, Product Services and Quality Department
Blue Circle Industries plc, UK

Abstract

ENV 197-1:1992 is reviewed and compared with British Cement Standards. It is shown that British Cement Standards are substantially covered by ENV 197-1 and that the use of the latter need not change current UK practises. It is also shown that ENV 197-1 introduces additional cement types which are unfamiliar to the UK.

1 Introduction

The preparation of a standard for cement was initiated by the European Economic Community (EEC) in 1969 and in 1973 the work was transferred to the European Committee for Standardization (CEN). Technical Committee TC 51 was entrusted by CEN with the task of preparing a cement standard for the countries of Western Europe, comprising the EEC and EFTA members.

The inquiry initiated by CEN/TC 51 in the mid-seventies identified at that time nearly 20 different types of cement and a second inquiry in 1990 resulted in some further 50 different types of cement, which had all been standardized on a national basis and which had proved satisfactory in common or special fields of application under local conditions.

CEN/TC 51 decided in the early eighties to include in ENV 197 only those cements which were intended for use in any plain and reinforced concrete and which were familiar in most countries in Western Europe because they had been produced and used in those countries for many years. This earlier view of CEN/TC 51 was that the more regional cements should continue to be standardized at the national level. The 1989 draft of ENV 197 followed this approach, but did not achieve the majority necessary for acceptance because a few countries wanted to incorporate all their nationally standardized cements and because the EEC Construction Products Directive appeared to require the incorporation of all traditional and well tried cements in order to remove technical barriers to trade in the construction field.

Euro-Cements: Impact of ENV 197 on Concrete Construction. Edited by R.K. Dhir and M.R. Jones. Published in 1994 by E & FN Spon, 2–6 Boundary Row, London SE1 8HN. ISBN: 0 419 19980 2.

In view of the large number of different kinds of cement involved, CEN/TC 51 then decided to divide ENV 197 into several parts with the first part, ENV 197-1, dealing only with "common cements". This concept was developed to a successful conclusion in ENV 197-1:1992 "Cement-Composition, specifications and conformity criteria - Part 1:Common Cements". In accordance with CEN rules, the development of the pre Standard ENV 197-1 into a full European Standard EN 197-1 will be considered in 1995.

2 The structure of ENV 197-1:1992

The pre-Standard is laid out in the following sequence:

1.Scope
2.Normative references
3.Cement
4.Constituents
5.Cement types, composition and standard designation
6.Mechanical requirements
7.Physical requirements
8.Chemical requirements
9.Conformity criteria

The normative references in 2. above all relate to test methods which are being dealt with in Paper No.6 in this Seminar and the conformity criteria in 9. above will be dealt with in detail in Paper No.11. Therefore, neither of these items will be dealt with in this Paper.

This Paper will deal with the Standard definitions and requirements of the constituents in 4. above but some aspects of constituents will be dealt with in greater depth in Papers No.4 and 5.

3 The scope of ENV 197-1:1992

This, reproduced in its entirety, is as follows:

"This European Prestandard specifies properties of the constituents of common cements and the proportions in which they are to be combined to produce a range of types and classes of cement. It then specifies the mechanical, physical and chemical requirements for these types and classes as characteristic values and states the rules for assessing their conformity to these requirements.

It is recognized that different cements have different properties and performance. Where performance tests are available (i.e. setting time, strength and soundness), they have already been taken into account in this European prestandard. In addition, work is being carried out by CEN/TC 51 to identify any additional tests which are needed to specify further performance of cement. In the meantime, and during the life of this prestandard, it is necessary that the choice of cement, especially the type and/or strength class in relation to the exposure class and type of construction in which it is incorporated, should follow the national standards and other regulations valid in the place where the cement is used.

In addition to these requirements, an exchange of additional information between the cement producer and user may be helpful. The procedures for such an exchange are not within the scope of ENV 197-1 but are to be dealt with in accordance with national standards or regulations or may be agreed between the parties concerned".

The development of the further performance tests referred to in the Scope is under way and good progress has been made in freeze-thaw testing and somewhat slower progress has been made in carbonation testing. The way in which performance requirements which call up these future test methods might be incorporated in a future EN 197-1 has not yet been worked out.

4 The definition of "Cement" in ENV 197-1:1992

A fairly general verbal definition of cement is given in the pre-Standard because the wide range of cement types covered prevents a more precise approach to definitions. One specific technical requirement is given:
Reactive calcium oxide (CaO) + reactive silicon dioxide (SiO_2) $\geq$ 50%
Footnotes describe the test methodologies for arriving at the reactive CaO and SiO_2 levels.

5 Permitted constituents

The various constituents of cement are described in Clause 4 of ENV 197-1. In some cases no specific technical requirements are called up and in other cases technical requirements are called up but not all are supported by test methods. The situation is summarised in Table 1.

Specific points arising from the Table deserve a special mention:

The "glassy slag" requirement for granulated blastfurnace slag is not supported by a specified test method and the wide range of results which can be obtained from different test methods diminish the value of this specific requirement.

National pozzolanas(P) have a long history of successful use in cement without specific technical requirements but industrial pozzolanas(Q), especially non-ferrous slag containing significant quantities of heavy metals, have a much shorter history of use and the lack of specific technical requirements is disappointing.

To arrive at the "reactive" CaO and SiO_2 requirements for siliceous fly ash(V) and calcareous fly ash(W), is necessary to make some adjustments to the CaO and SiO_2 values produced from conventional analyses but the pre Standard describes how to do this.

Table 1. ENV 197-1: Permitted constituents

Constituent	Designation	Specification requirement		
Portland cement clinker	K	C_3S+C_2S ≥66.7% $\frac{C_3S}{C_2S}$ ≥2.0 MgO ≤5.0%		
Granulated blastfurnace slag	S	"Glassy slag" ≥66.7% C+S+MgO ≥66.7% (C+MgO)÷S > 1.0		
Natural pozzolana	P			
Industrial pozzolan	Q			
Siliceous fly ash	V	Loss on ignition ≤5.0% "Reactive" C < 5% "Reactive" S ≥25%		
Calcareous fly ash	W	Loss on ignition ≤5.0% "Reactive" C ≥5% "Reactive" C ≤15% "Reactive" S ≥25% Expansion < 10mm 28 days strength –	or ≤5.0% >15% – – <10mm ≥10N/mm^2	
Burnt shale	T	28 days strength ≥25.0 N/mm^2 Expansion <10mm		
Limestone	L	$CaCO_3$ ≥75% Clay content (MBA) ≤1.2g/100g Organic material content (TOC) ≤0.20% ≤0.50% (national option)		
Silica fume	D	Amorphous S ≥85% Loss on ignition ≤4% Specific surface ≥15m^2/g		
Filler	F			
Calcium sulfate	–			
Additives	–			

The calcareous fly ash clause effectively covers two different calcareous fly ashes with a different set of requirements depending upon the 'reactive' CaO being above or below 15%. In the case of the higher lime material, a strength requirement is introduced which recognises the significant hydraulic activity of these materials even in the absence of cement.

Burnt shale(T) also has a strength requirement which recognises an even greater hydraulic activity than that of high lime calcareous fly ash.

Filler(F) has no specific technical requirements but their status as minor additional constituents limit their additional levels to 5% on cement. Additives are normally limited to 1% on cement.

6 Cement types

ENV 197-1 identifies 25 types of cement built around the constituents previously described and the wide range of national practices existing within Europe. The full list of cements is given in Table 2.

Table 2. ENV 197-1: Cement types

Cement type	Designation	Notation	Clinker K
I	Portland cement	I	95-100
	Portland slag cement	II/A-S	80-94
		II/B-S	65-79
	Portland silica fume cement	11/A-D	90-94
	Portland pozzolana cement	II/A-P	80-94
		II/B-P	65-79
		II/A-Q	80-94
		II/B-Q	65-79
II	Portland fly ash cement	II/A-V	80-94
		II/B-V	65-79
		II/A-W	80-94
		II/B-W	65-79
	Portland burnt shale cement	II/A-T	80-94
		II/B-T	65-79
	Portland limestone cement	II/A-L	80-94
		II/B-L	65-79
	Portland composite cement	II/A-M	80-94
		II/B-M	65-79
III	Blastfurnace cement	III/A	35-64
		III/B	20-34
		III/C	5-19
IV	Pozzolanic cement	IV/A	65-89
		IV/B	45-64
V	Composite cement	V/A	40-64
		V/B	20-39

In all cases, the non clinker component would consist of one or more of the constituent materials described in 5. "Permitted constituents". Also, in all cases the non clinker component might include up to 5% of filler(F).

For cement types II, the main non clinker component would be described by the final letter of the notations described in 5. "Permitted constituents". The exception is the designation M ("mixed") for Portland composite cement which might contain several different constituents.

The separate classification III for certain slag cements is necessary because uniquely low levels of clinker are sometimes possible in these cements.

Pozzolanic cements IV may contain mixtures of silica fume(D), natural pozzolana(P), industrial pozzolana(Q) and siliceous fly ash(V).

Composite cements V may contain mixtures of granulated blastfurnace slag(S), natural pozzolana(P), industrial pozzolana(Q) and siliceous fly ash(V).

An example of the actual ingredients in an industrially produced cement might be:

Portland fly ash cement II/B-V

	% used	% permitted
Clinker(K)	68	65-79
Siliceous fly ash(V)	28	21-35
Filler(F)	4	0-5
	100	
Calcium sulfate	5	-
Additive	0.1	0-1
	105.1	

It should be noted that the 100% total is considered as the "cement nucleous" and does not include calcium sulfate or addition. The preStandard places no limit on calcium sulfate addition as such but the amount is of course controlled by the cement SO_3 limits. The additive might typically be a grinding aid which would normally be used at considerably below the 1% maximum permitted level.

7 Cement strengths

ENV 197-1 adopts the increasingly accepted convention of both mimimum and maximum strength requirements at 28 days. The detailed requirements are in Table 3.

Paper No.11 will deal with the detailed statistical background to these numbers.

The preStandard permits all cement types to be supplied to all strength classes but in practice the most likely types of cements to be supplied to the different strength classes are indicated in Table 4.

This Table is illustrative and not definitive. Also, it should be noted that if the R (higher early strength) classification is reached, the lower classification is not claimed in the Table but a manufacturer might still choose to claim the lower early strength classification. For example, a coarsely ground cement Type I with 28 days strength greater than 32.5 N/mm^2 and less than 52.5 N/mm^2 i.e. Class 32.5, is highly likely to substantially exceed the 2 days strength requirement of 10 N/mm^2 for Class 32.5R. However, the cement

Table 3. ENV 197-1: Cement strength classes

Compressive strength (in N/mm^2)				
Class	Early strength		Standard strength	
	2 days	7 days	28 days	
32,5	–	≥ 16	≥ 32,5	≤ 52,5
32,5 R	≥ 10	–		
42,5	≥ 10	–	≥ 42,5	≤ 62,5
42,5 R	≥ 20	–		
52,5	≥ 20	–	≥ 52,5	–
52,5 R	≥ 30	–		

Table 4. ENV 197-1: Likely available strength classes

Cement notations	Likely strength classes available					
	32.5	32.5R	42.5	42.5R	52.5	52.5R
I		✓	✓	✓	✓	✓
II/A-S		✓	✓	✓	✓	
II/A-D				✓	✓	✓
II/A-P,Q,V,W,T,L,M		✓	✓			
II/B-S		✓	✓		✓	
II/B-P,Q,V,W,T,L,M	✓		✓			
III/A, III/B, IV/A						
III/C, IV/B, VA, V,B	✓					

manufacturer may choose to market the cement only claiming to meet the less onerous early strength requirement of Class 32.5 (16 N/mm^2 at 7 days is far easier to reach than 10 N/mm^2 at 2 days).

8 Cement physical and chemical requirements

The initial setting times of cements to strength classes 32.5 and 42.5 are required to be at least 60 minutes but this requirement is relaxed to 45 minutes for strength class 52.5 in recognition that higher strength cements can have faster setting times than lower strength cements.

Cements to ENV 197-1 are all required to meet classical soundness requirements in terms of expansion. These requirements are not onerous for modern cements.

The chemical requirements of ENV 197-1 are summarised in Table 5.

Table 5. ENV 197-1: Chemical requirements

Property	Test reference	Cement type	Strength class	Requirements[1]
Loss on ignition	EN 196-2	CEM I CEM III	all classes	≤ 5,0 %
Insoluble residue	EN 196-2	CEM I CEM III	all classes	≤ 5,0 %
Sulfate (as SO_3)	EN 196-2	CEM I CEM II,[2] CEM IV CEM V	32,5 32,5 R 42.5	≤ 3,5 %
			42,5 R 52,5 52,5R	≤ 4,0 %
		CEM III[3]	all classes	
Chloride	EN 196-21	all types[4]	all classes	≤ 0,10 %
Pozzolanicity	EN 196-5	CEM IV	all classes	Satisfies the test

[1] Requirements are given as percentages by mass.

[2] This indication covers cement types CEM II/A and CEM II/B including Portland composite cements containing only one other main constituent, e.g. II/A-S or II/B-V except type CEM II/B-T, which may contain up to 4,5% SO_3 for all strength classe.

[3] Cement type CEM III/C may contain up to 4,5% SO_3.

[4] Cement type CEM III may contain more than 0,10% chloride but in that case the actual chloride content shall be declared.

The lack of loss on ignition and insoluble residue requirements for CEM II, IV and V follows from the possibility that high loss on ignition materials, e.g. limestone or high insoluble residue materials e.g. fly ashes and pozzolanas might be in these cements.

The sulfate and chloride limits are similar to those recently agreed for British cement Standards.

The pozzolanicity requirement for CEM IV cement is helpful in ensuring that good quality pozzolanas are used, bearing in mind the relatively loose specifications applying to some pozzolanic constituents which were reviewed in 5. Permitted constituents.

9 ENV 197-1 and British Cement Standards

The main British Cement Standards were revised in 1991 to align as far as possible with the 1989 version of prENV 197-1 which had been approved by the UK. Close correspondence still exists between these British Standards and ENV 197-1:1992 and the National Foreword to DD ENV 197-1 will describe the exact relationship.

In terms of cement types, Table 6 shows where ENV 197-1 corresponds to British Standards. It can be seen that 8 out of the 25 Types of cement in ENV 197-1 are already covered by existing British Standards.

Table 6. Cement types in ENV 197-1 and British cement Standards

Cement type	Designation	Notation CEM	Clinker content %	Content of other main constituents %	Corresponding British Standard
I	Portland cement	I	95-100	–	BS12:1991
II	Portland slag cement	II/B-S	80-94	6-20	BS146:1991
		II/B-S	65-79	21-35	
	Portland silica fume cement	II/A-D	90-94	6-10	None
	Portland pozzolana cement	II/A-P	80-94	6-20	None
		II/B-P	65-79	21-35	
		II/A-Q	80-94	6-20	
		II/B-Q	65-79	21-35	
	Portland fly ash cement	II/A-V	80-94	6-20	BS6588:1991
		II/B-V	65-79	21-35	BS6588-1991
		II/A-W	80-94	6-20	None
		II/B-W	65-79	21-35	
	Portland burnt shale cement	II/A-T	80-94	6-20	None
		II/B-T	65-79	21-35	
	Portland limestone cement	II/A-L	80-94	6-20	BS7583:1992
		II/B-L	65-79	21-35	None
	Portland composite cement	II/A-M	80-94	6-20	None
		II/B-M	65-79	21-35	
III	Blastfurnace cement	III/A	35-64	35-65	BS146:1991*
		III/B	20-34	66-80	None*
		III/C	5-19	81-95	None*
IV	Pozzolanic cement	IV/A	65-89	11-35	None
		IV/B	45-64	36-55	BS6610:1991
V	Composite cement	V/A	40-64	36-60	None
		V/B	20-39	61-80	

* BS 4246:1991 covers a blastfurnance slag content of 50-85%

British Standards do not exactly copy all the chemical requirements of ENV 197-1 and an important exception is the requirement for sulfate (as SO_3). British Standards do not allow the 4.0% SO_3 limit in Table 5 and retain an effective limit of 3.5% SO_3 for all cements.

Whilst the UK takes a more conservative view than ENV 197-1 in terms of cement Types and sulfate levels, it takes a far more liberal view in terms of cement strength classes and this is summarised in Table 7. British Standards generally adopt the ENV 197-1 strength classes but add several more. These extra strength classes in British Cement Standards will almost certainly lapse when ENV 197-1 progresses to a full European Standard. The 62.5 strength class in BS 12 is of little practical value. The "L" classes in BS 146 and BS 4246 may well eventually appear in a future European Low heat cement Standard. The future of the special strength classes in BS 6610 and BS 6699 is unclear.

Table 7. Cement strength classes in ENV 197-1 and British cement Standards

Standard	Cement Class	Minimum N/mm^2 2d	7d	28d	Maximum N/mm^2 28d
ENV 197-1	32.5		16	32.5	52.5
	32.5R	10		32.5	52.5
	42.5	10		42.5	62.5
	42.5R	20		42.5	62.5
	52.5	20		52.5	
	52.5R	30		52.5	
BS12	62.5	20		62.5	-
BS146	52.5L	10		52.5	-
	42.5L		20	42.5	62.5
BS4246	32.5L		12	32.5	-
BS6610	22.5		12	32.5	-
BS6699	37.5		16	37.5	57.5
	47.5L		20	47.5	67.5

10 Conclusions

The 1991 series of British Cement Standards revisions relate closely to the requirements of one third of the cement types listed in ENV 197-1:1992. The adoption of ENV 197-1:1992 instead of equivalent British Standards should not create any technical risks but will introduce an administrative burden in that designations of familiar cements will change and require revisions of specification documentation.

The cement Types specified in ENV 197-1:1992 which are not currently covered in British Standards are clearly identifiable. This gives the Specifier or User the opportunity to choose whether or not to approve of or use these unfamiliar cements.

References

ENV 197-1:1992 Cement, composition, specification and conformity criteria - Part 1: Common cements
BS12: 1991 Specification for Portland cements
BS146:1991 Specification for Portland blastfurnace cements
BS4246:1991 Specification for High slag blastfurnace cement
BS6588:1991 Specification for Portland pulverized-fuel ash cements
BS6610:1991 Specification for Pozzolanic pulverized-fuel ash cement
BS7583:1992 Specification for Portland limestone cement

EMERGING SPECIFICATIONS FOR SPECIAL CEMENTS

P LIVESEY
Chief Chemist
Castle Cement Ltd, UK

Abstract
The work of CEN Technical Committee, TC 51, is reported as to the definition of Special cements, the development of performance tests for special properties and the production of standard specifications for these. The work to develop standard test methods for sulfate resistance, heat of hydration, resistance to freezing and thawing, resistance to carbonation and for chloride corrosion is described. The position in the development of specifications for Masonry cements, Sulfate-resisting cements, Low heat cements, Binders for road bases, as well as cements resistant to freezing and thawing, alkali-silica reactivity and corrosion of reinforcement and the latest on Calcium Aluminate and Oilwell cements is described.

Keywords: Calcium aluminate, Cements, Corrosion of reinforcement, Freeze thaw resistance, Low heat, Masonry, Road base binders, Sulfate resistance.

1.   Introduction

The European Standards Organisation Technical Committee responsible for cement standards, TC 51, has decided that in view of the large number of cements involved the cement standard, EN 197, will be divided into several parts. The first part, EN 197-1 (currently approved as a pre-standard [1]), has been restricted to those cements whose hardening mainly depends on the hydration of calcium silicates and which are provided for common uses. Other parts of the EN 197 series will be drafted for cements having different mechanisms of hardening or additional special properties. As the number EN 197-2 has now been assigned to the evaluation of conformity presumably special cements will be numbered from EN 197-3 onwards. Some special cements may be given numbers in other series e.g. EN 413 - Masonry cements. As the European Standards develop the UK will consider these, amending any

Euro-Cements: Impact of ENV 197 on Concrete Construction. Edited by R.K. Dhir and M.R. Jones. Published in 1994 by E & FN Spon, 2–6 Boundary Row, London SE1 8HN. ISBN: 0 419 19980 2.

relevant British Standards to align them with the new ENs or introducing new British Standards to incorporate any not previously standardized in the UK.

Cements utilising broadly the same constituents as ENV 197-1 cements but with special properties are Masonry cements, sulfate-resisting cements, low heat cements and Oilwell cements. Binders for road bases introduce some new constituents whilst the composition of cements resistant to freezing and thawing, corrosion of reinforcement and alkali-silica reaction have yet to be considered. Calcium aluminate cements are, to date, the only cements considered which have a different mechanism of hardening. In the cases of cements having special properties the development of a suitable performance test has generally pre-ceded the drafting of a cement specification.

2.   Masonry cements ENV 413-1 / BS 5224

The CEN Committee has completed a European pre-Standard for Masonry cement specification, ENV 413-1 [2], and a full European Standard for test methods, EN 413-2 [3]. The British Standard for Masonry cement, BS 5224 [4], is being revised to take account of these developments. Table 1 compares the properties of the old BS 5224 with that of class MC 12.5 cement in the ENV which is that closest to the traditional UK Masonry cement.

Table 1.   Comparison of requirements in BS 5224:1976 with those of
         ENV 413-1 for MC 12.5 cement

Cement	BS 5224:1976	ENV 413-1 MC 12.5
Sulfate	3.0 % max.	3.0 % max.
Chloride	No limit	0.10 % max.
Setting time - initial	45 mins. min.	60 mins. min.
final	10 hrs. max.	15 hrs. max.
Soundness	10 mm. max.	10 mm. max.
Mortar properties:		
Water retentivity	70 % min.	80 % min.
	95 % max.	95 % max.
Air entrainment	10 % min.	8 % min.
	25 % max.	20 % max.
Flow	80 % min.	Test to be
	120 % max.	investigated
Compressive strength		
at 7 days	4.0 N/mm^2	See Table 2
at 28 days	6.0 "	"
Sieve residue (90μm)	No limit	15 % max.

The CEN Standard for Masonry cement test methods was given approval as a full EN and therefore the UK is obliged to withdraw conflicting Standards and adopt the EN. This has been approved for implementation by BSI as BS EN 413-2.

The revised BS 5224 whilst excluding specification of test methods takes the new ones into account in the specification which has been extended to include the wider range of cement classes adopted in the ENV. In comparison with the previous edition it introduces a 90 μm sieve test; more tightly defines air content and water retention; includes a range of sulfate limits related to clinker content, a chloride limit and standard strengths based on EN 196-1 mortar [5]. Although the requirement for workability has been dropped TC 51 have approved a further work programme to look into a possible harmonised test. Whilst the test for compressive strength has been revised to that of the mortar prism test in EN 196-1 it can be noted that the limits for class 12.5 are comparable to the strengths of traditional BS 5224 cements. The new limits are set out in Table 2.

Table 2. Compressive strength limits for Masonry cements to BS 5224: 1994

Class	7 day strength N/mm^2	28 day strength N/mm^2	
MC 5	-	≥ 5	≤ 15
MC 12.5 MC 12.5 X	≥ 7	≥ 12.5	≤ 32.5
MC 22.5 X	≥ 10	≥ 22.5	≤ 42.5

An affix "X" applied to the class indicates ones which do not incorporate an air-entraining agent. Class 5 is not permitted without air-entraining and class 22.5 is not permitted with air-entrainment class 12.5 might be either with or without.

The revised BS 5224 will also include a guide to the use of Masonry cement under the requirements of EN 998-2 mortar. The details are set out in Table 3.
For MC 12.5X and MC 22.5X Masonry cements it is recommended in the UK that an air-entraining agent is added at the mixer. No recommendation is made for MC5.

Table 3.   The relationship of prescribed mortar mixes using BS 5224 Masonry cement to DD ENV 413-1 and the European specification for mortars EN 998-2.

Masonry cement ENV 413-1	EN 998-2		Masonry cement BS 5224			
Cement class	Mortar class	Mortar strength 28 days (N/mm^2)	Mortar designation	Proportions by volume		
					Masonry cement	Sand
MC 12.5	M 5	5	(ii)	1	2½ to 3½	
MC 12.5X	M 2.5	2.5	(iii)	1	4 to 5	
MC 22.5X	M 1	1	(iv)	1	5½ to 6½	

3.   Sulfate-resisting cements prENV 197-x / BSs 4027 / 6588 / 4246.

3.1   Specification of sulfate-resisting cement by composition

The particular need for this cement arises from specifications for concrete likely to be exposed to aggressive media containing sulfates. At present no standardized test for such a cement has been finalised and the initial drafts of this standard have drawn upon the experience of those countries where the durability of local cements has been proven in practice. The draft therefore specifies the common aspects of composition, chemical, mineralogical and physical requirements specified in the national standards and aligned as far as possible with the test methods in EN 196 and the format for specification approved for ENV 197-1. Cement types are based on composition and on the ENV 197-1 strength classification. It is accepted that some additional cements, recognised in some countries to have sulfate-resisting properties, but with insufficient general acceptability, can be included in the National Annexes to the (pre-)standard.

The current draft selects the following types for inclusion:

Type I   Portland cement with low C_3A content $\leq 3.0\%$ although $\leq 5.0\%$ is permitted providing that the SO_3 content is $\leq 2.5\%$. Otherwise the SO_3 limit is $\leq 3.5\%$ which is an increase on the current BS 4027   limit.

Types III   Blastfurnace cement where in the case of type III/B the granulated
/B & C   blastfurnace slag content could be as low as 63% compared with the current UK requirement for a minimum of 70%.
It also differs from current UK practice in that there is no restriction on alumina content of either slag or clinker.
The strength classes proposed create compliance problems for traditional UK materials in that being from ENV 197-1 they reflect the rate of hydration for Portland cements whereas that in BS 4246 took account of the lower early strength of High slag cements.

Type IV/B   Pozzolanic cement having $\geq$ 36% and $\leq$ 55% natural pozzolana or siliceous fly ash. This again is in conflict with the UK tradition of $\geq$ 26 and $\leq$ 40% pulverised-fuel ash.

It is envisaged that other cements would qualify for inclusion when they meet the requirements for type testing for sulfate-resistance under the test being developed.

3.2 Test methods for sulfate-resistance

A working group of TC 51 has been developing a test for sulfate-resistance and has completed one round-robin series of tests, has revised the method and is in process of a further round.

The basis of the test is a prism of dimension 20 x 20 x 160 mm of EN 196-1 mortar, cast on the jolting table, moist cured for 24 hours and stored in water to 28 days. Prisms are then immersed in 0.167 mol/l sodium sulfate solution and with control prisms in potable water. Prism lengths are measured at ages up to 52 weeks. No limits for acceptable performance have yet been agreed. The cements included in the present round are:

Moderate C_3A CEM-I
Low C_3A CEM-I
Low C_3A CEM-I with added SO_3

other cements included in the UK participating laboratory work include a High C_3A CEM-I, plus CEM-III/B, and CEM-II/B-V cements.

4.   Low heat cements

Work to date has concentrated on developing agreed test method(s) for heat of hydration. Two of the traditional tests have been approved by TC 51 to proceed for voting as full EN standard tests. These are based on the traditional UK heat of solution method [6] and a semi-adiabatic "hot-box" method [7] standardized in France which has a thermally calibrated calorimeter. There was insufficient experience in other countries to accept the isothermal calorimeter developed by C&CA.

4.1 Heat of solution

The principle of the test is that specified BS 1370 and in earlier editions of BS 4246. This test has fallen into dis-use in the UK with only one laboratory equipped for the test and with only one experienced operative remaining. Several European laboratories still use the test and have developed more modern equipment for it including Italy, Germany and one laboratory in Sweden.

The basis for calculation of heat of hydration is the difference in the heat of solution for anhydrous cement compared with that of partially hydrated cement paste, hydrated to the age of the test. The normal ages for test are 7 days or 28 days but as the heat of solution for hydrated cement, even at 28 days, is quite large the precision of the calculation suffers from being the difference between two large numbers. Hydration takes place in sealed containers at 20 °C and the relevance of this temperature compared with field conditions is questioned particularly for those cements containing secondary materials whose hydration is temperature dependent.

4.2 Semi-adiabatic calorimetry

The method is based upon that developed in France and standardized by AFNOR. It employs a calorimeter for which the thermal characteristics have been calibrated so that as the hydration takes place and the temperature rises the amount of heat escaping can be calculated. The heat of hydration determined is therefore that for fully adiabatic conditions. The test is based on EN 196-1 mortar and as the test progresses the temperature rise is continuously monitored. The method has a number of advantages:

- the heat of hydration can be continuously monitored throughout the test;
- the time to peak temperature in the calorimeter can be determined and the amount of heat generated up to that time can be calculated. This is important for relating the results to performance in a field structure;
- the thermal characteristics of the calorimeter are known and can be related to those of a field concrete structure, formwork, etc.;
- the effect of elevated temperature on the hydration characteristics of secondary materials is taken into account for a thermal system similar to that of the calorimeter.

The main dis-advantage is that the sensitivity of the temperature measurement and calorimeter calibration is such that hydration heat for ages greater than 7 days is too low to be accurately determined. Also because of the variable temperature of hydration absolute scientific data on the heat of hydration cannot be determined. Neither of these is relevant to performance in a field structure where the temperature varies with the state of hydration and the peak temperature is reached much earlier than 7 days.

No decision has yet been taken on which method would be preferred as the reference method or what limits would be applied to classes of low heat cements and how many classes there might be. The Working Group is about to start work on this aspect.

5.   Hydraulic binders for road bases ENV 197-xx

In Europe specially formulated, factory made products are frequently supplied as binders for the various stages of road construction. These include products for soil stabilization, capping layers, sub-bases and bases in addition to the traditional cement for any wearing course. TC 51 is preparing a specification for binders for these applications and which are limited to factory made products which harden by a hydraulic mechanism.

Table 4. Strength classes for hydraulic binders for road bases

Strength class	Compressive strength to EN 196-1 (N/mm²)		
	7 days	28 days	
5	-	≥ 5	≤ 15
12.5	≥ 7.0	≥ 12.5	≤ 32.5
22.5	≥ 10.0	≥ 22.5	≤ 42.5
32.5	≥ 16.0	≥ 32.5	≤ 52.5

The strength classes under consideration are set out in table 4.

The main constituents for such binders include Portland cement clinker, granulated blastfurnace slag, natural pozzolana, thermally activated clays and shales, fly ash (siliceous and calcareous), burnt shale and/or limestone. All of these are defined as in ENV 197-1 with the exception that the loss on ignition of fly ash can be up to 10%. Also all types of lime to ENV 459-1 are permitted. Minor constituents can be filler up to 5%, additives up to 1.5% and/or calcium sulfate.

Other physical requirements include a fineness test in which limits of 15% retained on 90 microns and 5% on 200 microns are proposed; a setting time minimum of 2 hours; a soundness limit of 10mm expansion which also requires binders with sulfate levels greater than 4% to comply with the DIN 1060 : Part 3 cold water stability test.

Chemical requirements proposed, but still to be finalised, are set out in table 5.

Table 5. Chemical requirements for hydraulic binders for road bases

Strength class	Maxima (% by mass)			
	Loss on ignition	CO_2	Insoluble Res	SO_3
5	?	?	?	?
12.5	23	18	18	4
22.5	?	?	18	4
32.5	5	3.5	18	4

Notes: 1) Insoluble residue may be relaxed to 30% when trass is included or to 50% if fly ash is included.
         2) SO_3 may be relaxed to 7% if burnt shale or calcareous fly ash is included and the additional SO_3 can be shown to come from these.

Table 6.   Comparison of the requirements of prENV 197-10 and BS 915:Part 2:1972

Cement	BS 915	ENV 197-10
Fineness	225 m²/kg	No limit
Alumina	≥ 32%	≥ 36% ≤ 55%
Strength	Mortar cubes	Mortar prisms
	1 day ≥ 42 N/mm²	6 hours ≥ 20 N/mm²
	3 days ≥ 49 "	24 " ≥ 42.5 "
Setting time - initial	≥ 2 ≤ 6 hours	≥ 60 mins.
- final	≤ initial + 2 hours	No limit
Soundness	≤ 1 mm expansion	No limit
Chloride	No limit	≤ 0.10%
Alkali	No limit	≤ 0.4% Na$_2$O$_{equiv}$
Sulfate	No limit	≤ 0.5%

6.   Calcium aluminate cement prENV 197-10 / BS 915

A draft standard has been produced by the working group of TC 51 and has been submitted for formal vote as a pre-standard. The UK accepts the specification for the cement which in Table 6 is compared with the requirements of BS 915:Part 2:1972 [8]. The problem for the UK is that the draft also contains guidance on the use of the cement for structural purposes. Whilst it does draw attention to the fact that the cement is not permitted in some countries this is not considered to be a sufficiently strong warning in view of the serious failures experienced here.

The major issue with calcium aluminate cement is that of conversion. The guide to use in structural applications claims that the principle results of conversion, increased porosity and reduced strength, can be controlled by limiting the water / cement ratio to not more than 0.4. The UK feel that this is not sufficient and that it does not make clear how critical this is for concrete which might be targeted at below 0.4 but which in practice is 0.41 or for sections of concrete where there could be locally high water concentrations. It is probable that the UK will vote against the draft on the basis that by linking the specification and the guide it will give the impression that it is now accepted in the UK for structural purposes.

7.   Cement resistant to freezing and thawing

Work to date has concentrated on the development of a test method(s) capable of differentiating between the performances of cements. Methods so far investigated have been assessed for their ability to differentiate between concretes of various resistance to freezing and thawing cycles. This has been a necessary first criteria in assessing the sensitivity of the method and the type of concrete to be used for assessment of cement performance. No discussion cement specification limits have been considered.

Table 7. Concretes used to evaluate freeze/thaw tests

Mix reference	Mix details			Concrete hardened properties		
	Cement (kg/m³)	Water/ cement	Entrained air (%)	Bulk density (kg/m³)	28-day Strength (N/mm²)	Total air (%)
1	350	0.45	5 to 6	2270	46.5	5.1
2	350	0.45	nil	2350	60.5	2.2
3	280	0.65	nil	2310	38.5	2.2

Cement used   : CEM-I class 32.5R
Aggregates   : natural sand / gravel max. size 16mm.

In all cases after casting concretes were kept moist at 20°C, demoulded at 24 hours, cured in water at 20°C for a further six days and then stored in air at 20°C and 65% RH for 21 days.

A draft method has been submitted to TC 51 and has been approved to proceed to voting as a pre-standard. It is based on the measurement of scaling when subjected to freezing and thawing cycles and is suitable for use with either water or 3% w/w sodium chloride solution as the freezing medium.

The draft method contains two alternative tests. The Scandinavian Slab test [9], which is proposed as the reference method, and the German Cube test [10]. There has also been debate on whether to include a test capable of assessing the degree of internal frost damage and the German CDF test [11] has also been included in the Round Robin series of investigations. Table 7 sets out the details of the concretes tested in the Round Robin series.

7.1 Scandinavian Slab test

Sample specimens were 150mm cubes, which at 21 days from casting are sawn to produce slabs 50mm x 150mm x 150mm from the centre of the cube. After washing the slabs are stored for a further 7 days in air at 20°C / 65% RH. Slabs are encased in rubber on five sides leaving one 150mm x 150mm face exposed and with the rubber sides protruding 20mm above that face. The test face is covered in a 3mm layer of water to allow re-saturation for a further 3 days.

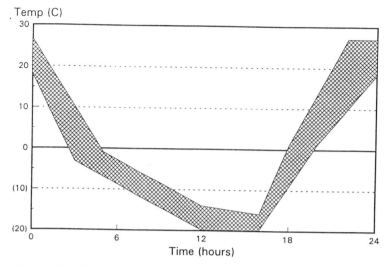

Figure 1A. Temperature cycle and ranges for the Scandinavian Slab test.

Before the start of the freezing tests all surfaces, except the test face, are insulated with 20mm of polystyrene. 15 minutes before the start of the freeze cycle the water on the test surface is replaced with 67mls of freezing medium (tap water or 3% NaCl) and, to prevent evaporation, the top is covered with a flat polyethylene sheet.

Samples are placed in the freezing chamber and subjected to the cycle illustrated in figure 1A, the temperature being that measured at the centre of the freezing medium. Samples are held above 0°C for between 7 and 9 hours in each cycle.

At the end of 7, 14, 28, 42 and 56 cycles material which has scaled from the test surface is collected by rinsing and lightly brushing with a small stiff-bristled brush. The scaled material is filtered off, dried and weighed. Results are expressed as the mass of scaled material (mg) per unit sample test area (mm^2).

7.2 German Cube test

The test uses 100mm cubes cast and cured to 27 days as for the Slab test. At 27 days the weights of the cubes are measured after which they are placed, in pairs, in brass or stainless steel containers which have a watertight lid and are fitted with temperature sensors. Containers are filled with the freezing medium (water or 3% NaCl) to cover the cubes by at least 20mm and after 24 hours the weights of the now saturated cubes are re-determined and the absorption in 24 hours calculated.

Containers with lids sealed are placed in the freezing chamber and subjected to the freezing cycle shown in figure 1B. Immediately after the 16 hour freezing phase the chamber is flooded with water at 20°C. and a thawing phase of 8 hours takes place during which the water is maintained at 20°C. The chamber is then drained and the cycle repeated.

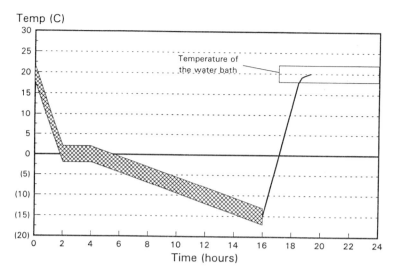

Figure 1B. Temperature cycle and ranges for the German Cube test

After 7, 14, 28, 42 and 56 cycles the cubes are checked for visual damage, brushed to remove scaled material, the liquid in the container emptied and filtered and the scalings dried and weighed. Results are expressed as the % mass of scaled material per mass of the air dried (27 days) cube. The % mass of absorbed medium is also expressed per mass of the air dried (27 day) cube

7.3 CDF test

Concrete cubes are cast and cured to 28 days as in the Slab test and are then sealed on each lateral surface by epoxy resin. Samples are then re-saturated by immersion in the freezing medium (water or 3% NaCl) for 7 days.

A container with sample cube covered in freezing medium is immersed in a liquid filled freezing chamber and subjected to the cycle shown in figure 1C. No range tolerances have yet been set for the cycle temperatures. The dynamic elastic modulus is measured at each set of cycles after which the scaled material can be removed from the cubes and the deterioration can be calculated as for other tests and expressed as the mass of scaling per area of test surface.

Conclusions on the Round Robin were that all scaling tests were able to differentiate clearly between the concrete with the high freeze/thaw resistance (mix 1) and the moderate one (mix 2). It was not possible to differentiate between the moderate and the poor freeze/thaw resistant (mix 3) concretes. Measurement of the dynamic elastic modulus did not produce a clear differentiation between concretes.

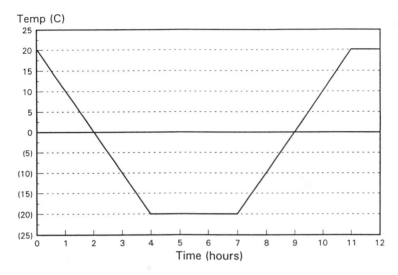

Figure 1C. Temperature cycle for the CDF test

Comments on the respective merits of the various tests were:

> The Slab test sample preparation is relatively complicated and the effect of using a cut face requires further examination. The test itself is simple and the costs of the equipment and the testing are low.

> The Cube test preparation and testing are simple but the equipment costs are high.

> The CDF test preparation and testing are simple and the temperature cycle can be maintained very accurately. The cost of the equipment is midway between the other two.

It remains to be seen as to whether the methods are sufficiently discriminating as to be able to differentiate between the freeze/thaw performance of different cements.

8.   Cements resistant to corrosion of reinforcement

The work has been undertaken on three separate fronts. An enquiry has taken place into the experience with different cement types for various applications in European countries; experimental work has been started to assess the suitability of the RILEM test for carbonation as a means of assessing the corrosion protection performance of cements; and a further work programme has just started to investigate chloride corrosion. Details are as follows:

8.1 Enquiry on the use of different cement types according to ENV 197-1 in plain, post-tensioned and pre-tensioned concrete in different countries

The conclusion of the enquiry is that except for a very few cases there were no discriminatory measures for cement with respect to prevention of corrosion of reinforcement. It states that this does not imply that all traditional and well tried cements are equally fit to prevent corrosion under all practical circumstances and it may well be that a cement which behaves well under Scandinavian conditions may not do so well under Mediterranean conditions, and vice versa. It also points out that a cement may be well tried under indoor conditions and never under outdoor or in reinforced and never un-reinforced concrete.

The report points out that it would be difficult, if not impossible, to define unique performance classifications which meet the experience in all European regions and that the freedom to select cements for given environmental conditions will be crucial to keep in line with local experience.

The report will be published as a CEN Technical Report in which it is hoped will be of value to TC 104 in the drafting of EN 206.

8.2 Development of a carbonation performance test for cements

The RILEM test [12] has been used as the basis of a Round Robin experiment. Four cement types CEM-I, CEM-II/A-L, CEM-III/A and CEM-IV/A have been tested in two concretes with 16mm maximum size aggregate and having cement and water/cement of 240 kg/m^3 and 0.70 w/c or 305 kg/m^3 and 0.55 w/c. After 3 days of moist curing in moulds prisms of section 100mm x 100mm were then stored in air at 20°C and 65% RH. At ages of 90, 180 days, 1, 2 and 4 years slices of 50mm length were split off and tested for carbonation depth by phenolpthalein indication. The test has currently run for 1 year and differences are just beginning to emerge.

9.   Cements resistant to alkali-silica reaction

It quickly became apparent that practices for selection of cements for use with aggregates containing reactive silica differed widely throughout Europe. Furthermore the various National practices related more to concrete specification than to any special performance of cement. A working group of RILEM has been given the task of investigating the variety of methods used throughout Europe to specify concrete on a local basis to resist damaging alkali-silica reaction. This group report is in preparation.

10.   Oilwell cements

There has been a move to standardize Oilwell cements through the various standards bodies in addition to the traditional American Petroleum Institute specification. cement Technical Committee TC 51 is liaising with TC 12 - Materials for petroleum and natural gas industries - to avoid duplication in this area. Meanwhile the main standardization activity is taking place in ISO Committee TC 67.

Within the British Standards Institute Committee PSE/17/3 dealing with oilwell materials work has commenced to produce a standard specification for ground granulated blastfurnace slag for mud to cement conversion applications.

11.   References

1   ENV 197-1 (1992). Cement - Composition, specification and conformity criteria - Part 1 : Common cements. British Standards Institution, London, UK.

2   prENV 413-1 (1992). Masonry Cement - Specification. British Standards Institution, London, UK.

3   prEN 413-2 (1992). Masonry cement - Test methods. British Standards Institution, London, UK.

4   Draft BS 5224 (1993). Specification for Masonry cement (revision of BS 5224:1976). DC 93/106580. British Standards Institution, London, UK.

5   EN 196-1 (1987). Methods of testing cement; Determination of strength. British Standards Institution, London, UK.

6   BS 4246:Part 2:1974. Low heat Portland-blastfurnace cement. Appendix A. Test for heat of hydration. British Standards Institution, London, UK.

7   NF P 15-436. September 1988. Measurement of hydration heat of cements by means of semi-adiabatic calorimetry. (Langavant method). Association Francais de Normalisation, Paris, France.

8   BS 915:Part 2:1972. High alumina cement. British Standards Institution, London, UK.

9   Swedish Standard SS 137244. Concrete testing - Hardened concrete - Frost resistance.

10   Prufung von Beton. Empfehlungen und Hinweise als Erganzungen zn DIN 1048. Deutscher Ausschuss fur Stahtbeton. Heft 422. Abschn.2.3, S 12/14, Beuth - Verlag, Berlin 1991.

11   Setzer, M.J. und V. Hartmann : CDF - Test Specifications. Betonwerk und Fertigteil - Technik 57 (1991), S. 83/86.

12   RILEM Recommendations. (1988) CPC-18 Measurement of hardened concrete carbonation depth. Materials and Structures. November 1988. pp 453 - 455.

MINOR ADDITIONAL CONSTITUENTS: PERMITTED TYPES AND BENEFITS

G MOIR
Chief Chemist
Blue Circle Industries plc, UK

Abstract
The types of minor additional constituents (mac) permitted by current British Standards and by ENV 197-1 : 1992 are reviewed. Their influences on cement early age and strength development properties are discussed. Practical benefits in enabling cement properties to be controlled are illustrated with reference to a UK cement works.
Keywords: Minor additional constituents, ENV 197-1, filler, cement quality, high efficiency separation

1 Introduction

The European pre-Standard for common cements ENV 197-1 : 1992 permits the incorporation of up to 5% by mass of a minor additional constituent (mac). The mac may be one of the main constituents, such as blastfurnace slag or fly ash, which are permitted at higher levels in designated cement types, or it may be an unspecified filler.

'Fillers are specially selected, natural or artificial inorganic mineral materials which, after appropriate preparation, on account of their particle size distribution, improve the physical properties of the cement (such as workability or water retention). They can be inert or have slightly hydraulic, latent hydraulic or pozzolanic properties. However, no requirements are set for them in this respect.'

Cements containing macs have a long history of satisfactory performance in a number of European countries. In some countries the current national standards limit the mac level to 3% or even 1%, rather than 5% and the range of permitted materials may be specified. Details are given in Table 1 [1].

Euro-Cements: Impact of ENV 197 on Concrete Construction. Edited by R.K. Dhir and M.R. Jones. Published in 1994 by E & FN Spon, 2–6 Boundary Row, London SE1 8HN. ISBN: 0 419 19980 2.

Table 1. European countries whose cement standards permit a minor additional constituent

Country	Level %	Specified materials
Austria	≤ 5	
Belgium	≤ 5	
Denmark	≤ 5	
France	≤ 3	Limestone
Germany	≤ 5	Inorganic mineral material (slag, trass or partially burnt raw materials used in the production of clinker)
Greece	≤ 3	limestone, pozzolan, slag etc
Luxembourg	≤ 3	Inorganic material which may be pozzolan or limestone
Netherlands	≤ 5	
Norway	≤ 5	
Portugal	≤ 5	
Spain	1-5	
Sweden	≤ 5	
Switzerland	≤ 1	Fly ash
United Kingdom	≤ 5	Granulated blastfurnace slag, natural pozzolana, fly ash or filler

The UK standard for Portland cement was revised extensively in 1991 to bring it in line with the expected European cement standard. Only minor differences exist between BS12 : 1991 and ENV 197-1 : 1992 and the available options for the incorporation of a mac are essentially unchanged.

2 Background to the revision of BS12 to permit a mac

In 1980 the UK Cement Makers Federation (now the British Cement Association, BCA) submitted a proposal to amend BS12 to permit the addition of up to 5% of fly ash or granulated blastfurnace slag.

This proposal was more conservative than the standards already in existence in several European countries, such as Germany, France and Holland which permitted a wider range of materials including limestone or filler.

BSI committee CAB/1/-/2 considered that further evidence concerning long-term performance was required and a joint investigation was initiated between the Building Research Establishment (BRE) and the UK cement manufacturers.

A comprehensive report containing cement performance and durability data collected over a two year period was submitted to the BSI in 1984. Although the report concluded that the study had produced no firm evidence to suggest that satisfactory ordinary Portland cement could not be produced with 5% fly ash or slag additions, the proposal was rejected on the grounds of objections from specifiers within the public sector who wished to retain the option to be able to specify pure Portland cement.

Concurrent with the investigation in the early 1980's the proposed European cement standard EN 197 was taking form.

The early drafts contained proposals for additions of up to 5% of 'minor additional constituents' to Type I (Portland cement) and for a new type of cement containing up to 20% limestone 'filler'.

In order to obtain information concerning the properties and long term performance of these cements the BRE/BCA working party was reformed in 1986. The core investigation involved cements produced by 5 cement works and containing 0, 5 and 25% of different sources of limestone. Additional cements were also prepared containing 5% cement making raw meal and 25% fly ash.

The results available at 2 years were presented at a seminar held at the BRE during November 1989 and updated versions of the papers presented were compiled in a BRE report [2] published in 1993.

Paper 8 from this current seminar will provide an update to the long term test data generated by this investigation. No significant adverse influences on concrete durability associated with the presence of 5% mac have been detected. The evidence from the joint investigation provided reassurance and in November 1991 the current version of BS12 was published which contains all the main elements of ENV 197-1 : 1992 including the option to introduce up to 5% of a mac.

The other cement standards revised at the same time for fly ash and slag containing cement, also contain the option to incorporate 5% mac, but this option was not extended to BS 4027 for sulfate resisting Portland cement.

3 Types of mac permitted by pr ENV 197-1 and current British Standards

3.1 ENV 197-1 : 1992

A mac is permitted up to a proportion not exceeding 5% by mass of all main and minor constituents, ie 5% by mass of the cement 'nucleus' excluding gypsum. For most cements this corresponds to approximately 4.8% of the total cement.

The mac may be one of the permitted main constituents of cement unless these are included as a main constituent in the cement, or it may be a filler. Options available are thus:

- granulated blastfurnace slag (two-thirds glass)
- natural pozzolana (normally volcanic in origin)
- industrial pozzolana (eg activated clays and air cooled slags)
- fly ash (LOI < 5%)
- burnt shale (containing C_2S and CA)
- limestone (of specified purity)
- silica fume (LOI < 4%)
- filler

The filler may be any specially selected natural or artificial inorganic material provided it does not increase the water demand of the cement appreciably, impair the resistence of the concrete or mortar to deterioration in any way or reduce the corrosion protection of the reinforcement.

Thus, for example a CEM II B-V cement containing 28% fly ash cannot contain an additional 5% fly ash as mac but it may contain up to 5% of granulated blastfurnace slag, filler or any of the other above materials either alone or in combination.

In practice the mac is most likely to be a limestone, cement making raw meal or partially calcined material generated during the cement making process.

3.2 BS 12 1991
BS12 only refers to 4 types of material which may be introduced as a mac

- granulated blastfurnace slag
- natural pozzolana
- fly ash
- filler

BS12 1991 differs from ENV 197-1 : 1992 in that there are no specific chemical or physical requirements for the designated macs. There is also a requirement in the British Standard for the cement manufacturer to provide, on request, information concerning the type and quantity of any mac.

In effect, however, materials such as artificial pozzolan are permitted under the designation of filler and the most likely type of mac in both BS12 and ENV 197-1 cements is limestone or cement making raw meal. Granulated slag and fly ash, whilst technically satisfactory in most respects as a mac, are unlikely to be attractive on economic grounds. In addition, limestone or raw meal offer certain technical advantages as discussed in Section 5.

4 Influence of mac on cement properties

4.1 Granulated slag and fly ash
The comprehensive investigation at the BRE in the 1980's utilised cements with 0, 2.5 and 5% fly ash. The differences between cements with and without the

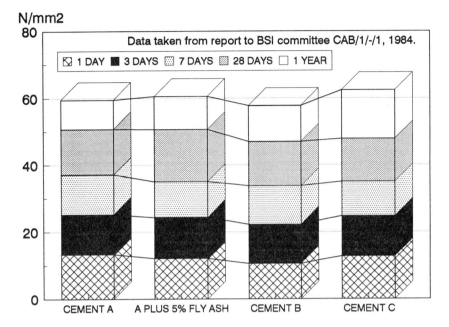

Fig. 1. Influence of 5% fly ash on strength growth

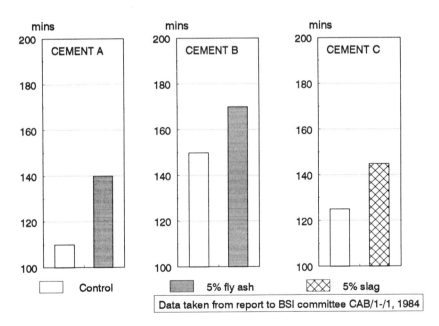

Fig. 2. Influence of fly ash and slag on initial set.

5% addition were generally well within the range of performance of the control cements with 0% ash or slag.

For example, for cements produced at any one works to give the same 28 day strength under standard laboratory conditions, it can be expected that cements containing either 5% ash or slag will give slightly lower strengths at early ages, but slightly higher strengths at ages beyond 28 days. These small changes in strength growth are rather less than the differences shown by 'pure' Portland cements from different works. The effect is illustrated for fly ash containing cements in Figure 1.

One property which was significantly influenced by the presence of 5% fly ash and slag was cement paste setting time. Figure 2 shows that the initial setting time was extended by 20-30 minutes by the incorporation of 5% of either material. This extension of set can be disadvantageous in certain applications.

4.2 Limestone or raw meal

4.2.1   Properties of fresh cement paste and concrete

Figure 3, illustrates the influence of 5% limestone/raw meal on the initial setting time of cement paste and of the mortar fraction removed from the BS 4550 concrete mix. The paste results are the average of determinations on cements from 9 works and the mortar results the average of determinations on cements from 5 works [2]. Setting times were shortened in both series of tests, the reduction being more pronounced in concrete than in paste.

Figure 4 illustrates that concrete bleeding is a function of cement surface area and is independent of the presence or absence of limestone/raw meal filler. This finding is very relevant to the use of filler to control cement strengths as discussed in Section 5 of this paper.

Figure 5, illustrating average data for cements from 5 cement works [2] shows that concrete water demand was unaffected in normal and relatively rich mixes, but was reduced in the lean mix (225 km m^{-3}). This effect can be attributed to the more stable paste phase generated by the higher surface area of the cements containing 5% filler.

4.2.2   Strength development characteristics

The influence of 5% limestone/raw meal on strength development is, not unexpectedly, rather small and tends to be obscured by testing error when results for single pairs of cement are examined.

A further complication is that the cement strength development properties are strongly influenced by the fineness of the clinker component. In order to isolate the influence of the presence or absence of 5% limestone/raw meal filler, data from the BRE/BCA investigation for cements prepared by blending, as opposed to intergrinding, have been averaged.

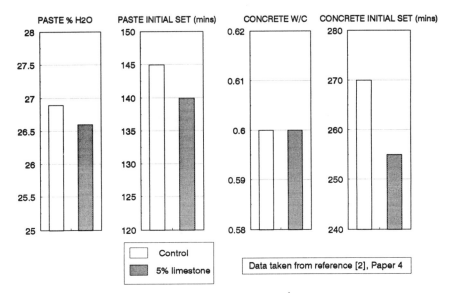

Fig. 3. Influence of 5% limestone on setting behaviour.

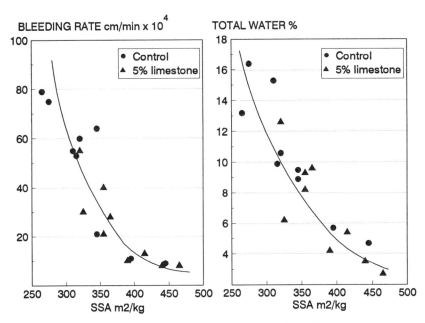

Fig. 4 Relationship between SSA and concrete bleeding.

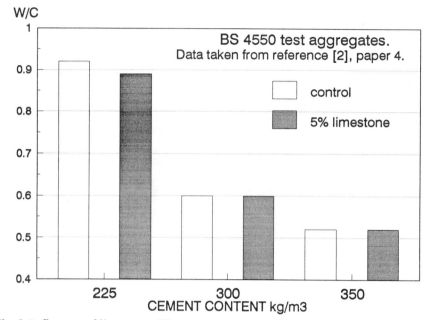

Fig. 5 Influence of limestone filler on w/c ratio for 60mm slump.

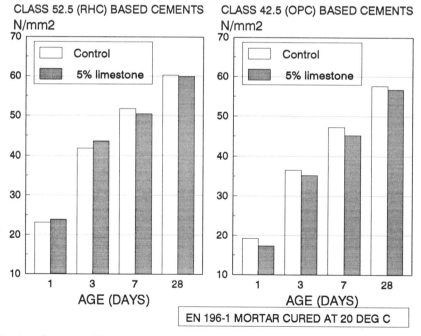

Fig. 6 Influence of limestone filler on strength development of EN 196-1 mortar

Figure 6 shows that the addition of 5% filler slightly reduced the EN 196-1 mortar strengths of the OPC based cements at all ages. The more finely ground rapid hardening cements showed a slight strength enhancement at 2 and 3 days.

Figures 7 and 8 illustrate the results obtained in Thames Valley gravel and BS 4550 concrete mixes. The OPC mixes showed small strength reductions at most test ages. In contrast, the rapid hardening cements showed a small strength enhancement at all ages.

4.2.3 Discussion of results

The presence of finely divided material in cement has an accelerating effect on cement hydration [3]. The acceleration is more pronounced the finer the material, and is particularly pronounced with $CaCO_3$ [4].

The increased hydration rate is attributed to the nucleation sites for $Ca(OH)_2$ crystallisation provided by the fine particles. In addition, $CaCO_3$ appears to interact with the hydrating C_3A to form a carboaluminate phase [5] and to become partially incorporated in the C-S-H phase [6]. The overall extent of reaction is, however, relatively small and even after 4 months hydration 80-90% of the $CaCO_3$ remains unreacted as determined by X-ray diffraction [5].

In the BCA/BRE investigations the presence of 5% fly ash or slag was actually found to lower the initial hydration rate, as indicated by the paste setting time. This effect with fly ash has been reported by other workers [7].

Ground limestone clearly behaves in a different manner from fly ash and slag. The acceleration of initial hydration was confirmed by the BCA/BRE investigations, and in the case of the more finely ground rapid hardening cements, the benefits to strength of 5% limestone persisted even at 1 year.

Thus, although finely divided limestone cannot be considered to be reactive in a hydraulic sense, it clearly interacts in a positive manner with hydrating cement.

As will be seen in Sections 5 and 6 of this paper, the greatest benefits which arise from the incorporation of a limestone filler are in allowing cement fineness (particle size grading), rheological properties and strength development to be adjusted and controlled.

5 Practical benefits of mac option

The practical benefits of the option to incorporate up to 5% of a mac are closely related to the introduction of cement grades with upper and lower strength limits in BS12 1991 and ENV 197-1 : 1992.

These strength grades are essential in order to control the escalation in cement strengths which has occurred since the 1950's and to thus facilitate the specification of durable concrete with stable cement contents, both at present and in the future.

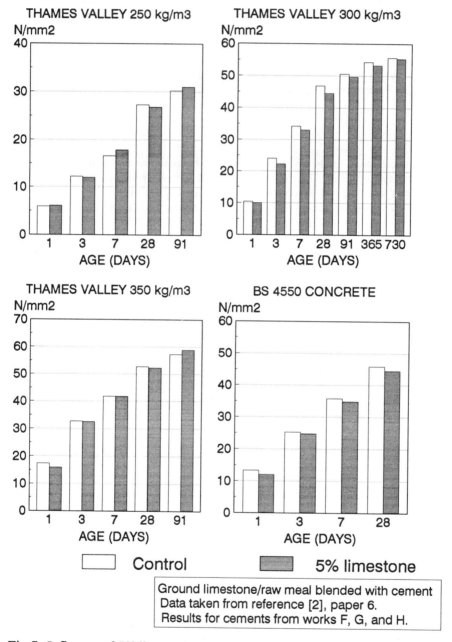

Fig. 7. Influence of 5% limestone on concrete strengths - class 42.5 cements.

CLASS 52.5 (RHC) BASED CEMENTS

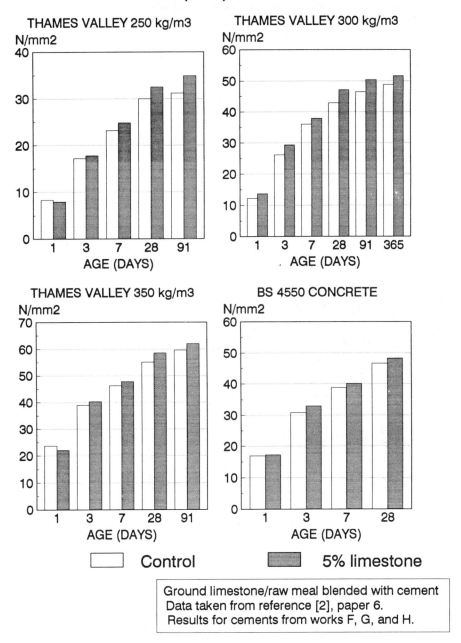

Fig. 8 Influence of limestone on concrete strengths - class 52.5 cements.

Over 90% of the Portland cement supplied in the UK is BS12 class 42.5. This is the strength grade which corresponds most closely to the OPC supplied according to BS12 : 1989, prior to the introduction of the revised standards.

In order to comply with the maximum strength requirements of class 42.5, and also be competitive in the market, it is necessary to produce cement with a mean strength (EN 196-1 mortar prisms) of approximately 58 Nmm^{-2}. This assumes a standard deviation of 28 day strength results of 2 Nmm^{-2} or better.

For cement with open circuit milling systems, or relatively inefficient closed circuit systems, the achievement of this target strength level at an acceptable cement fineness of 330 - 380 m^2 kg^{-1} does not normally present a problem. These cements have relatively wide particle size gradings and consequently a relatively high proportion of coarse particles which remain partially hydrated, even after a considerable period of curing.

Figure 9 is a scanning electron photomicrograph of a polished cement paste which has been hydrated for 90 days.

Completely hydrated   Anhydrous centre of large
15 micron particle   (70 micron) particle.

◄——►
20 microns

Cement 45 micron residue 13.6 %.
Curing temperature 20 deg C.
Paste w/c 0.3

Fig . 9   An SEM image of cement paste hydrated for 6 months

The cement was produced in an open circuit cement mill and 14% of the cement was coarser than 45 microns. It can be seen that the particles larger than approximately 15 microns are only partially hydrated, and that the depth of hydration of the coarsest particles is approximately 7 microns.

If the cement grains are assumed to be spherical and all react at the same rate, it is possible to estimate the influence of particle size grading on the proportion of cement hydrated at a given age [8].

Modern milling systems equipped with so-called high efficiency separators enable specific grinding power to be reduced and higher outputs to be achieved from a given size of unit. A further advantage is that cement temperatures are significantly lower. Associated with the more efficient grinding the cement has a steeper particle size grading and a lower proportion of coarse particles. This results in higher 28 day strengths for a given specific surface area (SSA), as more of the cement particles are accessible to hydration.

One obvious solution is to reduce the cement surface area to lower the strength, but, as illustrated in Figures 3 and 4 the tendency for concrete to bleed increases progressively at lower SSA. Practical experience indicates that an SSA of 300 $m^2 kg^{-1}$ represents the lowest practical limit for a cement which will have acceptable rheological and bleeding characteristics.

A change in clinker chemistry to reduce 28 day strength is normally precluded by the requirements of the market in terms of strength growth (particularly early strength), composition (eg silicates content, eq Na_2O) and by economic consideration such as the cost of raw materials and the need to operate the kilns at maximum efficiency.

The introduction of up to 5% limestone filler enables overall cement fineness to be maintained and 28 day strengths controlled at the required level. A further benefit is that the limestone tends to bring about some shortening of initial set which is normally longer in cements with steeper particle size gradings. The user gains the additional benefits of a more consistent cement produced by a modern milling system. The lower cement temperatures may also be advantageous in certain applications.

There are also overall environmental benefits associated with the introduction of efficient milling systems, as less electrical power is required to grind the cement, thus lowering CO_2 emissions from power stations, and less clinker is required, thus reducing CO_2 emissions from the cement plant. These benefits are quantified with an example in the following section.

6 Example of mac usage to control cement properties

The Blue Circle cement works at Aberthaw was equipped with 8 old and relatively inefficient open circuit cement mills.

Electrical power and maintenance costs were high and quality control was complicated by the number of different mills and their different grinding characteristics. In August 1992 a new 2340 kW closed circuit mill was installed equipped with a high efficiency separator.

The product produced by the open circuit mills had a wide particle size grading with a typical 45 micron residue of 20% for a SSA of 350 $m^2 kg^{-1}$. The new mill was expected to give a 45 micron residue of approximately 3% for a SSA of 350 $m^2 kg^{-1}$. It was clear that a limestone mac addition would be required to control strength and to optimise cement rheological and setting behaviour.

Table 2. Characteristics of open and closed circuit cements

	Open Circuit	Closed Circuit		
	Mean Jan–June '92	Trial Samples August '92		Mean Sept '92 – May '94
% limestone	nil	nil	nil	4.1
SSA m^2 kg^{-1}	349	340	280	340
45 micron residue %	19.9	3.5	12.4	7.7
SO$_3$ %	2.7	2.9	2.9	2.9
Initial set (mins)	120	175	230	170
Compressive Strength Nmm^{-2} EN 196 mortar				
2d	25.2	26	23	26.6
7d	43.5	46	40	42.6
28d	58.8	64	59	58.8
BS 4550 concrete				
3d	23.1	–	–	22.4
7d	33.0	–	–	31.5
28d	45.4	–	–	43.8
Slump mm	50	–	–	65

Table 2 summarises the characteristics of cement produced with the old and the new milling system.

The trial sample results have been obtained by the interpolation of data generated during mill commissioning to enable comparisons to be made at the same SSA and 28 day strengths with and without a limestone mac.

It can be seen that without a limestone mac, in order to meet the strength requirements of class 42.5 the fineness of the cement has to be reduced to a level which would be unacceptable in the market in terms of concrete bleeding (see Figure 4) and setting behaviour.

Table 3 compares the particle size distribution of typical 'old' and 'new' cements. The distribution of the limestone filler has been determined by analysing fractions separated using a Bahco classifier.

Figure 10 illustrates the size distribution of the open and closed circuit cements and also illustrates the approximate distribution of limestone within each size fraction. It can be seen that the limestone is mainly concentrated in the size fraction 5-20 microns.

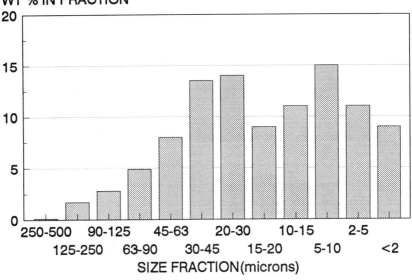

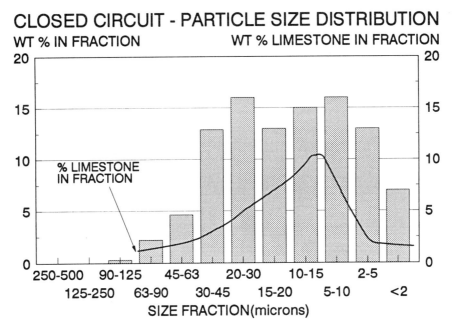

Fig. 10 Weight fraction of cement in different size fractions.

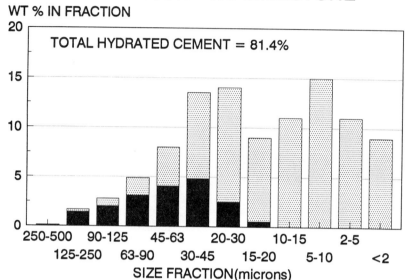

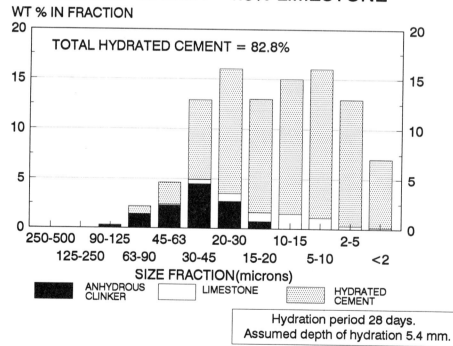

Fig. 11 Estimated proportions of cement hydrated in different size fractions.

Table 3. Particle size distribution of typical open circuit
and closed circuit cements

	Open Circuit	Closed Circuit		
	%	%	%	
	Finer	Finer	CaCO$_3$ in Fraction	
500 microns	100	100		
250	99.9	100		
125	98.2	100		
90	95.4	99.7		
63	90.5	97.5		
45	82.5	92.9	45 microns	1.9
30	69	80	30-45 microns	3.4
20	55	64		
15	46	51	17-30 microns	5.6
10	35	36	5-17 microns	11.7
5	20	20	<5 microns	2.2
2	9	7		
SSA m^2 kg^{-1}	365	340		

As indicated in Section 5, it is possible to estimate the proportion of cement which has hydrated at a given age [8]. The relevant equation is

$$\alpha = \sum f \times [1 - (1 - 2h/d)^3]$$

where α = fraction of cement hydrated
  f = weight fraction of anhydrous cement
  d = diameter of anhydrous cement particles in microns
  h = depth of hydration in microns

If a mean depth of hydration of 5.4 microns at 28 days is assumed [9] the results illustrated in Figure 11 are obtained.

The proportion of hydrated cement in both the open and closed circuit cements is estimated to be approximately the same (81% and 83% respectively). This is consistent with both cements giving the same 28 day strength [10].

The closed circuit cement has a higher proportion of readily hydrated particles, in the size range 5-20 microns, but this is compensated for by the higher concentration of limestone in this size range. The open circuit sample contains a significant proportion of particles, coarser than 45 microns which, in most circumstances, will never fully hydrate. These anhydrous clinker particles represent a wastage of energy used to manufacture the clinker and cement.

The saving in electrical power and the environment benefits (in terms of reduced CO$_2$ emissions) of the closed circuit cement containing a limestone mac are summarised in Table 4.

Table 4. Reduction in electrical power consumption and CO_2 emissions

	Open Circuit	Closed Circuit
Annual production (tonnes)	400,000	400,000
Cement grinding $kWht^{-1}$	65	40
CO_2 from electrical power for cement grinding	26,000	16,000
CO_2 from other electrical power	36,000	36,000
CO_2 from clinker production	328,000	313,000
Total	390,000	365,000
∴ % reduction = 6.4%		

The benefits of the new mill in terms of quality control are summarised in Table 5.

Table 5. Variability of key cement quality parameters - daily average samples

	Open Circuit Jan-June '92	Close Circuit Jan-June '94
	sd	sd
SSA $m^2 kg^{-1}$	13.5	7.7
45 micron residue %	2.1	0.8
LOI %	0.18	0.19
SO_3 %	0.17	0.10
Initial Set (mins)	17	11
Compressive Strength Nmm^{-2}		
2d	1.5	1.5
7d	2.0	1.8
28d	2.6	1.8

A notable achievement has been the tight control of mac level as indicated by the low sd for loss on ignition (LOI). Figure 12 illustrates the step change which occurred. The graph is a moving average of 25 results, and the band width represents ± 2 sds. It can be seen that cement loss on ignition is no more variable than was the case where no addition was being made. The changes in level are as a result of deliberate target changes to fine tune cement strengths.

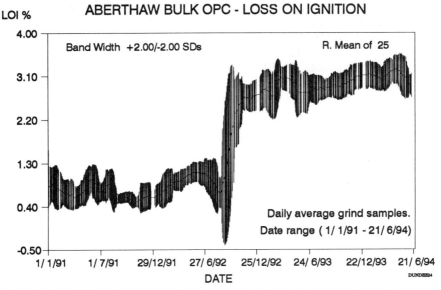

Fig. 12 Variability of loss on ignition before and after the introduction of limestone.

7 Conclusion

The option to introduce a mac into Portland cement is essential if progress is to be made in reducing the electrical power consumed when grinding cement.

Finely divided limestone is likely to be the preferred mac on both technical and economic grounds. The introduction of a controlled level of limestone enables both strength development and rheological properties to be modified. Class 42.5 and 52.5 cements can thus be produced from the same clinker and the specification of durable concrete with stable cement contents facilitated. Cement variability can also be reduced, with obvious benefit to the user.

8 References

1. Cembureau (1991) *Cement Standards of the World,* 8th Edition
2. Building Research Establishment (1993) *Performance of limestone-filled cements.* BRE Report, BR245
3. Soroko, I. and Setter, N. (1977) The effect of fillers on the strength of cement mortars. *Cement and Concrete Research,* Vol 7, pp 449-456
4. Ramachandran, V. S. and Zhang Chun-mei (1986) Cement with calcium carbonate additions, 8th International *Congress on Chemistry of Cement,* Vol 4, pp 197-20
5. Klemm, W. A. and Adams, L. D. (1990) An investigation of the formation of carboaluminates. *Carbonate Additions to Cement,* ASTM STP 1064, pp 60-72
6. Ramachandran, V. S. and Zhang Chun-mei (1986). Influence of $CaCO_3$ on hydration and microstructural characteristics of tricalcium silicate. *Il Cemento,* 83, 3, pp 129-152

7. Halse, Y. et al (1984). Development of microstructure and other properties in fly ash OPC systems. *Cement and Concrete Research,* 14, pp 491-498
8. Taylor, H. F. W. (1990) *Cement Chemistry, Academic Press Ltd,* pp 99-100
9. Andevegg, F. O. and Hubbell, D. S. (1930) The rate of hydration of cement clinker. Proceedings of ASTM, 29, pp 554-569
10. Ritzmann, H. (1968) On the relation between particle size distribution and the strength of Portland cement. *Zement Kalk Gyps,* 21, pp 390-396.

ADDITIONAL MATERIALS AND ALLOWABLE CONTENTS IN CEMENT

R K DHIR
Director, Concrete Technology Unit
University of Dundee, UK

Abstract

The types of materials that can be added to cement to the European Standard ENV 197 are presented together with their allowable quantities. Additions are the most significant of the permitted materials which can introduced to CEM cements and should clearly be seen as distinct from 'fillers' and 'additives', which are described in other papers in these Proceedings. Some allowable materials for additions are familiar in current BS 5328 mixes such as fly ash and granulated blastfurnace slag. While there is some overlap with existing British Standards, in general terms, the allowable quantities are different in ENV 197 and new additions are permitted, for the first time in the UK. Some problems are highlighted and possibly the most important of which is whether fillers in any way affect the performance of additions.

Keywords: *Additions, burnt shale,* calcareous and siliceous fly ash, granulated blastfurnace slag, limestone, natural and industrial pozzolanas, silica fume.

1 Introduction

The introduction of ENV 197[1] could be regarded as heralding a new era in cement specification whose implications could be the most far reaching there have ever been in a single standard. In the short-term, many in the UK will regard the Standard as a fad and that the status quo will be preserved and the portland cement will be essentially no different to what has always been available. The likelihood, however, is that the real situation will be some where between these two views. If required portland cement, which would have in the past been termed OPC, will be available and likewise engineers will be able to select materials which can be used for blending which can provide a whole range of performance

Euro-Cements: Impact of ENV 197 on Concrete Construction. Edited by R.K. Dhir and M.R. Jones. Published in 1994 by E & FN Spon, 2–6 Boundary Row, London SE1 8HN. ISBN: 0 419 19980 2.

in concrete. Clearly, this has the potential to cause some difficultly and has shifted emphasis, at least in the short-term, for engineers to specify the correct blend of materials for the required performance. In the long-term, a shift toward performance based specifications for concrete will remove some of these problems, with the responsibility for the choice of materials shifting back to the producer.

This paper is concerned with the main method with which cement performance can be varied i.e. through the use of 'additions'. These materials will be partially familiar to UK specifiers and include PFA, now termed fly ash, and GGBS, now termed as granulated blastfurnace slag. However, there are also permitted a number of new materials that can be used to blend with portland cement clinker. These include silica fume, which is available, and a number of other materials, such as burnt shale, which are not likely to be used in the UK, at least not in the short-term.

A further problem with pan-European standardisation is the differences in the manner in which materials have been used. In the UK, typical practice is to blend at the mixer, usually at a ready mixed concrete plant, using a selected ratio of portland cement and addition. In continental Europe, additions are more commonly used pre-blended with portland cement at a fixed ratio. However, ENV197 must be seen in the light that it is only one of a whole range of European standards which will cover both cement and additions in their own right as well as for concrete. However, there is the potential for some conflict either with national standards or typical practice until all these standards finally emerge.

2 Nomenclature

ENV 197 uses a series of letters to identify the different additions, as follows:

Burnt Shale	T
Fly Ash	
- Calcareous	W
- Siliceous	V
Granulated Blastfurnace Slag	S
Industrial Pozzolana	Q
Limestone	L
Natural Pozzolana	P
Silica Fume	D

While some of these letters appears to make some sense in English, for example S for slag, L for limestone etc, the others are less obvious and some care will be necessary to ensure that assumptions are correct of what is contained for example in a CEM II/B-Q cement (portland pozzolana cement with between 21 and 35% industrial pozzolana).

3 Permitted Additions

ENV197 : Part 1 allows for a total of 8 additions, as shown above, to be used in CEM cement and details of these and their allowable quantities are given in Table 1. The following sections examine the individual requirements for these cement in more detail. Figure 1 compares the key compositional characteristics of the main additions with portland cement.

3.1 Burnt Shale

Burnt shale is produced by heating oil shale in a special kiln at a temperature of approximately 800°C and in some respects it can be regarded as similar in nature to blastfurnace slag. This results in the material being weakly cementitious, due to the production of clinker-like phases, mainly dicalcium silicate and monocalcium aluminate. It also contains, besides small amounts of free CaO and calcium sulphate, larger proportions of pozzolanically reacting oxides, especially SiO_2. One of the problems of the material is that the SO_3 content can be very high. If the SO_3 content of the burnt shale exceeds the permissible upper limit, then this has to be taken into account for the manufacturing of the cement by appropriately reducing its calcium sulphate-containing constituents.

Burnt shale is finely ground and must have a compressive strength of at least 25 N/mm^2 at 28 days when tested in accordance with EN 196[2], except that the mortar is prepared with burnt shale alone instead of with cement. The mortar specimens are demoulded 48 hours after preparation and cured in a moist atmosphere of at least 90% RH until tested.

The expansion of burnt shale must be less the 10 mm, when tested in accordance with EN 196, using a mixture of 30% by mass of ground burnt shale and 70% by mass of reference portland cement.

3.2 Granulated Blastfurnace Slag

Granulated blastfurnace slag is a latent hydraulic material and possesses pozzolanic properties when suitably activated. The requirements for use in as an addition in cement are that it should contain at least two-thirds by mass of glassy slag and at least two-thirds by mass of the sum CaO, MgO and SiO_2. In addition, the ratio by mass of CaO + MgO/SiO_2 must exceed 1.0. The remaining material in slag is mainly Al_2O_3 together with small amounts of other oxides. Granulated blastfurnace slag should be made by rapid cooling of a slag melt of suitable composition, as obtained by smelting iron ore in a blastfurnace.

Non-ferrous slag contents are limited to 15% by mass. Although now allowed in ENV 197, it should be noted that some authorities are concerned about the use of non-ferrous slag, as it can contain heavy and potentially toxic metallic species which could be leached out. Therefore, local regulations will have to be checked if non-ferrous slag containing concrete is used in proximity to water courses and aquifers.

3.3 Fly Ash

Two very different types of fly ash can be used i.e. silico-aluminous or silico-calcareous in nature. The former, derived from bituminous coal burning, has pozzolanic properties and is the type of fly ash that is available in the UK. The latter, derived from sub-bituminous and lignite coal burning, may have, in addition, intrinsic hydraulic properties by virtue of its free lime content.

All fly ash for use as an addition must be obtained by electrostatic or mechanical precipitation of dust-like particles from the flue gases from furnaces fired with pulverized coal. Ash obtained by any other method cannot not be used.

The specification for fly ash, EN 450[3], has reduced the loss on ignition (LOI) to 5% by mass (cf 7% in BS 3892[4]) in line with other materials. However, the biggest change as far as the UK is concerned is the increased coarseness of ash, up to 40% retained on a 45μm sieve, that is now allowed. At this stage, however, the implications of these changes, if any, are not known. Indeed, this subject is a matter of current investigation at the University of Dundee.

Table 1. Cement Types and Composition, (% mass)

CEMENT TYPE	DESIGNATION	NOTATION	CLINKER	SLAG	SILICA FUME	POZZOLANA Natural	POZZOLANA Industrial	FLY ASH Siliceous	FLY ASH Calcareous	BURNT SHALE	LIMESTONE
I	Portland Cement	I	95-100	-	-	-	-	-	-	-	-
	Portland Slag Cement	II/A-S	80-94	6-20	-	-	-	-	-	-	-
		II/B-S	65-79	21-35	-	-	-	-	-	-	-
	Portland Silica Fume Cement	II/A-D	90-94	-	6-10	-	-	-	-	-	-
	Portland Pozzolana Cement	II/A-P	80-90	-	-	6-20	-	-	-	-	-
		II/B-P	65-79	-	-	21-35	-	-	-	-	-
		II/A-Q	80-94	-	-	-	6-20	-	-	-	-
		II/B-Q	65-79	-	-	-	21-35	-	-	-	-
II	Portland Fly Ash Cement	II/A-V	80-94	-	-	-	-	6-20	-	-	-
		II/B-V	65-79	-	-	-	-	21-35	-	-	-
		II/A-W	80-94	-	-	-	-	-	6-20	-	-
		II/B-W	65-79	-	-	-	-	-	21-35	-	-
	Portland Burnt Shale Cement	II/A-T	80-94	-	-	-	-	-	-	6-20	-
		II/B-T	65-79	-	-	-	-	-	-	21-35	-
	Portland Limestone Cement	II/A-L	80-94	-	-	-	-	-	-	-	6-20
		II/B-L	65-79	-	-	-	-	-	-	-	21-35
	Portland Composite Cement	II/A-N	80-94	-	-	-	-	6-20	-	-	-
		II/B-N	65-79	-	-	-	-	21-35	-	-	-
III	Blastfurnace Cement	III/A	35-64	36-65	-	-	-	-	-	-	-
		III/B	20-34	66-80	-	-	-	-	-	-	-
		III/C	5-19	81-95	-	-	-	-	-	-	-
IV	Pozzolanic Cement	IV/A	65-89	-	-	-	11-35	-	-	-	-
		IV/B	45-64	-	-	-	36-55	-	-	-	-
V	Composite Cement	V/A	40-64	18-30	-	-	16-30	-	-	-	-
		V/B	20-39	31-50	-	-	31-50	-	-	-	-

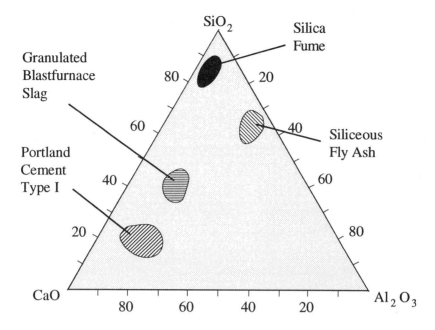

Figure 1 Comparison of key compositional characteristics of main additions.

3.3.1 *Siliceous Fly Ash*
Siliceous fly ash is defined in ENV 197 as a fine powder of mainly spherical particles having pozzolanic properties and consisting of mainly reactive SiO_2 and Al_2O_3 with minor amounts of Fe_2O_3 and other oxides. The proportion of reactive CaO (free) must be less than 5% by mass and the reactive SiO_2 content of siliceous fly ash must be not less than 25% by mass.

3.3.2 *Calcareous Fly Ash*
Calcareous fly ash is defined as a fine powder, having intrinsic hydraulic (i.e. self-setting) and/or pozzolanic properties consisting essentially of reactive CaO, silica SiO_2 and alumina Al_2O_3 with minor amounts of Fe_2O_3 and other oxides. The proportion of reactive CaO must be greater than 5% by mass. Calcareous fly ash containing between 5% and 15% of reactive CaO must contain not less than 25% by mass of reactive SiO_2.

Finely ground calcareous fly ash containing more than 15% of reactive CaO, must have a compressive strength of at least 10 N/mm^2 at 28 days when tested in accordance with EN 196. The expansion of calcareous fly ash must be less than 10 mm using a mixture of 30% by mass of ground fly ash and 70% by mass of reference cement. Before testing, the ash is ground and the fineness, expressed as the proportion by mass of the ash retained when wet sieved on a 40μm mesh sieve, should be between 10% and 30% by mass. It should be noted that this sieve size differs from the more usual 45μm sieve size. The reasons for this change are not clear, particularly as ENV 450[3] still retains the quantification of ash fineness by use of the 45μm sieve.

As with burnt shale, if the SO_3 content of the fly ash exceeds the permissible limit then this has to be taken into account for the manufacture of the cement by appropriately reducing its calcium sulphate-containing constituents.

The mortar for testing standard compressive strength is prepared with calcareous fly ash only instead of blending with portland cement. The mortar specimens are demoulded 48 hours after preparation and then cured in a moist atmosphere of at least 90% RH until tested.

3.4 Industrial Pozzolanas
Industrial pozzolanas are thermally treated and activated clays and shales and air-cooled slags from lead, copper, zinc and other products from the ferro-alloys industry.

One critical requirement that may limit the use of some materials is that should not increase the water demand of the cement appreciably, impair the resistance of the concrete or mortar to deterioration in any way or reduce the corrosion protection of the reinforcement.

3.5 Natural Pozzolanas
Natural pozzolanas are usually substances of volcanic origin or sedimentary rocks with suitable chemical and mineralogical composition. Once ground they behave in much the same way as fly ash. They have a long history of use in southern Europe and Greece and can claim to have the longest history of being used as an addition, and are able to be traced back to Roman and even pre-Roman times. The name pozzolana is derived from the use of volcanic soil found around the town on Pozzuoli in southern Italy.

The types of material that are included in this group are tuffs, trass, zeolytes, Santorin earth and calcined clays and oil shales. ENV 197 treats this group of additions in much the same way as fly ashes, with the same allowable contents in cement.

3.6 Pozzolanic Materials
Pozzolanic materials are natural substances or industrial pozzolanas, siliceous or silico-aluminous, or a combination thereof. Although fly ash and silica fume have pozzolanic properties, they are covered by separate clauses in ENV 197.

Pozzolanic materials do not harden in themselves when mixed with water, but when finely ground and in the presence of water, they react at normal ambient temperature with dissolved calcium hydroxide $(Ca(OH)_2)$ to form strength-developing calcium silicate and calcium aluminate compounds. These compounds are similar to those which are formed in the hardening of hydraulic materials. Pozzolanas must consist mainly of reactive SiO_2 and Al_2O_3. The remainder contains Fe_2O_3 and other oxides. The proportion of reactive CaO should be negligible and the reactive SiO_2 content must be greater than 25% by mass.

3.7 Limestone
In addition to the general requirements for the use of limestone as a filler, when used in a proportion exceeding 5% by mass (i.e. a main constituent) it also has to meet the following requirements:

Limestone content as CaCO₃	*≥ 75% by mass*
Clay content *(measured using the methylene blue adsorption test)*	*≤ 1.20 g/100g*
Organic material content (TOC)	*≤ 0.20% by mass*

The procedure for the methylene blue adsorption test is described in detail in the experimental standard AFNOR P 18-592[5].

Limestone with an organic material content (TOC) between 0.2% and 0.5% by mass may also be suitable for producing satisfactory cement with acceptable performance. Until adequate performance tests are developed by TC 51/WG 12, cements containing these limestones are permitted to be specified in national standards and other regulations valid in the place where the cement is used. This is, however, unlikely to be the case in the UK

The procedure for determining the total organic content (TOC) in limestone was prepared by a European Cement Association (CEMBUREAU) working group[6].

3.8 Silica Fume

Silica fume, produced from the reduction of high purity quartz with coal in electric arc furnaces in the production of silicon and ferro-silicon alloys, can be used and is defined in ENV 197 as consisting of very fine spherical particles with a high content of amorphous silica.

If the proportion of silica fume in the cement exceeds 5% by mass (i.e. a main constituent) then it should meet the following requirements :

Amorphous Silica (SiO$_2$)	*$\geq$ 85% by mass*
Loss on Ignition	*$\leq$ 4% by mass*
Specific Surface (BET) untreated	*$\geq$ 15m^2/g*

The procedure for determining the specific surface uses the BET method as described in DIN Standard 66131[7] or the adsorption of nitrogen method to DIN Standard 66132[8].

For intergrinding with clinker and gypsum, the silica fume may be in its original state or compacted or pelletized (with water).

4. Additions Relevant to the UK

4.1 Fly Ash Additions
The development of the use of fly ash in the UK has occurred mainly through direct addition at the concrete mixer rather than through blended cements[9]. This has meant that the quality of fly ash has been strictly controlled through BS 3892 : Part 1[4], rather than the cement standard itself covering the quality of both the portland cement and the fly ash.

It is wothwhile noting that ENV 197 differentiates between calcareous and siliceous fly ashes by having a reactive CaO either above or below 5% by mass respectively. This limit is different to that in ASTM C618 where this differentiation figure is 10%.

4.2 Review of Current British Standards for Blended Fly Ash Cement
The first British Standards covering blended fly ash cements i.e. BS 6588[10] and BS 6610[11] were introduced in 1985. These were then reissued in 1992 to align themselves with the first draft of ENV197 of 1989. Table 2 shows the parallel development of both ENV 197 and the British Standards.

Before ENV 197 was submitted for CEN voting in 1989, BSI committee CAB/1 had taken the decision, based on the assumption that ENV 197 would achieve a positive vote and would, therefore, be introduced into the UK, to revise the British Standards for cements to bring them more closely into line with ENV 197.

In the event, the first draft of ENV 197 received a negative vote by CEN but BSI continued to work on the revision of these standards using the existing ENV 197, rather than various subsequently amended versions, as a model. It should be noted that in both BS 6588 and BS 6610, the cement is permitted to be manufactured either by intergrinding the constituents or by dry blending. The fly ash is required to comply with all the requirement of BS 3892 : Part 1 except that if the cement is produced by intergrinding, the fineness requirement of BS 3892 : Part 1 is not applicable.

BS 6588 was closely aligned with ENV 197 (1989), including the introduction of strength classes, and covers two types of Portland fly ash cement with permitted fly ash contents of (i) 6-28% and (ii) 0-40%. The cements are distinguished by the latter being required to comply with a pozzolanicity test. However, earlier work at BRE[10] had demonstrated that, especially with ash of the high quality required to manufacture cement to BS 6588, ash contents of 25% upwards would enable a cement to satisfy the pozzolanicity test. In order, therefore, to allow a continuous compositional range of Portland fly ash cement to be produced without the onerous need for pozzolanicity testing, cements of type (ii) above with fly ash contents in the range 29-40% are deemed to satisfy the pozzolanicity test.

It is perhaps unfortunate that, since the revision of BS 6588 was finished, the compositional ranges for fly ash cements given in ENV 197 (1992) have undergone change. Thus, whilst the ranges of fly ash content of 6-28% and 0-40% were aligned with the compositions of Type II-C and Type IV cements in the 1989 version of ENV 197, the version of ENV 197-1 which recently gained a positive vote has different compositional requirements as indicated in Table 1.

BS 6610 now covers a cement containing 41-53% fly ash (the figure of 53% being approximately equivalent to the previous upper limit of 50% calculated as percentage by mass of *total* constituents including calcium sulphate) which is also deemed to satisfy the pozzolanicity test. The nearest equivalent to this cement in the European Standard is Type IV for which the range of fly ash contents has altered from a single range of 0-40% in ENV 197 (1989) to two separate ranges of 10-35% and 36-55% in ENV 197 (1992).

4.3 Blended Fly Ash Cement to ENV 197

It can be seen from Table 1 that various fly ash cements are defined. Firstly, it is noteworthy that calcareous fly ashes, as well as siliceous fly ashes, are permitted in Type II cements. However, the use of such ashes is largely confined to countries such as Spain and Greece and they are not available in the UK and it seems unlikely that such fly ash will be used in the near future.

The main cements containing siliceous fly ash are Type II-V, sub-type A permitting 6-20% fly ash and sub-type B 21-35% fly ash, and Type IV, sub-types A and B permitting 10-35% and 36-55% fly ash (or pozzolana) respectively. Type IV cements must pass the EN 196 test for pozzolanicity.

Cement compositions are expressed as a percentage of the total mass of the constituents but excluding calcium sulphate and any additives, which differs from the traditional UK method of expressing composition as a percentage of the total mass of all of the components of the cement.

Each cement type is theoretically available in all the different strength classes, denoted by 32.5, 42.5 or 52.5, which are the minimum 28-day strengths in N/mm^2 when determined by the new mortar prism test method. Classes 32.5 and 42.5 also have maximum 28-day strengths of 52.5 and 62.5 N/mm^2 respectively. In addition, each strength class is divided into two sub-classes depending upon early strength, the letter R being used to denote cement with high early strength.

Table 2 Comparison of UK and ENV 197 Specifications for Fly Ash Cements

PROPERTY	PORTLAND FLY ASH CEMENTS				POZZOLANIC CEMENTS			
	BS 6588 (1985)	BS 6588 (1991)	ENV 197 (1989)	ENV 197-1 (1992)	BS 6610 (1985)	BS 6610 (1991)	ENV197 (1989)	ENV 197-1 (1992)
Composition (%)								
Clinker	65-85	(i)72-94 (ii)≥60	72-94	(A)80-94 (B)65-79	50-65	47-59	60-100	(A)65-90 (B)45-64
Fly ash	15-35	(i) 6-28 (ii)≤40	6-28	(A) 6-20 (B)21-35	35-50	41-53	0-40	(A)10-35 (B)36-55
Minor additional constituents	Not permitted	(i) 0-5 (ii)0-5	0-5	(A) 0-5 (B) 0-5	Not permitted	0-5	0-5	(A) 0-5 (B) 0-5
Fineness (m²/kg) min	225	Unspecified	Unspecified	Unspecified	225	Unspecified	Unspecified	Unspecified
Chemical Composition max								
Sulphate (SO₃) (%)	3.0	3.0	3.5	3.5	3.0	3.0	3.5	3.5
Magnesia (MgO) (%)	4.0	Unspecified†	Unspecified†	Unspecified†	4.0	Unspecified†	Unspecified†	Unspecified†
Loss-on-ignition (%)	4.0	Unspecified	Unspecified	Unspecified	4.5	†	Unspecified	Unspecified
Chloride (%)	Unspecified	0.10	0.10	0.10	Unspecified	0.10	0.10	0.10
Setting Times								
Initial min	45 mins	60 mins	60 mins	60 mins	45 mins	60 mins	60 mins	60 mins
Final max	10 hrs	Unspecified	Unspecified	Unspecified	10 has	Unspecified	Unspecified	Unspecified
Compressive Strength (N/mm²)	(concrete)	(mortar)	(mortar)	(mortar)	(concrete)	(mortar)	(mortar)	(mortar)
3 days min	8	Unspecified	Unspecified	Unspecified	Unspecified	Unspecified	Unspecified	Unspecified
7 days min	Unspecified	16	16	16	8	12	16	16
28 days min	22	≥32.5;≤52.5	≥32.5;≤52.5	≥32.5;≤52.5	16	22.5	≥32.5;≤52.5	≥32.5;≤52.5
Pozzolanicity	Unspecified	(i) Unspecified (ii)Deemed to satisfy if fly ash ≥29%	Unspecified	Unspecified	Pass	Deemed to satisfy	Pass	Pass

It is likely, however, that Type II cements will occupy the 32.5 and 42.5 grades. Indeed, given the high strength per unit weight values of typical UK portland cements, blending with fly ash may be the only way of achieving these grades. A difficulty posed for the UK here is that the lowest strength class specified in ENV 197 is 32.5, which is considered by the UK as too high for a cement containing 50% fly ash (BS 6610 effectively has a single strength class of 22.5). When TC 51 goes on to consider `special´ cements as opposed to the `common´ cements given in ENV 197 Part 1, the UK has notified its intention to seek the inclusion of a high fly ash content cement, with composition to match BS 6610, a strength class of 22.5 (which currently only appears in the draft European standard for masonry cement) and no requirement for pozzolanicity.

Apart from strength requirements, all cements are required to comply with limits on initial setting time, soundness, loss on ignition, insoluble residue, sulphate and chloride. As noted above, Type IV cements are additionally required to comply with the pozzolanicity test. These properties are the ones to which the autocontrol procedures apply, and are subject to minimum testing frequencies given in ENV 197. These procedures are discussed in other papers in these Proceedings.

There are additional `requirements´ given in definitions of the components of cement. For example, Portland cement clinker has requirements for the minimum value of the $CaO:SiO_2$ ratio and for the maximum MgO content, whilst siliceous fly ash has requirements for loss on ignition, reactive CaO and reactive SiO_2. These properties are, however, relevant to the constituents of cement not the finished cement and are not, therefore, part of the autocontrol procedures.

4.4 Granulated Blastfurnace Slag Additions

Blastfurnace slag to BS 6699[13] and mixer-combinations with portland cement are well established in the UK and are accepted equivalents to composite slag cements manufactured to BS 146[14] and BS 4246[15]. Many European countries use slag cements but in contrast to the UK few use slag in mixer-combinations.

The standards for blended slag cement, as with fly ash, they have recently been completed revised to align with the ENV 197[16](1989). Again as has occurred with fly ash, the latest version of ENV 197 (1992) includes a much wider range of CEM slag cements with much higher slag contents allowable than has been previously used in the UK.

BS 146 and BS 4246, for Portland blastfurnace and high slag blastfurnace cements respectively, are compared with the allowable slag contents of CEM cement in Table 3. Virtually any slag content can be used right up to a 95% replacement with CEM Type III/C blastfurnace cement.

4.5 Silica Fume Additions

For the first time silica fume cement is recognised in the UK, outside of its application in highway structures. This does raise some questions regarding its application, since internationally it is normally used in slurrified form as a mixer blend, due to the difficulty of its dispersion in concrete. The standard allows silica fume to be used in a densified or pelletized state and it has to be questioned as whether this will result in the material being dis-agglomerated and uniformly distributed throughout a concrete mix.

Another aspect of concern is whether fillers should be used with silica fume, effectively reducing the clinker content of the cement. Silica fume is a very reactive pozzolana and has the potential for reducing the resistance to carbonation. The reduction in clinker content, which is the source of alkalinity for the pore fluids, by replacement with limestone filler may have the effect of depleting pore fluid alkalinity further.

Table 3 Comparison of UK and ENV 197 Specifications of Slag Cement

SLAG CEMENT	CLINKER (%)	SLAG (%)
British Standard		
BS 146	35 to 94	6 to 65
BS 4246	15 to 50	50 to 58
ENV 197		
II/A-S	80 to 94	6 to 20
II/B-S	65 to 79	21 to 35
III/A	35 to 64	36 to 65
III/B	20 to 34	66 to 80
III/C	5 to 19	81 to 95

5 Conclusions

There is more choice of binder additions recognised in ENV 197 then has ever been the case with British Standards. There are also advantages in drawing together all cements and additions under a single standard. In the short-term, however, it is likely that what will be available will be cements that are currently familiar to engineers ie fly ash and slag blends. With time, and perhaps more through demand from specifiers, a wider range of materials will be available. This will give the opportunity to further tailor cements for particular requirements, such as low heat of hydration, pump mixes, low carbonation and chloride ingress rates.

There some unknowns regarding the performance of unfamiliar additions. Perhaps more importantly some aspects of performance of even familiar additions, such as fly ash, slag and silica fume, with filler cements remains unclear.

Undoubtable, there are changes, some significant, from current UK standards and adoption of ENV 197 will not be aided while the national standards are allowed to stand alongside. As has be seen with EC2, the use of 'voluntary' European Standards will be virtually nil and until ENV 197 becomes a full standard, the current status quo is likely to remain.

References

1.   European Committee for Standardization. ENV 197. Cement - Composition, Specification and Conformity Criteria. Part 1 : Common Cements. 1992.
2.   European Committee for Standardization. ENV 196. Methods for Testing Cement.
3.   European Committee for Standardization. ENV 450. Specification for Fly Ash.
4.   British Standards Institution. BS 3892: Part 1. Specification for PFA for Use as a Cementitious Component in Structural Concrete. 1982.

5.   AFNOR. Experimental Standard P 18-592. Aggregates.   Methylene blue test. July 1980 (Revised 1990).

6.   ZEMENT-KALK-GIPS. Procedures for the Determination of Total Organic Carbon Content (TOC) in Limestone. No 8, 1990. pp 409-411.

7.   DIN Standard 66131. Determination of specific surface area of solids by gas adsorption using the method of Brunauer, Emmett and Teller (BET).

8.   DIN Standard 66132. Determination of specific surface area of solids by adsorption of nitrogen; single-point differential method according to Haul and Dumbgen.

9.   Dhir, R K. Pulverized-Fuel Ash. Chapter 7, Cement Replacement Materials. ed R N Swamy. Pub Surrey University Press. 1986

10. British Standards Institution. BS 6588. Specification for Portland Pulverized-fuel Ash in Cements. 1991.

11. British Standards Institution. BS 6610. Specification for Pozzolanic Pulverized-fuel Ash Cement. 1991.

12. Matthews, J D. Standards and Specifications. Proceeding of the National Seminar, The Use of PFA in Construction. Ed R K Dhir and M R Jones. University of Dundee, 25-27 February 1992, pp 283-297.

13. British Standards Institution. BS 6699. Specification for Ground Granulated Blastfurnace Slag for Use with Portland Cement. 1992.

14. British Standards Institution. BS 146. Specification for Portland Blastfurnace Cement. 1992.

15. British Standards Institution. BS 4246. Specification for High Slag Blastfurnace Cement. 1991.

16. Dewar, J D. UK and European Standards. Proceeding of the National Seminar, The Use of PFA in Construction. Ed R K Dhir and M R Jones. University of Dundee, 25-27 February 1992, pp 283-297.

KEY TEST METHODS AND LIMITS

M G TAYLOR
Standards Manager
British Cement Association, UK

Abstract

National methods for testing cement are slowly being withdrawn where they conflict with the provisions of developed European Standards. However, useful informative methods are being retained in National Annexes to the Standards as they are implemented nationally. In addition, shortcomings in several of the European testing standards are identified in the appropriate Annexes, and guidance given for their remediation.

The most important test method for the testing of compressive strength has introduced testing based on the mortar prism rather than on the concrete cube. The implications for traditional practice are here considered, together with a detailed review of the other key physical and chemical methods necessary for testing cement against autocontrol requirements. The difference between the values for the limiting criteria for autocontrol results and the limit value conformity of individual results (or for acceptance inspection) is briefly explored and the limits presented. The particular test methods which are required for autocontrol purposes are clearly identified.

In addition, individual physical and chemical test methods which fall outside the scope of autocontrol requirements are described and discussed.

Finally, test methods and limit values specifically required for limestone as a main constituent of cement, are presented and considered.

Keywords: Cement, standard tests, mechanical, physical, chemical, limiting criteria, autocontrol, limit value conformity, EN 196, EN 197, limestone.

Euro-Cements: Impact of ENV 197 on Concrete Construction. Edited by R.K. Dhir and M.R. Jones. Published in 1994 by E & FN Spon, 2–6 Boundary Row, London SE1 8HN. ISBN: 0 419 19980 2.

1   Introduction

The recent (March 1994) re-drafting of EN(V) 197-1[1], (the European Prestandard for common cements) according to the CEN/PNE rules, presages the next stage; transformation into a draft EN.

In fact, the effect that this, or the eventual implementation of EN 197-1, will have on the day-to-day testing regimes in the U.K. cement industry will be fairly minor. It should be understood that since the 1991/1992 alignment of the BS specifications for the industry's main products, with an earlier draft (June 1989) of EN(V) 197-1[2], test results have been determined and reported according to the relevant EN 196 methods of testing cement. In addition, the limiting criteria adopted in the revised specifications are mainly those of the European Prestandard but with some additional criteria which reflect traditional U.K. practice and which were considered to be both of continued value to customers and of help with control of product quality.

The implementation of the various parts of EN 196 as British Standards in the U.K. continues, although now considerably behind the agreed schedule. However, all the parts of the standard were "made available" in the U.K. many years ago (some as long ago as 1987) and have become familiar to manufacturers, users and testing laboratories, if not perhaps, to the ultimate customer.

It cannot be denied that not all of the changes required of the cement industry in order to proceed towards harmonization in Europe, have been welcomed. However, significant further change is unlikely in the short-term, given the legal interdependence and integration of harmonized specifications, test methods and EC directives, the mandate to remove technical barriers to trade and the overriding requirement to demonstrate conformity with the 'essential requirements' of the Construction Products Directive (CPD)[3].

The Euro-hierarchy of documentation for the construction industry is coherent and will eventually be complete. The cement industry's products, their quality/fitness for purpose are of fundamental importance to the construction process and so deserve consideration in depth.   The changes to the requirements for conformity, the expression of limiting criteria and associated test methods need to be explained and understood in order both to avoid confusion and to confirm to users that, although the documents have changed, the products remain, by and large, as they were, with the exception of the most recent developments in air-entrained general purpose cements appearing principally in the bagged sector but available, on request, in bulk.

2   General

2.1   Performance vs. prescription

Amongst the provisions of the CPD is the following for test methods which are to be incorporated in a harmonized European standard ..."[test methods should be]... expressed as far as possible in terms of product performance...". In fact, in common with CEN Member States' national standards specifications for cements, the Prestandard ENV 197-1 expresses its requirements in terms of performance and prescription. This will remain the case even when the ENV is adopted nationally as a full EN, although work is being carried out by CEN/TC51/WG12[4] to identify any additional test methods which may be needed to specify further performance characteristics of cement. Whether there will ever be a point at which prescriptive requirements can be dispensed with is a matter for speculation.

2.2 'Key' performance tests
European standards (ENs) for the three 'key' performance tests of, strength[5], soundness[6], and setting time[7], have been made available in the U.K. since 1987, although implementation of them as British Standards (BS ENs) is still awaited. However, implementation is fully expected within 1994 in light of the positive outcome of a 'second final vote' in CEN and the recent endorsement by the relevant BS committee, of draft National Forewords and National Annexes for inclusion in Parts 1, 2[8], 3 and 5[9].

2.3 'Key' prescriptive tests
The 'key' prescriptive characteristics of EN(V) 197-1 cements are expressed as chemical requirements for loss on ignition (LOI in EN 196-2), insoluble residue (IR in EN 196-2), sulfate (as SO_3 in EN 196-2) and chloride (Cl⁻, now in BS EN 196-21). In addition, a performance test, but still a chemical requirement, for pozzolanicity has been standardised in EN 196-5.

2.4 Conformity
It should be understood that conformity of a cement with the European Prestandard is assumed if statistical conformity criteria (clause 9) are met for <u>specific</u> mechanical, physical and chemical requirements. These requirements expressed in terms of characteristic values are defined in clause 7 of the PNE version of EN(V) 197-1[1] (or in clauses 6, 7 and 8 in the 1992 Final Draft) and are reproduced in table 1 simply as properties.

Table 1. Mechanical, physical and chemical properties of cement to European Prestandard EN(V) 197-1

Property of cement		Standard test method
Mechanical	Standard strength Early strength	EN 196-1
Physical	Initial setting time Soundness	EN 196-3
Chemical	Loss on ignition Insoluble residue Sulfate (as SO_3)	EN 196-2
	Chloride	EN 196-21 (now a BS EN[10])
	Pozzolanicity	EN 196-5

The properties listed in table 1, together with their defined numerical requirements, were the only properties given in the current documents as being subject to autocontrol (continuous quality control of the cement) procedures by the manufacturer. However, an additional autocontrol requirement for the periodic monitoring of composition is proposed for inclusion in clause 9 (Conformity criteria) but the test method(s) to be used will be chosen by the manufacturer and agreed between the manufacturer and a certification body.

2.5   Acceptance inspection and conformity

It should be understood that EN(V) 197-1 does not deal directly with acceptance inspection at delivery. Acceptance inspection, i.e. the testing of 'spot' samples by the customer or his agent, is a traditional part of U.K. practice and is included in the current BS cement specifications. However, in the March 1994 (PNE version) of EN(V) 197-1, a 'note' is included which states ..."It is recommended that any acceptance inspection at delivery of CEM-cement should be at least in accordance with the [limit value] conformity criteria specified in clause 9.2.3. These latter limits are in addition to the statistical (autcontrol) conformity criteria and impose a requirement that ..."each test result remains within the limits specified in clause 9.3, table 8". Accordingly, these limits can be treated as being applicable, also, to acceptance inspection.

2.6   Additional requirements

In addition to the properties associated with the conformity of cement, listed in table 1, there are many other properties and associated requirements specified in EN(V) 197-1 which could appear to be mandatory. These appear in clauses 4 and 5 of the PNE version, are indicated by the word ..."shall"... and are given in Annex 1 to this paper. Most of these are requirements of the constituents but around five are associated with the cement itself. For several of the requirements, no test method is given and for others, no numerical criteria are specified against which to test. Although this is currently unsatisfactory, review/revision of the specification at scheduled dates should allow for the appropriate amendments.

The subject matter of this present paper will concern itself mainly with the conformity properties and their requirements, i.e. the 'key test methods and limits', together with those given below in table 2.

3.   Mechanical/physical test methods and associated limiting criteria

3.1   Mechanical test methods and requirements - standard and early strength
3.1.1   Introduction

The major change to traditional testing practice, that the attempts to harmonize European cement specifications has introduced to U.K. cement manufacturers, is the requirement to determine compressive strength using EN 196-1 mortar prisms rather than BS 4550 concrete (or mortar) cubes.

The EN 196-1 mortar prism test gives numerical values which are different from those given by the equivalent concrete cubes and, since the inclusion of the new system in the 1991/1992 revisions of the U.K. cement specifications, both

Table 2. Additional properties subject to test

Property of cement or constituent		Standard test method
Physical	Fineness N.B. No requirement in ENV 197-1	EN 196-6 (now a BS EN)[11]
	Alkalis N.B. No requirement in ENV 197-1	EN 196-21 (now a BS EN)
Chemical	Reactive calcium oxide (of cement)	EN 196-2
	Reactive silicon dioxide (of cement)	plus EN 196-21
	Composition (of cement)	ENV 196-4[12]
	CaCO$_3$ content (of limestone)	EN 196-2
Chemical	Clay content (of limestone)	EN XXX (National Annex to BS EN 196-2 (when published)
	Total organic carbon (TOC) content (of limestone)	EN 196-XX (National Annex to BS EN 196-2 (when published)

the manufacturer and customers have had to become familiar with these differences. The relationship between the results from cube and prism tests is cement dependent, but a general relationship has been derived. Particular relationships can be obtained from the appropriate manufacturer.

Introduction of the mortar prism strength test has not been without some problems for the cement industry. Works laboratories and technical services laboratories have had to re-equip with the appropriate mixing, compacting and testing equipment, in addition to evaluating sources of CEN Standard sand and buying-in new moulds. As a result, the industry can now boast many years of testing to the 'Euro-regime' and has gained complete confidence in its ability to control product quality within the required limits.

3.1.2   Test methods; description of EN 196-1 compressive strength

The mortar prism test, which has been for many years the standard method of testing cement in continental European countries, uses specimens which are 40mm x 40mm x 160mm in dimensions. These are cast from a mix of 3 parts of a CEN Standard sand, 1 part of cement and 0.5 parts of water. The mortar is compacted by using a jotting table, according to the standard reference method, but alternative methods are permitted, subject to acceptable conformity with measurements using the jolting table.

The U.K. cement industry has decided to use a vibrating table which is quieter and so environmentally more acceptable.

After curing in water for the specified time, the prisms are broken in half in a flexure test or, more usually, by some other suitable means and the two halves then tested in compression across their 40mm widths. In fact, three specimens are made concurrently and a test result is defined as the arithmetic mean (expressed to the nearest $0.1 N/mm^2$) of six strength determinations made on the set of three prisms.

If one result within the six determinations varies by more than $\pm 10\%$ from the mean of the six, the result is discarded and the mean of the remaining five is calculated. If a further result within the five varies by more than $\pm 10\%$ from the mean, the entire set of results is discarded.

All the individual results must be recorded but only the calculated mean and an indication of whether any result has been discarded, need actually be reported.

3.1.3   Implementation of EN 196-1 as BS EN 196-1

Implementation of EN 196-1, in the U.K., should take place within 1994. At the same time, clause 1 of BS 4550: Part 3: Section 3.4: 1978 - compressive strength of concrete cubes - must be withdrawn, since it conflicts with the EN. However, clause 2 of the British Standard - compressive strength of mortar cubes - which is currently called up in BS 915, BS 1370 and BS 4248, will not be withdrawn until these specifications are revised.

BS EN 196-1 will consist of the verbatim text of EN 196-1, together with a 'National Foreword' and five 'National Annexes'. Four of these will be 'Normative', i.e. mandatory in the U.K., whilst the remaining one will be 'Informative'. National annexes NA, NB and NC give the normative requirements for CEN Standard sand, for the alternative vibration compaction procedure and for the verification of the mass requirements for the jolting table, respectively. National annex ND provides additional recommendations for the application of the test procedure in the U.K. and national annex NE lists the technical comments submitted by the U.K. at the final voting stage.

It cannot be said that the text of EN 196-1 has been drafted with the rigour traditionally associated with a BS document. However, the inclusion of the national foreword and annexes in BS EN 196-1 will compensate for most of the ambiguities which appear.

The major outstanding shortcoming, when one considers that the ..."removal of technical barriers to trade..." is a principal aim of European standardisation, is the following. There is still no co-operative testing scheme in place through which assurance can be given that the properties of, i.e. CEN Standard sand from producers in different countries are comparable. Hence, there can equally be no assurance that users of the standard are working to a uniform pan-European strength testing level.

There are many other matters of detail to attend to which indicate that a full review of the EN is overdue and, indeed, a decision on this is expected within 1994.

3.1.4 Precision of test method and proficiency testing

3.1.4.1 *Precision*

In keeping with the recommendations of ISO 5725 (BS 5497: Part 1)[13], precision estimates for repeatability (r) and reproducibility (R) are quoted, but both in terms of coefficients of variation and only for compressive strength testing at 28-day (standard strength). The values quoted were obtained from the results of a comprehensive precision experiment conducted in Europe @ 1977. Laboratories (ten in total, including the U.K.) were at liberty to choose, in an unqualified way, from the range of available jolting tables and compression testing machines. Four cements were used, together with a Belgian sand, centrally distributed.

General dissatisfaction with the rather poor reproducibility estimate obtained, was expressed in the CEN working group drafting EN 196-1 but no follow-up investigations were carried out in order to identify/isolate those elements of the test method contributing mostly to the variability. However, it was acknowledged that continued international co-operative testing should be undertaken and such a requirement was included in the standard for laboratories involved in the certification testing of CEN Standard sand.

The precision estimate for reproducibility is given in clause 10.6 of EN 196-1: "For the 28-day compressive strength the reproducibility under these conditions between well-experienced laboratories expressed as the coefficient of variation may be expected to be less than 6%".

The precision estimate for repeatability is given in clause 11.5: "For the 28-day compressive strength, the repeatability under these conditions within a well-experienced laboratory, expressed as the coefficient of variation, may be expected to lie between 1% and 3%".

The above estimates can be re-expressed in several ways, assuming a mean 28-day strength of, say, 60N/mm². Examples are given in table 3.

Table 3. Precision estimates for 28-day compressive strength derived from EN 196-1

Age at test	Mean strength (assumed)	Std. dev. S_R	R $(2.8S_R)$	Std. dev. S_r	r $(2.8S_r)$
[d]	[N/mm²]	[N/mm²]	[N/mm²]	[N/mm²]	[N/mm²]
28	60	3.6	10.1	1.8	5.0

It is clear from the estimates for R and r in table 3 that there is room for improvement in the standard method and, indeed, application of the aforementioned national annexes in BS EN 196-1 will assist in this.

Investigations within the U.K. cement industry, subsequent to the 1977 experiment, have indicated that the most likely source of a major element of the observed variability was in the very variable performance of the different designs of jolting table used; all of which appeared to comply with the requirements of the standard. However, other possible contributing factors should not be dismissed.

In the absence of a follow-up investigation, the only realistic and convincing way of improving the overall performance of testing laboratories is for the requirement in sub-clause 11.6.1 of EN 196-1 to be implemented. This makes international collaboration in co-operative testing schemes mandatory for "certification laboratories" undertaking the "certification testing of CEN Standard sand". Such investigations would eventually reveal any inadequacies in the drafting of the standard and in the variability of any stage of a laboratory's mixing, making, curing and testing operations or in its equipment.

3.1.4.2 *Proficiency testing*
There is no requirement in either EN(V) 197-1 or EN 196-1 for laboratories which undertake strength testing of cement to participate in proficiency testing. However, the CEN European Cement Certification Scheme embodied in an as yet unapproved document entitled "Cement - Conformity evaluation"[14] (which may eventually be published as EN(V) 198) does specify such a requirement for a testing laboratory which undertakes the testing of audit samples taken at a factory or depot. However, at present this cannot be a mandatory requirement, since the harmonised European hierarchy of standardisation is still being developed. When it is all in place, it is more than likely that such proficiency testing will become one more mandatory (requirement) in order to attest the conformity of cement with the essential requirements of the CPD and allow for the affixing of the CE mark.

In the case where cements hold a product certificate of conformity (Kitemark) with BSI Product Certification (BSI PC), then proficiency testing to BSI's scheme[15] has already been mandated for laboratories carrying out third party product testing of 'audit' samples on its behalf.

Proficiency testing is unlikely to become centralised as a single pan-European activity. However, within a given Member State, its establishment should both set an agreed industry testing level for strength and allow participants to demonstrate whether their accuracy or precision is better or worse than indicated in EN 196-1. In the latter case, a properly organised scheme should include a feed-back system for investigating discrepancies and for achieving an improvement in performance.

3.1.5   Limiting criteria - standard and early strength
3.1.5.1 *Definitions of standard and early strength*
The standard strength of a cement is defined as the compressive strength determined in accordance with EN 196-1 at 28 days. It must conform to all the requirements reproduced in table 4 below, relevant to the strength class declared.

The early strength of a cement is the compressive strength determined in accordance with EN 196-1 at either 2 days or 7 days. It also must conform to the requirements reproduced in table 4 relevant to the sub-class declared.

3.1.5.2   *Characteristic and limit value conformity criteria*
In the latest draft (PNE version) of EN(V) 197-1, criteria for conformity are given as 'requirements defined as characteristic values' (autocontrol statistically-based requirements), together with 'limit value conformity criteria'. These latter apply to individual test results and require that each remains at or above the limits specified. The limiting criteria are reproduced in table 4.

Table 4. Mechanical requirements, defined as characteristic values, together with limit values for individual results.

Strength class	Compressive strength [N/mm²]			Strength lower limit [N/mm²]		
	Early strength		Standard strength	Limit values		
	2 day	7 day	28 day	2 day	7 day	28d
32.5	-	≥ 16.0	≥ 32.5 ≤ 52.5	-	14.0	30.0
32.5 R	≥ 10.0	-		8.0	-	30.0
42.5	≥ 10.0	-	≥ 42.5 ≤ 62.5	8.0	-	40.0
42.5 R	≥ 20.0	-		18.0	-	40.0
52.5	≥ 20.0	-	≥ 52.5 -	18.0	-	50.0
52.5 R	≥ 30.0	-		28.0	-	50.0

Other papers presented at this Seminar will deal more fully with the implications of the limits for both the cement manufacturer and the customer.

3.15.3   *Standard mortar prism vs. concrete cube compressive strength*
The relationship between the results from standard prism and cube tests varies with the cement. However, a general relationship has been derived applicable to the standard ages of test and is given below:

$$\text{Log}e\ (\gamma/x) = 0.28/d + 0.25 [16]$$

where x = concrete cube compressive strength (N/mm²)
γ = mortar prism compressive strength (N/mm²)
d = age at test (days)

This relationship has been established from extensive laboratory testing but should only be invoked in the absence of particular data for a given cement.

An additional complication introduced with the Prestandard is that early strength is measured at 2 days rather than at 3 days as was the U.K. tradition. Where it is desired to convert three day concrete cube strengths to two day mortar prism strengths for CEM I cements, the general formula to apply is:

$$\gamma_2 = 1.3\varkappa_3 - 4$$

where $\varkappa_3$ = concrete cube strength at 3 days (N/mm²)
γ_2 = mortar prism strength at 2 days (N/mm²)

No relationships have been derived for cement types other than CEM I.

The factors which affect the relationships between prism/cube strengths at the different ages of test are not fully understood but must be associated with cement fineness, specific differences in cement chemistry or perhaps a combination of both.

More generally, the factors which affect (or control) the relationship between standard prism strength (28 day) and standard concrete cube strength of the same age, for CEM I cements, is also not fully understood. However, when testing to both regimes is adequately controlled, there is a good and useful relationship between them for individual CEM I cements. Accordingly, the cement industry has re-affirmed its intention to phase-out BS 4550 testing at its works laboratories.

The relationship(s) which exist between standard prism strength and customer-type concrete strength testing are much more difficult to address. It is clear, however, that standard prism strength alone is entirely inadequate in ranking CEM I cements for their expected performance in 'real concretes'. Even a combination of standard prism strength and water demand of a cement has proved to be inadequate. Indeed, as an additional complication, the apparent ranking of a cement can vary with the grade (w/c ratio) of the concrete. There are clearly many interrelated factors to consider theoretically, and currently only practical performance tests will indicate the relative strength performance of different CEM I cements.

3.2   Physical test methods and requirements
- initial setting time and soundness
3.2.1   Test methods; description of EN 196-3 provisions

The performance test methods for initial setting time, final setting time and soundness, are provided in EN 196-3. It should be noted, though, that only the first and last mentioned properties are actually subject to autocontrol and limit value conformity requirements in ENV 197-1. The principles of each of the tests are the same as currently drafted in BS 4550: Part 3: Sections 3.6 and 3.7. Setting time is determined by observing the penetration of a Vicat needle into a paste of standard consistence until it reaches a specified value. Soundness is determined by observing the volume expansion of a paste of standard consistence as indicated by the relative movement of two needles forming part of the Le Chatelier apparatus.

Any differences in methodology introduced in the standard are matters of detail rather than substance but taken together, were sufficiently significant for the U.K. to register a negative vote on the document. Badly written instructions or required tolerances which cannot actually be met in practice have marred what should have been a relatively simple drafting exercise.

When EN 196-3 is implemented as BS EN 196-3, it will include a National Foreword and three informative National Annexes. The final annex (NC) records the U.K.'s technical comments submitted at the final voting stage, whereas the first two compensate for several shortcomings by providing guidance for the practitioner.

Implementation of EN 196-3 is expected in 1994 but its provisions are already called-up in the revised British Standard cement specifications.

3.2.2 Limiting criteria - initial setting time and soundness

Conformity criteria for setting time and soundness are given in terms of statistical requirements defined as characteristic values and limit values applicable to individual test results. The limiting values are reproduced in table 5.

Table 5. Physical requirements, defined as characteristic values, together with limit values for individual results

Characteristic values			Limit values	
			Lower limit	Upper limit
Strength class	Initial setting time [min]	Expansion [mm]	Initial setting time [min]	Expansion [mm]
32.5				
32.5 R				
42.5	≥ 60		45	
42.5 R		≤ 10		10
52.5	≥ 45		40	
52.5 R				

The characteristic values recorded in table 5 for both performance requirements are no different to those in the current British Standards for the same strength class cements. This is to be expected since the British Standards have been revised to align with EN(V) 197-1. In fact, although the requirements for initial setting time in the 1989 edition of BS 12 (prior to alignment) may seem to be different and is expressed as an absolute limit rather than a characteristic, in practice the performance of the products has not changed at all.

The limit(s) for the soundness expansion test have remained numerically the same at 10mm throughout the revisions to BS 12. In terms of the effect on performance of cement, it is purely academic whether these have been quoted as absolutes or characteristics; typical expansions (@ 1mm) are so far below the 'safety' limit that unsoundness in U.K. cements is no longer encountered.

3.3 Additional physical test method - fineness

3.3.1 Introduction

There is no requirement in EN(V) 197-1, or in the current revised British Standards, for fineness of a common cement. However, in the 1991 edition of BS 12, there exists a provision for the specification of a 'controlled fineness Portland cement'. Essentially,this is a special cement for use where easy removal of excess water from a concrete is required. It is defined as a 'Portland cement having a specific surface controlled within a small agreed range'. The range has to be agreed between the manufacturer and the purchaser. This cement will still be available in the U.K. even though EN(V) 197-1 makes no specific mention of it.

3.3.2   Test method(s); description of BS EN 196-6 fineness methods

BS EN 196-6 describes three methods of determining the fineness of cement. Two appear in the body of the transposed EN 196-6, whilst the third is documented in an informative national annex (NB).

As a consequence of a number of quite major shortcomings in the EN, the U.K. registered a negative vote at the final voting stage but under the later CEN Rules, was bound to abide by the majority decision and implement EN 196-6.

The shortcomings of the standard, together with the preferred practices for the U.K., documented in a suite of national annexes, are explored in the next few sections.

3.3.2.1   *Sieving method*

The first method in the EN is a simple sieving (90μm mesh) method which serves only to demonstrate the presence of coarse cement particles. The method is of value to the manufacturer for checking and controlling his production process. A reference material is required for checking the sieve but none is specified in the EN; a major omission. However, U.K. informative annex, NA, identifies a suitable material for use, produced by the former Community Bureau of Reference (BCR)[18].

3.3.2.2   *Air permeability method - Blaine, secondary standard method*

In the air permeability method for determining fineness as specific surface (mass related surface), measurement is made by comparison of a test sample with a reference cement sample. The method is therefore comparative rather than 'absolute', as was previously the case for the 'Lea and Nurse' method in the British Standard[19] which has had to be withdrawn. The Blaine apparatus is used which operates on the principle of 'constant volume air permeametry'. The fineness of cement is measured by observing the time taken for a fixed quantity (constant volume) of air to flow through a compacted cement bed of specified dimensions and porosity. Under standardised conditions, the specific surface is proportional to $\sqrt{t}$, where t is the time for the given quantity of air to flow through the compacted powder bed. The number and size range of individual pores in the compacted bed are a function of the cement particle size distribution, which also determines the time taken for the air to flow through.

The shortcomings of this method, as drafted in the EN, are indicated in National Annex NB to BS EN 196-6 together with the full but revised text of the former BS Lea and Nurse primary standard method which has been retained for the purpose of certifying or checking a reference cement.

A fundamental step in the determination of fineness, is the prior determination of particle density; no documented method is given in the EN. For U.K. purposes, National Annex NC describes in full a revised procedure which was formerly given in BS 4550: Part 3: Section 3.2: 1978[20], until it was withdrawn.

In addition, the reference cement for use, NBS-SRM 114, which is indicated (but not specified directly as the sole reference cement) in the EN, is less than ideal, since there is a question mark over its certified level and characterisation history[21].

National Annex (ND) gives the preferred method of reporting results (in m²/kg) in the U.K., simply in an attempt to preserve traditional practice.

3.3.3 Fineness - additional information

In practice, although there is no actual requirement for a value of fineness in the standards, the cement manufacturers will continue to provide one as additional information if it is requested at the time of ordering. In such cases, the actual method

employed could vary with manufacturer, since there is no requirement to use the BS EN 196-6 method. The manufacturer will declare the method used, upon request.

4.   Chemical test methods and associated limiting criteria

4.1   Chemical test methods and requirements - Loss on ignition, insoluble residue, sulfate (as SO₃), chloride and pozzolanicity

4.1.1   Introduction

The chemical test methods for the chemical requirements specified in EN(V) 197-1 are little different to those still documented, or previously documented, in BS 4550: Part 2[22]. Where they differ in detail, they do so in a way which will only marginally affect the results that would have been obtained by the provisions of the pre-1991/1992 BS 12. They do, however, differ in their application in that not all the requirements/tests can be sensibly applied to all the types of cement (CEM I - CEM V) specified in EN(V) 197-1. This is self-evident for the pozzolanicity requirement, but less so for loss on ignition (LOI) and insoluble residue (IR); the sulfate requirement(s) applies to all cement types.

Requirements for LOI and IR have been included in cement specifications in order to safeguard the compositional quality of the product. For example, a test which revealed a high value for LOI for a traditional OPC type cement would have indicated either an 'air-set' cement or one which, perhaps, contained unspecified quantities of unreactive carbonate species (limestone, for instance). Similarly, a high value for IR would have indicated the presence of unspecified quantities of acid-insoluble (unreactive) species. However, in continental Europe, composite cements (CEM II and CEM V) have traditionally contained constituents which could exhibit high values for either or both of LOI and IR. Consequently, the tests and requirements are inapplicable to such products and have been retained for cements to which they can be logically applied. In addition, the limits for some of the chemical requirements (LOI, IR and SO₃) have been raised from their traditional BS levels and expressed as characteristic values. In the cases of LOI and IR, this is a consequence of a provision in EN(V) 197-1 which permits the inclusion of up to 5% minor additional constituent (mac) into most cement types. Mac's contain, or are based upon, materials which, when incorporated into cement, would give values for LOI and IR outside the pre-1991/1992 BS 12 limits, thereby no longer giving any indication of the cement's compositional quality. The raised limits include an allowance for the contributions expected from these additional constituents.

In the case of sulfate as SO₃ (not as total sulfur as in the pre-1991/1992 BS), the requirement has always been imposed in order to minimize the potential for internal sulfate expansion of the hardened cement by restricting SO₃ content, whilst yet allowing the manufacturer the flexibility to optimise SO₃ content for purposes of setting time adjustment, strength development and resistance to sulfate attack. On the basis of consensus and experience within the CEN Member States, limits for SO₃, for

OPC type cements to the pre-1991/1992 BS 12, have been raised by around 0.5%. However, a simple single comparison is difficult given that permitted %SO$_3$ takes on values which can depend on strength class or, in some cases, on the individual cement type.

The requirement for chloride ion (0.10%) is the same as that in the pre-1991/1992 BS for OPC type cements and is specified simply to limit the intrinsic access of chloride ion in concrete, from the cement component.

The pozzolanicity requirement is only applicable to CEM IV (Pozzolanic cements) and takes the traditional form, although changes to the test method makes evaluation of a result a little different to that which would have been obtained using BS 4550: Part 2.

4.1.2   Chemical test methods - LOI, IR, SO$_3$, Cl⁻ and pozzolanicity

The test methods for LOI, IR and SO$_3$ are given in EN 196-2. Its implementation in the U.K. as a BS EN is imminent, wherein it will be supplemented by the addition of a national foreword and seven national annexes. However, none of these annexes bears directly upon the chemical properties which are specified in EN(V) 197-1, as requirements. It should be noted, though, that other unspecified methods can be used as alternatives to the reference procedures in EN 196-2, provided that they give results equivalent to those given by the reference methods. Unfortunately, "equivalence" is not defined and, in any case, in the event of a dispute, only the reference procedures are to be used. The determination of LOI in clause 7 of
EN 196-2 is adequate for most cements but could lead to different values being quoted for cements containing oxidisable sulfide, dependent on which of the two correction systems are applied. Of the two, the <u>sulfate</u> correction is the more technically correct. In the case of the <u>sulfide</u> correction, the assumption is made that all the sulfide initially present is oxidised to sulfate under the conditions of the test. This is rarely the case for ignition in the normal range of muffle furnaces and is therefore an invalid assumption. However, this latter system confers the benefit of simplicity. Accordingly, upon method revision, a choice should be made between accuracy and simplicity and then only a single correction system documented.

In EN 196-2 there are two methods documented in clauses 9 and 10 for the determination of IR. In EN(V) 197-1, no indication is given as to which clause the 'test reference' calls up. In fact, clause 9 (solubility in hydrochloric acid and sodium carbonate) is appropriate for CEM I and CEM III cements and is the clause called up in the 1991/1992 BS 12 specification for Portland cement. Any revision of the Euro-standard should address this point.

The sulfate (as SO$_3$) determination differs only in detail from earlier standard gravimetric determinations of SO$_3$ as barium sulfate but differs in principle from the pre-1991/1992 BS 12 specification, in that total sulfur was specified. Total sulfur also included sulfide-sulfur which would have been present if an un-permitted blastfurnace slag constituent had been inadvertently (or deliberately) incorporated. Now that blastfurnace slag could be present in almost any EN(V) 197-1 cement as a mac (or main constituent in some cements), specifying sulfate as 'total sulfur' is no longer appropriate.

The test method for chloride determination is now given in BS EN 196-21 and in principle has much to recommend it, although in detail it could be improved; indeed, has been improved in AMD 5713[23] an amendment to BS 4550; Part 2, now withdrawn. When EN 196-21 is approved for review, the U.K. will advance AMD 5713 as a suitable basis for improvement to the EN chloride determination. At the same time the revised test methods of EN 196-21 should be subsumed into a revised EN 196-2, since Part 21 was only published in order to document three test methods (chloride, carbon dioxide and alkali content) which had been overlooked during the drafting of Part 2.

The pozzolanicity test is to be found in EN 196-5 and suffers from poor drafting although, in principle, it is little different from the current method in BS 4550: Part

2. EN 196-5 is ready for implementation as a BS EN, wherein a national annex will draw the user's attention to the method's shortcomings whilst offering suitable guidance.

4.1.3   Limiting criteria - Loss on ignition, insoluble residue, sulfate as (SO_3), chloride and pozzolanicity

In common with the mechanical/physical criteria for conformity. chemical requirements are given as characteristic values for autocontrol purposes, together with 'limit value conformity criteria' for individual results or which can be for acceptance inspection testing. The limiting criteria are reproduced here in table 6.

4.2   Quantitative determination of constituents of cement
4.2.1   Introduction

In EN(V) 197-1 'Type' and 'Designation' of cement are defined by reference to composition, expressed as proportions of constituents by mass, on the basis of the nucleus (free of set regulator and additives) of the cement.

The composition of the cement types must be in accordance with the associated table of limiting values (Table 1 in EN(V) 197-1). However, there is no autocontrol, (or other) requirement in the March 1994 PNE version of the standard for actually testing the cement in order to check conformity. Instead, assurance is provided by ..."The cement manufacturing process and its control shall ensure that the composition of CEM cements is kept within the limits etc. ...". However, an additional autocontrol requirement for the periodic monitoring of composition is proposed for inclusion in clause 9 (Conformity criteria). The assessment of composition will only relate to a demonstration of compliance within the compositional limits, for the relevant cement type, not to the attainment of any 'target' composition, within the limits. The test methods to be used will be chosen by the manufacturer and agreed between the manufacturer and a certification body. It should be noted that such a requirement for CEM I types will only apply to CEM I's which contain an mac. A CEM I without an mac will, according to the definition applied to composition, consist only of 100% cement clinker. Of course, in reality the final cement despatched will consist of clinker plus calcium sulfate (set regulator) plus any additives.

The methods of analysis which a manufacturer will choose for monitoring composition will probably not be the classical methods documented in ENV 196-4. The manufacturer will almost certainly develop a more rapid and quantitatively

Table 6. Chemical requirements, defined as characteristic values, together with limit values for individual results

Characteristic values					Limit values
Property	Test reference	Cement type	Strength class	Require-ments[1]	
Loss on ignition	EN 196-2	CEM I CEM III	All	≤5.0%	No specified limit
Insoluble residue	EN 196-2	CEM I CEM III	All	≤5.0%	No specified limit
Sulfate (as SO₃)	EN 196-2	CEM I CEM II[2] CEM IV CEM V	32.5 32.5 R 42.5	≤3.5%	4.0
			42.5 R 52.5 52.5 R	≤4.0%	4.5
		CEM III[3]	All		CEM III/A & B CEM III/C 5.0
Chloride	EN 196-21	All[4]	All	≤0.10%	0.10
Pozzolan-icity	EN 196-5	CEM IV	All	Satisfies the test	Positive at 15 days

[1]   Requirements are given as percentage by mass.

[2]   This indication covers cement types CEM II/A and CEM II/B including Portland composite cements containing only one other main constituent, e.g. CEM II/A-S or CEM II/B-V except type CEM II/B-T, which may contain up to 4.5% SO₃ for all strength classes.

[3]   Cement type CEM III/C may contain up to 4.5% SO₃.

[4]   Cement type CEM III may contain more than 0.10% chloride but in that case, the actual chloride content shall be declared.

1. Cement type CEM II/B-T may contain up to 5% SO₃ for all strength classes.
2. Cement type CEM III may contain more than 0.10% chloride but in that case, the actual chloride content shall be declared.

accurate procedure around the benefits offered by his existing analytical equipment of wavelength dispersive X-ray fluorescence spectrometry (WD XRF).

4.2.2   ENV 196-4 - Quantitative determination of constituents of cement

After approximately 25 years, work on ENV 196-4 is reaching completion within CEN committee TC51/WG4. Following the final precision experiment of 1993/1994, the convenor has sent his proposals for amendments to the standard for endorsement by the parent technical committee, TC51. In addition, consideration will then need to be given to transforming the ENV into an EN at some future date. Such a transformation will require a deliberate policy decision, since the results of the schedule of investigatory work have not entirely fulfilled the original objectives.

The original brief sought to develop simple analytical methods which could, ideally, be used to identify and quantify the constituents of any cement type or designation, described and defined in EN(V) 197-1, and thereby identify an unknown cement.

In the event, the compositional complexity of, and wide range of, potential constituents has militated against such an easy outcome. However, the brief has been fulfilled, to an acceptable degree, for specific cements within types I, II and III. These are reproduced in table 7.

Table 7. Cement types which permit an accurate identification, using the reference methods of ENV 196-4

Type of cement	Designation	Notation
I	Portland cement	I
II	Portland-slag cement	CEM II/A-S CEM II/B-S
	Portland-silica fume cement	CEM II/A-D
	Portland-pozzolana cement	CEM II/A-P CEM II/B-P
	Portland-fly ash cement	CEM II/A-V CEM II/B-V
	Portland-limestone cement	CEM III/A CEM II/B-L
III	Blastfurnace cement	CEM III/A CEM III/B CEM III/C

It should be noted that the reference methods of clause 6 of the standard have been subject to most investigation and are to be preferred on grounds of simplicity, economy and reliability to those documented in clause 7 for 'cements containing only three constituents'.

In the case of cements containing constituents other than those indicated in table 7, the best that can be achieved will be to obtain, by empirical calculation, a percentage of the cement which reacts to the test reagents in a similar way to an undiscriminated mixture of slag, siliceous and calcareous fillers, calcium sulfate (set regulator) and clinker. It will be impossible to either accurately identify the components of the mixture or to derive their relative proportions.

The particular cements which create difficulties are either those which incorporate calcined schist, high-lime fly ash or industrial pozzolans of the non-ferrous slag types or those of the 'composite type, which can contain a range of constituents of variable composition.

Criticism of the failure to achieve full compliance with the original brief would be unjustified. The selective dissolution techniques (alkaline-EDTA and dilute acid) employed in the methodology can only be expected to discriminate broadly between calcareous and siliceous constituents. In fact, cement clinker and calcium sulfate are soluble in both media. A fuller indication of the relative solubility of some of the constituents of cement is reproduced here in table 8.

Table 8. Relative solubilities of some of the constituents of cement to the selective dissolution media of ENV 196-4

Reagent	Essentially soluble	Essentially insoluble
Alkaline-EDTA solution	Set regulator(s) Clinker Carbonate containing filler(s)	Blastfurnace slag Natural pozzolana Siliceous fly ash Silica fume Siliceous filler(s)
Dilute nitric acid	Set regulator(s) Clinker Blastfurnace slag Carbonate containing filler(s)	Natural pozzolana Siliceous fly ash Silica fume Siliceous filler(s)

Constituents, permissible in common cements, but which are not included in table 8, tend to react as mixtures of both calcareous and siliceous additions, to varying degrees.

In addition to the procedures which employ selective dissolution media and empirical calculation to quantity contents of constituents, sulfide, sulfate and carbon dioxide analyses may be required. The latter two allow quantification of calcium sulfate (set regulator) and calcareous filler content, respectively, whilst the former, sulfide, permits a more accurate determination of blastfurnace slag content when present at higher levels.

As a consequence of the anomalous behaviour of some cements/constituents to the reference methods, "further investigations" are recommended as follows:

"6.2.5.4 Further investigations
If results are anomalous, i.e. when:
- *some of the constituents quantified are different from those which should be present on the basis of the designated type and/or class declared by the supplier;*
- *the content measured for some constituents normally present in the cement leads to its identification within a type and/or class other than those declared by the supplier;*

- the use of a new addition for which experience of the quantitative determination by the present method is considered as yet insufficient,

an inspection body or, failing this, any independent body commissioned by the interested parties to carry out the analyses will proceed, prior to issuing a report of the analysis, to additional investigations with the cement manufacturer.

It can be seen from the above that the methods provide results which are useful and informative rather than definitive and should, therefore, be treated with considerable caution for the purposes of acceptance inspection testing.

On the other hand, the manufacturer has available to him the individual constituents, in addition to the known final cement.   This confers a most significant and fundamental advantage where accurate quantification is required, irrespective of analytical procedure.   Accordingly, a manufacturer's autocontrol records are very unlikely ever to be inferior to the best semi-quantitative estimates of composition derived from the ENV 196-4 procedures.

4.3   Additional chemical test methods for cement
4.3.1   Alkali content [Sodium oxide (Na_2O) and potassium oxide (K_2O)]
Considerable interest has been focused on the determination of alkalis in cement (and additions) over the last two decades. This has, of course, been a direct consequence of the ASR and the precautions advised in order to minimise any associated risk of deterioration to concrete. However, this 'alkali culture' has taken directions in the U.K., which although detailed and coherent, were not overly important to the drafting committee of the European test standard (now BS EN 196-21) for the determination of the alkali content of cement. Consequently, for purposes in the U.K., the methods fail to provide information in a way which is easily assimilated by the engineer. They would, however, provide the basis from which a cement chemist could develop the necessary information, if it were not for the fact that the EN 196-21 methods ..."give values for Na_2O equivalent of cement higher by approximately 0.025% absolute than those obtained using either the former BS 4550: Part 2 methods (*now officially withdrawn but retained in Annex NA to BS EN 196-21*) or the ASTM methods which have been used in the U.K. for the purpose of calculating the 'reactive' alkali content of concrete".

In fact, neither the former BS methods nor the European methods have ever attempted to distinguish directly by measurement, between 'reactive alkali' and unreactive alkali, for the wide range of cement types (or combinations) either used in practice or standardised in EN(V) 197-1. This should not be surprising given the somewhat empirical nature of the guidance which has evolved in the U.K. for taking into account, for example , the reactive/effective alkali contributions of just two of cement's possible additional constituents; fly ash and granulated blastfurnace slag.

The methods of determining alkali contents of cements are rather more 'introspective' and aim essentially to quantify the total amounts of Na_2O and K_2O in the final cement, although even this is to over-simplify the case for 'OPC' type CEM I cements.

The former shortcoming, alkali content over-estimation, has been addressed and resolved in BS EN 196-21 by including an informative national annex entitled ..."Test method for the alkali content of cement to be used for the purpose of calculating the reactive alkali content of concrete". The title makes no reference to reactive alkali content of cement but is, in fact, a slightly revised text of the former BS 4550: Part 2 method. It should be understood that it was this latter method which formed the basis of measurement for the 'nominal 3 kg/m³ $Na_2O(e)$' limit for concrete and the value of '0.6% certified maximum acid soluble alkali content' of a cement.

The latter shortcoming, feasible discrimination between reactive and unreactive alkali will, as a consequence of developments in the understanding of ASR and the poor selectivity and specificity of the alkali determinations available, remain outside standardisation. The provision of relevant information for either current engineering requirements or for developments, should be agreed between the cement manufacturer and the other parties. The U.K. manufacturer can supply alkali information on a variety of bases given his experience and access to the individual constituents of a cement.

In conclusion, it should be noted that there is no specified requirement for alkali content of any cement within the scope of EN(V) 197-1. However, a guaranteed low alkali (LA) sulfate-resisting Portland cement (SRPC) is specified in the current edition of BS 4027[24].

4.4   Reactive calcium oxide and reactive silicon dioxide
4.4.1   Introduction
EN(V) 197-1 has introduced, for the first time in the U.K., a requirement (but not autocontrol) for the sum of the proportions of reactive calcium oxide (CaO) and reactive silicon dioxide (SiO_2). The requirementss is expressed in the 1994 PNE version as "at least 50% by mass [in CEM cement] when the proportions are determined in accordance with EN 196-2". Although such a requirement is almost certainly unnecessary in any definition of performance or quality of a common cement, its inclusion aims to restrict the scope of the specification to cements which are very broadly 'Portland-based'. That is, those for which the hydraulic hardening is primarily due to the hydration of calcium silicates but for which other chemical compounds, e.g. aluminates, may also participate.

4.2.2   Reactive calcium oxide
Reactive calcium oxide (CaO) is defined as: "That fraction of the CaO which under normal hardening conditions can form calcium silicate hydrates or calcium aluminate hydrates. To determine this fraction, subtraction of two quantities of CaO are made from the determined total CaO content. The first subtraction corresponds broadly to the CaO component of any carbonate-containing calcareous constituent (e.g. limestone) which may be present and which is considered to be inert. It is derived by stoichiometric calculation from determined carbon dioxide (CO_2) content (BS EN 196-21), although the actual calculation is not given. The second subtraction corresponds broadly to the CaO component of the calcium sulfate set regulator, although the calculation may over-estimate the quantity. Again, a stoichiometric relationship between the various quantities is indicated but the actual calculation step required to obtain the 'CaO-equivalent' to calcium sulfate ($CaSO_4$) from a measurement of sulfate

(SO$_3$), has been omitted. However, this is a very minor point and does not relate to the earlier mentioned over-estimate. This latter would be a consequence of assuming all the measured sulfate is combined as calcium sulfate, whereas in some cements, these could be a significant quantity combined as alkali sulfate. Even so, this is really only of theoretical interest to a cement chemist rather than conferring any significance at all to the quality of the product.

4.4.3   Reactive silicon dioxide (SiO$_2$)

The concept of what constitutes reactive silicon dioxide in a common cement is even more abstruse than that of reactive calcium oxide. Reactive silicon dioxide is defined empirically by reference to the solubility of a cement to hydrochloric acid and boiling potassium hydroxide (KOH) solution. Unfortunately, the definition in the English is incorrect, either as a result of a mistranslation or, more likely, as a result of a misunderstanding on the part of the drafting panel. This is evidenced by the "Note" in the PNE version which explains the derivation/determination of the quantity in a logical fashion but by cross-reference to the definition, shows the latter to be wrong.

The definition given, is as follows:

"Reactive silicon dioxide (SiO$_2$): That fraction of the silica which, after treatment with hydrochloric acid (HCl), is soluble in boiling potassium hydroxide (KOH) solution".

To be logically correct and consistent with its stated derivation, it should more properly be defined as:

"That fraction of the silica which is rendered soluble by treatment of the cement with hydrochloric acid (HCl), plus that rendered soluble by treatment of the insoluble residue with boiling potassium hydroxide (KOH) solution".

The essence of the determination is that silicon dioxide (silica) present in cementitious calcium silicates (C$_3$S and C$_2$S) or present in, for example, the glassy phases of granulated blastfurnace slag or fly ash, counts as 'reactive silica' for the purposes of the standard. Only 'inert' siliceous components such as silica sand, quartz, mullite, etc. will remain insoluble under the conditions of the test, thereby corresponding to their perceived reactivity in a cement. Yet again, the complete methodology is not given. Strictly speaking an additional test is required for the determination of the silica fraction of the insoluble residue which is not soluble in boiling KOH. This quantity is required for subtraction from the total silica present in the cement, determined according to Clause 13.9 of EN 196-2.

When the necessary calculations for both reactive CaO and reactive SiO$_2$ have been carried out, the quantities are summed as mass percentages and must be greater than or equal to 50%.

4.5   Additional chemical test methods on limestone as a main constituent (CaCO$_3$, clay and TOC)

4.5.1   Introduction

When limestone is used as a main constituent in cement, it must meet three specific chemical requirements (not subject to any statistical autocontrol procedures) in addition to the more general stipulations relating to fillers.

There is a minimum requirement on the calcium carbonate (CaCO$_3$) content, a maximum limit for clay content and a maximum limit for total organic carbon (TOC).

The limiting values are reproduced in table 9:

The term, limestone, is rather unspecific in that it can be applied to a large, petrographically and polygenetic diverse group of sedimentary rocks in which carbonate species exceed non-carbonate; these extend from the soft chalks to the hard carboniferous limestones.

Selected limestone is required for use in a Portland limestone cement in order to

Table 9. Chemical requirements in EN(V) 197-1 for limestone, when used as a main constituent

	EN(V) 197-1 Specification requirements
% $CaCO_3$	≥ 75%
% Total organic carbon[*]	≤ 0.20%
Methylene blue sorption (g/kg)	≤ 12.0

[*] Limestone with a TOC content between 0.20% and 0.5% by mass may also be suitable for producing satisfactory cement with acceptable performance. Until adequate performance tests are developed by TC 51/WG12, cements containing such limestones are permitted to be specified in national standards and other regulations valid in the place where the cement is used.

meet the properties and performance requirements of the specification for the cement. The placing of a lower limit of 75% on the calcium carbonate content of the limestone ensures that this will be the principal component, whilst limiting the possible amounts of sand-sized quartz, magnesium carbonate and clay.

In fact, only a very small quantity of clay-like materials can be tolerated given their propensity to increase water demand (high sorptivity), increase shrinkage, reduce strength by forming impermeable layers around cements grains, and probably impair durability.

The total organic carbon content is determined in order to provide a measure of the oil shale content of the limestone. From previous studies, poor frost resistance has been associated with this component.

4.5.2   Calcium carbonate (CaCO₃) content

The $CaCO_3$ content is calculated from a determination of the total calcium oxide (CaO) content of the limestone. Although no actual test method is specified, the cement manufacturer will almost certainly use his calibrated wavelength dispersive X-ray fluorescence (WDXRF) technique. He could, however, use one of the determinations for cements and constituents given in EN 196-2, starting from clause 13.5 'Decomposition with hydrochloric acid and ammonium chloride etc'. In fact, a variety of analytical methods could be used and, if carefully carried out, would each give equivalent results.

4.5.3   Clay content

The clay content of a selected limestone is to be determined using the methylene blue adsorption test in the French experimental standard AFNOR P18-592, December 1990[25] (a revision of the July 1980 version), according to the final draft (January 1992) of EN(V) 197-1. The March 1994 PNE version of the standard refers to an, as yet, undrafted EN XXX which "will be elaborated by TC 154", the CEN technical committee for aggregates.

It should be apparent from the above that the actual methodology to be applied to limestone as a constituent of cement, is in a process of development. Accordingly, the manufacturer has adopted, in practice, the position documented in Annex NE (normative), to be published in BS EN 196-2, which maintains co-ordination with the revised British Standard, BS 7583: 1992 for Portland limestone cement. Hence, the 1980 version of the French experimental standard is retained in the Annex since the BS was drafted to align with the June 1989 pr ENV 197-1, which also called up the 1980 version. As part of Annex NE, an English translation of P18-592 will be provided. However, the object of the method is the determination of the "blue value" of the fine faction of a sand not a crushed limestone. Accordingly, the details seem to require some modification and, in particular, a sample of crushed limestone should be ground to pass a 90µm sieve and a much reduced test sample mass (approx. 2g) should be taken.

The purpose of the methylene blue (MB) test is to measure the capacity of 'fines' to adsorb a solution of methylene blue dye. Since MB is adsorbed preferentially by clays, organic matter and iron hydroxides, the test offers an overall indication of the surface activity of these species in the limestone. The test is 'titrimetric' in that fixed aliquots of a standard MB dye solution are injected into an aqueous bath containing the sample. The adsorption of MB is checked after each addition by staining a filter paper (stain test).

4.5.4   Total organic carbon (TOC) content

The final draft (January 1992) of ENV 197-1 includes a 'footnote 12)' which calls up a test method for TOC. The method is not currently available in the European documentation but was developed by a working party set up by WG6 (Specifications) of CEN TC51 and subsequently published in the technical journal ZEMENT-KALK-GIPS[26]. The intention within CEN is to either develop the method(s) further or to transcribe them verbatim and standardize the text in a part of the EN 196 series. Indeed, the March 1994 PNE version of EN(V) 197-1 refers to a proposed EN 196-XX indicating that this will be a transcription of the aforementioned paper. In order to make the method(s) available to standards users in the U.K., a National Annex NF (informative) has been prepared for inclusion in BS EN 196-2. Annex NF reproduces the text of the original paper in the journal verbatim, thereby describing a reference method and two alternatives.

The reference method utilises a classical 'wet' oxidation procedure, in which carbon dioxide (carbonate) in the limestone is first liberated by phosphoric acid. The remaining organic carbon is subsequently oxidised to carbon dioxide by treatment with a powerful oxidising mixture. The carbon dioxide evolved is absorbed into a suitable absorbent and determined gravimetrically.

The first alternative method describes a similar procedure, except that the oxidation stage involves treatment in a furnace at 900°C in an oxygen atmosphere.

Alternative method number two describes the principle of an automatic determination using commercially available gas analyzers. In common with the former classical procedures, carbonate CO_2 is first removed using a mineral acid. The carbon content of the residue is then oxidized with oxygen in a high frequency furnace at approximately 1500°C, in the presence of an accelerator. The gas evolved is a mixture of oxygen, carbon dioxide, carbon monoxide, sulfur dioxide and water. Sulfur dioxide is absorbed by treatment with manganese dioxide. Carbon monoxide is oxidised to carbon dioxide using copper oxide and water is absorbed into magnesium perchlorate. The liberated (and generated) carbon dioxide is first absorbed onto a molecular sieve, liberated again and quantitatively determined by a thermal conductivity meter.

Comparison tests have been carried out for all three procedures which indicated that deviations from mean values were not statistically significant.

References

1. European Committee for Standardisation, pr EN 197-1 (PNE version) - *Cement - composition, specifications and conformity criteria - Part 1: Common cements*, First Draft, March 1994, CEN/TC51/WG6 rev.
2. European Committee for Standardisation, pr ENV 197 Final Draft, June 1989, *Cement: Composition, specifications and conformity criteria.*
3. Construction Products Directive (Council Directive of 21 December 1988 on the approximation of laws, regulations and administrative provisions of the Member States relating to construction products (89/106/EEC), Official Journal of the European Communities (No L40 of 11.2.1989, pages 12-26).
4. European Committee for Standardisation. Sub-committee CEN/TC51/WG12: *Additional performance tests.*
5. European Committee for Standardisation. EN 196: Part 1, May 1987, Methods of testing cement; *Part 1: Determination of strength.*
6.&7. European Committee for Standardisation. EN 196: Part 3, May 1987, Methods of testing cement; *Part 3: Determination of setting time and soundness.*
8. European Committee for Standardisation. EN 196: Part 2, May 1987. Methods of testing cement; *Part 2: Chemical analysis of cement.*
9. European Committee for Standardisation. EN 196: Part 5, May 1987, Methods of testing cement; Part 5: *Pozzolanicity test for pozzolanic cements.*

10. British Standards Institution. BS EN 196-21: 1992, Methods of testing cement, Part 21, *Determination of the chloride, carbon dioxide and alkali content of cement.*
11. British Standards Institution. BS EN 196-6: 1992, Methods of testing cement. Part 6. *Determination of fineness.*
12. European Committee for Standardisation. ENV 196-4, Final Draft, March 1993 (English version), (supersedes ENV 196-4: 1989), Methods of testing cement. Part 4: *Quantitative determination of constituents.*
13. International Standards Organisation. ISO 5725-1986 (BS 5497: Part 1: 1987). Precision of test methods: Part 1: *Guide for the determination of repeatability and reproducibility for a standard test method by inter-laboratory tests.*
14. European Committee for Standardisation. Cement - Conformity evaluation. CEN/TC51/WG13, Doc. N31, Rev. 3. (17/3/94) Final version.
15. British Standards Institution. The Kitemark Scheme for Cement; Quality Plan Doc. P00077. BSI QA. 14 January 1992.
16. BCA Eurocements Information Sheet 2, November 1990, *New Test Method for Cement Strength.*
17. International Standards Organisation. ISO/DIS 9277. *Determination of the specific surface area of solids by gas absorption using the BET-Surface.*
18. Commission of the European Communities. Community Bureau of Reference BCR (DGX11), Rue de la Loi 200, B-1049, Brussels (Now part of the Measurements and Testing Programme of DGX11).
19. British Standards Institution. BS 4550: Part 3: Section 3.3, 1978. Methods of testing cement. Part 3. Physical tests, Section 3.3. Fineness test [Withdrawn].
20. British Standards Institution. BS 4550: Part 3: Section 3.2: 1978. Methods of testing cement. Part 3. Physical tests. Section 3.2. Density test [Withdrawn].
21. Hills, L. M. and Kanare, H. M. Fineness Testing of Renewal SRM 114P. NIST Contract No. 43NANB 116945. Report to the U.S. National Institute of Standards and Technology. Submitted by Construction Technology Laboratories Inc., Skokie, IL 60077- U.S.A.
22. British Standards Institution. BS 4550: Part 2: 1970. Methods of testing cement. Part 2. Chemical Tests (Text now withdrawn for chloride and alkali determinations).
23. British Standards Institution. AMD 5713. Amendment No. 3 published and effective from 29 July 1988 to BS 4550: Part 2: 1970. Methods of testing cement. Part 2. Chemical tests. [Withdrawn].
24. British Standards Institution. BS 4027: 1991. Specification for sulfate-resisting Portland cement.
25. ZEMENT-KALK-GIPS. Procedures for the determination of total organic carbon content (TOC) in limestone. No. 8. 1990. pp409-411.
25. AFNOR. Experimental standard P18-592. Aggregates. Methylene blue test. July 1980 (Revised 1990).

Annex 1

Requirements in clauses 4 and 5 of the PNE version (March 1994) of prEN(V) 197-1 indicated by the word "shall"

prEN(V) 197-1	Test method
4. Cement	-
- Cement conforming to this European Standard, termed CEM cement, shall, when appropriately batched and mixed with aggregate and water, be capable of producing concrete or mortar which retains its workability for a sufficient time	
- and shall after defined periods attain specified strength levels and also possess long-term volume stability.	-
- The sum of the proportions of reactive calcium oxide (CaO) and reactive silicon dioxide (SiO_2) in CEM cement shall be at least 50% by mass.	pr EN 197-1, definitions 3.1 + 3.2 (EN 196-2) (EN 196-21)
CEM cements consist of individual small grains of different materials but they shall be statistically homogenous in composition.	-
- A high degree of uniformity in all cement properties shall be obtained through continuous mass production process, in particular, adequate grinding and homogenization processes.	-
- The cement manufacturing process and its control shall ensure that the composition of CEM cements is kept within the limits fixed in this European Standard.	(Certification Scheme)
5.1 Portland cement clinker (K)	-
- Portland cement clinker is a hydraulic material which shall consist of at least two-thirds by mass of calcium silicates $((CaO)_3 \cdot SiO_2$ and $(CaO)_2 \cdot SiO_2))$, the remainder containing aluminium oxide (Al_2O_3), iron oxide (Fe_2O_3) and other compounds.	
- The ratio by mass $(CaO)/(SiO_2)$ shall be not less than 2.0.	(EN 196-2)

prEN(V) 197-1	Test method
The content of magnesium oxide (MgO) <u>shall</u> not exceed 5.0% by mass.	(EN 196-2)
- The raw meal, paste or slurry <u>shall</u> be finely divided, intimately mixed and therefore homogenous.	-
5.2 <u>Granulated blastfurnace slag (S)</u>	-
- It <u>shall</u> contain at least two-thirds by mass of glassy slag.	
- The granulated blastfurnace slag <u>shall</u> consist of at least two-thirds by mass of the sum of CaO, MgO and SiO_2.	(EN 196-2)
- The ratio by mass $(CaO + MgO)/(SiO)_2$ <u>shall</u> exceed 1.0.	(EN 196-2)
5.3 Pozzolanic material (P, Q) 5.3.1 <u>General</u>	prEN 197-1, definition 3.2 (EN 196-2)
- Pozzolanas <u>shall</u> consist essentially of reactive SiO_2 and Al_2O_3.	
- The reactive SiO_2 content <u>shall</u> not be less than 25.0% by mass.	prEN 197-1, definition 3.2 (EN 196-2)
- Pozzolanic materials <u>shall</u> be correctly prepared, i.e. selected, homogenized, dried and comminuted, depending on their state of production or delivery.	-
- They <u>shall</u> not increase the water demand of the cement appreciably, impair the resistance of the concrete or mortar to deterioration in any way or reduce the corrosion protection of the reinforcement.	-
5.4 <u>Fly ash (V,W)</u> 5.4.1 <u>General</u>	EN 196-2
- The loss on ignition of fly ash determined in accordance to EN 196-2 but using an ignition time of 1 hour <u>shall</u> not exceed 5.0% by mass.	

prEN(V) 197-1	Test method
- Ash obtained by other methods <u>shall</u> not be used in cement that conforms to this European Standard.	- A test is not relevant
5.4.2 <u>Siliceous fly ash (V)</u> - It <u>shall</u> consist essentially of reactive SiO_2 and Al_2O_3.	prEN 197-1, definition 3.2 (EN 196-2)
- The proportion of reactive CaO <u>shall</u> be less than 5.0% by mass.	prEN 197-1, definition 3.1 (EN 196-2), (EN 196-21)
- The reactive SiO_2 content of siliceous fly ash conforming to this European Standard <u>shall</u> be not less than 25.0% by mass.	prEN 197-1, definition 3.2 EN 196-2
5.4.3 <u>Calcareous fly ash</u> - It <u>shall</u> consist essentially of reactive calcium oxide CaO, reactive silica SiO_2 and alumina Al_2O_3.	prEN 197-1, definitions 3.1 + 3.2 (EN 196-2) (EN 196-21)
- The proportion of reactive calcium oxide CaO <u>shall</u> not be less than 5.0% by mass.	prEN 197-1, definition 3.1 (EN 196-2), (EN 196-21)
- Calcareous fly ash containing between 5.0% and 15.0% of reactive calcium oxide CaO <u>shall</u> contain not less than 25.0% by mass of reactive silica SiO_2.	prEN 197-1, definitions 3.1 + 3.2 (EN 196-2) (EN 196-21)
- Finely ground calcareous fly ash containing more than 15.0% of reactive calcium oxide CaO <u>shall</u> have a compressive strength of at least 10.0 N/mm^2 at 28 days when tested in accordance with EN 196-1.	EN 196-1
- Before testing, the fly ash <u>shall</u> be ground and the fineness, expressed as the proportion by mass of the ash retained when wet sieved on a 40μm mesh sieve <u>shall</u> be between 10% and 30% by mass.	EN 196-6

prEN(V) 197-1	Test method
- The mortar <u>shall</u> be prepared with ground calcareous fly ash only instead of cement. The mortar specimens <u>shall</u> be demoulded 48h after preparation and then cured in a moist atmosphere of relative humidity at least 90% until tested.	EN 196-1
- The expansion of calcareous fly ash (soundness) <u>shall</u> be less than 10mm when tested in accordance with EN 196-3 using a mixture of 30% by mass of calcareous fly ash ground as described before and 70% by mass of reference cement.	EN 196-3

5.5 Burnt shale (T)

EN 196-1

- Finely ground shale <u>shall</u> have a compressive strength of at least 25.0 N/mm² at 28 days when tested in accordance with EN 196-1. The mortar <u>shall</u> be prepared with finely ground burnt shale only instead of cement. The mortar specimens <u>shall</u> be demoulded 48h after preparation and cured in a moist atmosphere of relative humidity at least 90% until tested.

- The expansion of burnt shale (soundness) <u>shall</u> be less than 10mm tested in accordance with EN 196-3 using mixture of 30% by mass of ground burnt shale and 70% by mass of reference cement.	EN 196-3

5.6 Limestone (L)

- The limestone content ($CaCO_3$) calculated from the CaO-content <u>shall</u> be at least 75% by mass.	(EN 196-2)
- The clay content determined with methylene blue test in accordance with EN XXX <u>shall</u> not exceed 1.20 g/100 g.	EN XXX
- For this test the limestone <u>shall</u> be ground to a fineness of approximately 5000 cm²/g determined as specific surface in accordance with EN 196-6.	EN 196-6
- The total organic carbon content (TOC) <u>shall</u> not exceed 0.20% by mass when tested in accordance with EN 196-XX.	EN 196-XX

prEN(V) 197-1	Test method

5.7 Silica fume (D) —

- The amorphous silica (SiO$_2$) content shall be at least 85% by mass.

| - The loss on ignition shall not exceed 4.0% by mass. | (EN 196-2) |

| - The specific surface (BET) of the untreated silica fume shall be at least 15.0 m^2/g when tested in accordance with ISO/DIS 9277. | ISO/DIS 9277 |

5.8 Filler (F) —

Fillers shall be correctly prepared, i.e. selected, homogenized, dried and comminuted depending on their state of production or delivery.

| - They shall not increase the water demand of the cement appreciably, impair the resistance of the concrete or mortar to deterioration in any way or reduce the corrosion protection of the reinforcement. | - |

5.9 Calcium sulfate   (alternative: is added)

- Calcium sulfate shall be added in small quantities to the other constituents of cement during its manufacture to control setting.

5.10   Additives   - A test is not relevant

- If it does, the quantity shall be stated on the packaging and/or on the delivery note.

- These additives shall not promote corrosion of the reinforcement -
  or impair the properties of the cement or of the concrete or
  mortar made from the cement.

CEMENT - CONFORMITY EVALUATION
THE PRESTANDARD ENV 197-2: 1994

P BROOKBANKS
Quality Controller, Technical Services
Rugby Cement, UK

Abstract
The EC Construction Products Directive of 1988 specifies a number of essential requirements which must be taken into account when European standards for construction materials are written. The CEN committee for cement, TC51, has prepared the European prestandard for common cements ENV 197-1. Clause 9 of that prestandard, relating to conformity criteria, has been revised and incorporated into the draft standard prEN 197-1: 1994. For attestation that a cement conforms to the clause 9 criteria, a scheme has been developed which leads to certification of conformity by an approved certification body. The scheme is based upon autocontrol testing and factory production control operated by the manufacturer and assessed by the approved certification body, together with independent testing of audit samples. The early, draft version of the scheme has been adopted in a number of countries, and in the UK, forms the basis of the BSI Kitemark Scheme for Cement. The final draft of the scheme was awarded the status of a European prestandard - ENV 197-2 at the June 1994 meeting of CEN/TC51. The eventual, harmonised standards, EN 197-1 and EN 197-2 will, together, form a coherent system for attestation of conformity, leading to CE marking of cements.
Keywords: Approved certification body, attestation of conformity, audit testing, autocontrol testing, CE marking, certification of conformity, factory production control, inspection body.

1 Introduction

The creation of the single European market, has produced a consumer market that is the largest in the world. The total gross national product of the European countries and the sales in the construction industry exceed those of the United States or Japan.

Euro-Cements: Impact of ENV 197 on Concrete Construction. Edited by R.K. Dhir and M.R. Jones. Published in 1994 by E & FN Spon, 2-6 Boundary Row, London SE1 8HN. ISBN: 0 419 19980 2.

This fact demonstrates the great importance of the developments in Europe aimed at achieving an open market for construction products and eliminating barriers to trade.

Since 1985, the European Commission has been formulating harmonisation directives for a variety of product types to enable products from different countries of origin to be compared unambiguously. In order for a manufacturer to place his product on the market within Europe, he must demonstrate that it meets the requirements of the relevant directive. Demonstration of compliance with a directive is known as "attestation" and leads to application of the CE mark (Conformité Européenne - see Fig.1).

Figure 1: Certification mark of the European market.

The directive concerning construction products [1] appeared in 1988 and should have been implemented, or incorporated into national legislation in 1991. A number of countries, however, did not put it into force until 1993. In addition, the interpretation of this directive is not uniform and, in consequence, there are a number of problems associated with its implementation.

The Construction Products Directive (CPD), is based on satisfying a number of essential requirements:-

1. Mechanical resistance and stability.
2. Safety in case of fire.
3. Hygiene, health and environment.
4. Safety in use.
5. Protection against noise.
6. Energy and heat retention.

These requirements apply directly to construction works but may influence the technical characteristics of constituent products.   Accordingly, a number of interpretative documents have been prepared to elaborate on the essential requirements and which must be taken into account when European standards for construction materials are formulated. The European Commission has set up a Standing Committee for Construction (SCC) to deal with implementation of the CPD, and to this end, the SCC has also published a number of guidance papers [2].   The very general requirements of the CPD have to be translated into verifiable specifications for construction products.   For this purpose, the European Commission has given the European standardisation body, CEN, a mandate to formulate harmonised European standards. A harmonised standard:

1. Defines the relevant characteristics of the product.
2. Develops the relevant methods to measure these characteristics.

3. Defines levels or classes.
4. Indicates the procedure for attestation of conformity.

In the case of "Cement and Building Limes", this task has been given to CEN/TC51. With regard to cements, this committee has produced the European standard EN 196 - "Methods of testing cement" and the prestandard for common cements ENV 197-1, detailing composition, specifications and conformity criteria for the traditional and well tried cements used in Europe. CEN has also given its Technical Committees the task of preparing, as part of the standards, the requirements and rules for evaluation of conformity (Resolution BT 129/1991). At a later stage, corresponding CEN guidelines were published [3]. CEN/TC51 welcomed this development and accordingly, in mid 1991, set up Working Group 13 (Assessment of Conformity).

The European Cement Association, Cembureau, had already taken an initiative in respect of assessment of conformity, and had produced a draft scheme for certification of European cements. This scheme document was taken by Working Group 13 and developed over the subsequent two years. The final draft of the document was awarded the status of a European prestandard at the CEN/TC51 meeting of June 1994 and became: ENV 197-2 "Cement - Conformity evaluation". This prestandard forms the subject of this paper. It should also be noted, that, in May 1992, CEN/TC51 WG13 was further charged with the task of revising clause 9, conformity criteria, of ENV 197-1: 1992, in order to make it fully complimentary to the certification document. Opportunity was also taken to simplify the clause and to remove redundant terminology. Thus, standardisation and certification have been brought together to form a complete and coherent scheme. The eventual EN 197-1 will give the conformity criteria and EN 197-2 will detail the procedures for evaluation of conformity.

2 Attestation of conformity

2.1 CE marking
The CE mark on a product, affixed via an EC Certificate of Conformity, demonstrates that the product conforms to the requirements of the relevant harmonised European Standard, and that the necessary formal procedures to demonstrate compliance have been followed. It should be noted, that, the CE mark is not of itself a quality mark and that marks of certification bodies (eg. BSI Kitemark) may co-exist with it. The CE mark, indicates only a presumption of conformity with European legislation, enabling the manufacturer to place his product on the market. Cements bearing the CE mark will be permitted free movement throughout the EEC.

2.2 Choice of attestation procedure
Under the CPD, a manufacturer is responsible for attestation that his product conforms to the requirements of the relevant harmonised standard. Annex III of the CPD gives various levels of attestation, depending upon the importance of a product in construction works. Basically, a distinction is made between the following two systems of conformity attestation:-

1. Certification of conformity by an approved certification body.
2. Declaration of conformity by the manufacturer.

The essential objective of a conformity assessment procedure is to enable public authorities to ensure that products placed on the market conform to the requirements expressed in the provisions of the directives, in particular with regard to the health and safety of users or consumers. What the CPD requires to be addressed, therefore, in setting levels of attestation, are the consequences to health and safety of a product's failure in construction works. Article 13 of the CPD names the European Commission as responsible for the specification of procedures for products or families of products. Unfortunately, the Commission has not yet adopted a position with regard to attestation of conformity of building products, especially common cements! In the absence of a Commission decision, the SCC asked CEN/TC 51 to take their guidance paper 8, as the basis for considering a preferred system of conformity attestation for cement.

Because of the important role played by cement in respect of the essential requirements for construction works, CEN/TC 51 considered that certification of conformity was required and that manufacturer's declaration would be inadequate. This viewpoint was reached after the following considerations:-

1. In terms of the essential requirements, cement plays an important role, particularly in respect of "Mechanical resistance and stability".
2. Cement is purchased for a variety of applications, more or less demanding, frequently unknown to the manufacturer.
3. Cement is the most active constituent of concrete and it is important that control of its conformity should be based on a strict procedure.
4. A review of producers in CEN member countries showed that product certification by an approved body was the norm

This view was endorsed by the European trade associations for ready mixed concrete (ERMCO) and precast concrete (BIBM). CEN/TC 104 "Concrete" took a similar view. The SCC has, therefore, recommended to the Commission, that third-party product certification is required for common cements.

3 European cement certification

3.1 Development
Following the publication of the CPD, the European cement industry trade association, Cembureau, took the initiative in 1989, to prepare a possible single scheme for attestation of conformity of European cements, based on the highest level of attestation. The very first draft was prepared by UK members and represented a synthesis of UK and continental practice, in that it combined elements of a quality system (factory production control) with third party product certification, based on autocontrol and audit testing. After initial refinement, a draft was submitted to the EC

in 1990. As described in 2.2 several parties gave advice on the level of attestation that should be adopted for cement.

Working Group 13 of CEN/TC 51, was set up in mid 1991 to consider assessment of conformity for cements. The Cembureau document, then titled "the European Cement Certification Scheme" was taken as a basis for development into an eventual harmonised standard. The document has been through several redrafts, taking account of comments received from member countries. The final draft of March 1994, was approved as a prestandard by CEN/TC 51 in June 1994 and became ENV 197-2 - "Cement - Conformity evaluation". The document has been produced in parallel with the revision of clause 9 of ENV 197-1 and refers to that revised clause, incorporated in the draft standard prEN 197-1:1994.

ENV 197-2 is designed to be rigid enough to give users confidence in the conformity evaluation scheme, yet retaining sufficient flexibility to accommodate different situations and practices.

3.2 Principles of the scheme

The system embodied in ENV 197-2, provides the highest level of attestation under the CPD, based on the procedure given in Section 2(i) of Annex III of that document and resembles a number of schemes currently operating in CEN member countries. The scheme also takes account of the Global Approach to Certification and Testing [4], the SCC guidance papers and relevant clauses of EN 29002 [5].

The scheme incorporates two principal elements:-

1. Factory production control and its assessment.
2. Testing of the finished cement (autocontrol and audit testing).

The responsibilities for these elements are divided between the manufacturer and the approved certification body as follows:-

a) Tasks for the manufacturer:-

1. The manufacturer shall operate factory production control, taking account of those clauses of EN 29002, that are relevant to the manufacture of cement.
2. Conformity of the cement shall be continuously assessed by means of autocontrol testing of samples as per prEN 197-1, clause 9.

b) Tasks for the approved certification body:-

1. Surveillance, assessment and acceptance of factory production control.
2. Evaluation of the results of autocontrol testing of samples.
3. Audit testing of samples taken at the factory (or depot).

It must be emphasised, that, although assessment of factory production control is seen as an essential part of the scheme, it is secondary to testing of the cement. It is the product that is certified and not the system of factory production control. Figure 2 gives an overview of the certification scheme.

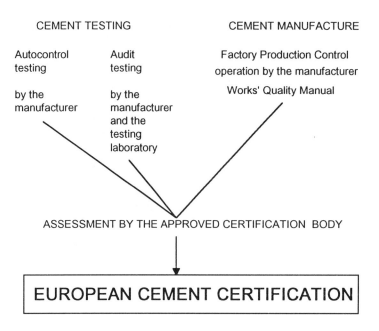

Figure 2. Overview of the European Cement Certification Scheme

3.2.1 Factory production control

Factory production control, is the control of production by the manufacturer to enable the required product characteristics to be achieved. This is, in effect, a management system and the manufacturer is required to produce a Works' quality manual, taking account of those clauses of EN 29002 that are relevant to production and process control of cement. The manufacturers documentation and procedures are given in, or referenced from, the Works' quality manual, which shall, amongst other things, adequately describe:-

1. The quality aims and organisational structure, responsibilities and powers of management with regard to product quality and the means to monitor achievement of the required product quality and the effective operation of factory production control.
2. The manufacturing and quality control techniques processes and systematic actions that will be used.
3. The examinations and tests that will be carried out before, during and after manufacture and their frequency.

As the quality of the finished cement is of primary importance within the scheme, cement grinding is given highest priority in the production process.

The tasks of the approved certification body, concern the surveillance, assessment and acceptance of factory production control as follows:-

1. Verification that the Works' quality manual complies with the requirements of ENV 197-2.
2. Verification that the factory production control is in accordance with the Works' quality manual.
3. Inspection of the manufacturers management reviews of the quality control system.

An inspection body nominated by the approved certification body may be used for this purpose. On-going factory inspection will normally be at a frequency of once per year.

The above tasks apply to established cement production. For a new factory or a new type or class of cement, initial testing and factory inspection are required, according to the relevant clauses.

3.2.2 Autocontrol and audit testing

The manufacturer is required to carry out autocontrol testing on spot samples taken at the point of release from the factory or depot, in accordance with the requirements of clause 9 of prEN 197-1. The results of autocontrol tests must be reported to the approved certification body (or nominated inspection body) for evaluation. The number of evaluations is from 1 - 3 per year and the control period (period over which autocontrol data are assessed) is set at 12 months. Depending on the number of evaluations, control periods may, thus, be consecutive or rolling.

Each evaluation is made on the totality of autocontrol results within the control period and leads, for each property examined, to a single conclusion in respect of the test results as a whole. Provided that each predetermined evaluation demonstrates conformity in respect of statistical criteria (prEN 197-1 clause 9.2.2), then the cement may be deemed conforming, as long as no individual results are outside of limit values (prEN 197-1 clause 9.2.3).

The manufacturers test results are verified by audit testing. The approved certification body arranges for audit samples to be taken (between 6 and 12 per year by agreement) and tested by an approved, independent, testing laboratory. Each audit sample is tested by both the manufacturer and the testing laboratory.

The manufacturers audit test results are checked for representativity against his autocontrol results for the appropriate control period. They are also checked against the testing laboratory results for the same samples, in order to estimate the accuracy of the autocontrol testing. Procedures for these evaluations are given in Annex A of ENV 197-2. For the present, the parameters given, apply only to 28 day compressive strength. Other properties may be checked by suitable statistical methods.

In order to ensure satisfactory application of the scheme, requirements need to be specified for approved certification bodies, inspection bodies and testing laboratories. Such bodies should be expected to comply with the relevant parts of the EN 45000 [6] series of documents and Cembureau has prepared recommendations representing the consensus view of the cement industry. For the present, these recommendations are not included in the certification document. Within the UK, approved testing laboratories for the Kitemark Scheme for Cement are required to be NAMAS accredited in respect of the relevant EN 196 test methods. ENV 197-2 does require testing laboratories to participate in proficiency testing in respect of at least, compressive strength determination.

Appendix 1 of this paper, reproduces table 1 of ENV 197-2, giving the test properties, methods and frequencies.

3.3 Certification

Following satisfactory assessment of the initial testing (autocontrol and audit) and factory inspection, the approved certification body will issue a certificate of conformity to the manufacturer. The certificate will give the standard designation of the cement and contain statements that the cement conforms to the requirements of the technical specification and the certification scheme. The certificate will remain valid unless withdrawn or cancelled as a result of actions taken in the event of non-conformity.

The certificate of conformity will entitle the manufacturer to apply the CE conformity mark to his product. CE marking will only be possible, of course, when the eventual harmonised standard EN 197-1 is implemented.

3.3.1 Intermediaries and Dispatching Centres

Additional requirements are included in the scheme to cover dispatching centres -ie: bulk cement handling facilities not located at the factory, where an intermediary has full responsibility for the cement dispatched. The intermediary may use the conformity mark applied by the manufacturer, provided that he complies satisfactorily with the requirements of clause 10. The requirements specified in that clause, include quality control (incorporating a quality manual), and confirmation autocontrol testing, to ensure that the cement retains its properties.

Appendix 2. of this paper reproduces Table 3. of prEN 197-1, giving properties, methods and minimum testing frequencies for samples taken at dispatching centres.

3.4 Non-conformity

ENV 197-2 includes procedures to be followed by the approved certification body in the event of non-conformity. These procedures cover measures to be taken in the event of non-conformity of the results of autocontrol or audit testing. Actions relate to non-conformity in respect of both statistical and limit value conformity criteria. The procedures are clearly specified in order to achieve uniform implementation by all certification bodies.

Appendix 3 of this paper reproduces table 2 of ENV 197-2, listing actions to be taken by the approved certification body in the event of non-conformity.

4 Future developments

As previously stated, CE marking of cements will not be possible until the technical specification has been developed into the harmonised standard EN 197-1. The certification scheme has now been approved as the prestandard ENV 197-2 but the status of EN cannot be conferred until the Commission finally decide upon the level of attestation of conformity for cement.

In the meantime, a number of member countries have partly or wholly aligned their national standards with ENV 197-1 and in the UK and Belgium, new certification schemes have been introduced, based on the European schemes. In the UK, the BSI Kitemark Scheme for Cement was launched in May 1992. This scheme was based on the early, draft version of the European scheme with BSI Quality Assurance (now BSI Product Certification) as the approved certification body. The Kitemark Scheme is currently being updated to bring it in line with the requirements of ENV 197-2, although certification is still in respect of the 1991 British Standards for cement, which were aligned with the draft, 1989 version of ENV 197. In other countries (including Norway, Spain, Germany and the Netherlands) the national certification scheme is being modified in line with the European scheme.

It is also worth noting, that, the CEN/TC51 Working Groups 10 (Masonry cement) and 11 (Building lime) are to formulate certification procedures on the basis of ENV 197-2, to complement the European prestandards ENV 413 (Masonry cement) and ENV 459 (Building lime), respectively.

In the run up to the implementation of harmonised standards, the European Cement Certification Scheme can be expected to gain ground within Europe, perhaps at a faster pace, now that it has gained the status of an ENV. The co-development of specification and conformity evaluation documents, has produced a complete and coherent scheme, dealing with all aspects of certification.

References

1. Construction Products Directive: European Council Directive of 21.12.88 on the approximation of laws, regulations and administrative provisions of the Member States relating to construction products (89/106/EEC).
2. Guidance papers prepared by the European Commissions' Standing Committee for Construction.
   Guidance paper No.5: Information to accompany the EC mark for construction products.
   Guidance paper No.6: Guidelines for the designation of approved bodies in the field of the Council Directive 89/106/EEC on construction products.
   Guidance paper No.7: Guidelines for the performance of the factory production control for construction products.
   Guidance paper No.8: Guidelines for the choice of conformity attestation procedure.
   Guidance paper No.9: Guidelines for the certification of construction products by an approved certification body.
   Guidance paper No.10: Guidelines for the assessment and certification of the factory production control by an approved body.
3. CEN/CS, TC Guidelines on requirements in European standards concerning the evaluation of conformity (dd.5.2.1993).
4. Global Approach to Certification and Testing Communication from the European Commission to the Council (COM (89) 209 final - SYN 208). Approved in principle by the Council on 21.12.89 and Council decision of 13.12.90 concerning

the modules for the various phases of the conformity assessment procedures which are intended to be used in the technical harmonisation directives (90/683/EEC).

5. European Standard EN 29002 "Quality Systems - Model for quality assurance in production and installation".

6. European Standard EN 45001 "General criteria for the operation of testing laboratories".
European Standard EN 45011 "General criteria for certification bodies operating product certification".

Appendix 1. Cement testing : Properties, Methods and Minimum Testing Frequencies (1) (Table 1. of ENV 197-2)

Property	Type(s)/strength class(es) of cement to be tested (2)	Test Method (3)	Minimum frequency of testing				
			By the manufacturer — Autocontrol testing			By the testing laboratory — Audit testing	
			As a rule (Clause 5.2.1) (4)	For 2 months following receipt of a warning (Clause 8.2.1) (5)	Initial period for a new type of cement (Clause 5.2.1)	as a rule (Clause 6.4)	initial period (Clause 6.6)
Strength after							
- 2 days	All except 32,5	} EN 196, Part 1	2/week	4/week	4/week	} 6-12/year	Number of samples as agreed with the certification body to be collected over the initial period
- 7 days	32,5	}				}	
- 28 days	All	}				}	
Initial setting time	All	EN 196, Part 3	2/week	4/week	4/week	}	
Soundness	All	EN 196, Part 3	1/week	2/week	4/week	}	
Loss on ignition	CEM I, CEM III	EN 196, Part 2	2/month (6)	4/month	1/week	}	
Insoluble residue	CEM I, CEM III	EN 196, Part 2	2/month (6)	4/month	1/week	}	
Sulfate content	All	EN 196, Part 2	2/week	4/week	4/week	}	
Chloride content	All	EN 196, Part 21	2/month (6)	4/month	1/week	}	
Pozzolanicity	CEM IV	EN 196, Part 5	2/month	4/month	1/week	}	
Composition	All	(7)	1/month	-	1/week	}	

(1) The methods used to take and prepare samples shall be in accordance with the requirements of EN 196, Part 7.
(2) See ENV 197-1 for description of cement types/strength classes.
(3) Where allowed in the relevant EN 196 standard, other methods may be used provided they give results equivalent to those obtained with the reference method.
(4) Frequencies are as in ENV 197-1 *). Control period for assessment of conformity = 12 months.
(5) Frequencies are doubled compared with those for "as a rule" testing.
(6) When none of the test results exceeds 50% of the characteristic value the frequency may be reduced to 1 per month.
(7) Appropriate test method chosen by the manufacturer and agreed by the certification body.

*) Until ENV 197-1 is revised, references to clause 9 of ENV 197-1 are to the revised version of clause 9 in prEN197-1, First Draft, January 1994, prepared by CEN/TC51/WG6 rev.

Appendix 2. Testing of cement samples taken at dispatching centres: Properties, Methods and Minimum Testing frequencies (1) (Table 3. of ENV 197-2)

Property	Types / Strength class(es) of cement to be tested (2)	Test method (3)	Minimum testing frequencies		
			By the intermediary (Confirmation autocontrol)		By the testing laboratory (Audit testing)
			Cement stored at the dispatching centre	Cement transhipped at the dispatching centre	
Strength after					
- 2 days	All except 32,5	}	}	}	}
- 7 days	32,5	} EN 196, Part 1	1/week	}	}
- 28 days	All	}	}	} 1/delivered lot	} } 3/year
Initial setting time	All	EN 196, Part 3	1/week	} but at least 1/500 tonnes	}
Loss on ignition		}	}	}	}
	CEM I, CEM III	} EN 196, Part2	1/week	}	}
Insoluble residue		}	}	}	}
Pozzolanicity	CEM IV	EN 196, Part 5	2/month	}	}

(1) The methods used to take and prepare spot samples shall be in accordance with the requirements of EN 196, Part 7.
(2) See ENV 197-1 for description of cement types/strength classes.
(3) Where allowed in the relevant EN 196 standard, other methods may be used provided they give results equivalent to those obtained with the reference method.

Appendix 3. Actions to be taken by the Certification Body in the event of Non-Conformity of the Results of Autocontrol and/or Audit Testing (Table 2. of ENV 197-2)

	Item		Non-conformity of test result(s) (1)	Action to be taken by Certification Body		
				Issue of a Complaint	Issue of a Complaint plus Warning (2)	Withdrawal of Certificate of Conformity (4)
Characteristic value	Autocontrol testing	All results in control period	Non-conformity of the test results with the requirements of ENV 197-1, clause 9.2.2	First non-conformity of the test results	Non-conformity of the test results for the same property in 2 consecutive statistical assessments	Non-conformity of the test results for the same property in 3 consecutive statistical assessments
Limit value		Individual results	Non-conformity of any result with the requirements of ENV 197-1, clause 9.2.3	First non-conformity of a test result	Second non-conformity of a test result for the same property within 12 months (3)	Third non-conformity of a test result for the same property within 12 months (3)
	Audit testing	Individual results (6-12) samples	Non-conformity of any result with the requirements of ENV 197-1, clause 9.2.3	First non-conformity of a test result	Second non-conformity of a test result for the same property within 12 months (3)	Third non-conformity of a test result for the same property within 12 months (3)

(1) Non-conformities for different properties are treated separately.

(2) The minimum frequency of autocontrol testing shall be doubled for a period of 2 months following receipt of a complaint plus warning (see also Table 1.).

(3) Only if information on the preceding non-conforming test result has been available at the time of sampling.

(4) Withdrawal is always based on a case by case assessment of the history.

PERFORMANCE OF LIMESTONE FILLER CEMENT CONCRETE

J D MATTHEWS
Head, Silicate Chemistry Section
Building Research Establishment, UK

Abstract
This paper reports the results of five-year durability tests carried out
on concretes made with limestone filler cements. A wide-ranging
programme was established by a joint Building Research
Establishment/British Cement Association Working Party to test the
properties and the effects on concrete durability of cements containing
additions of 5% and 25% limestone filler. Short-term data were presented
at a public seminar held at BRE in 1989 and some of the key results,
covering concrete water demand, oxygen permeability and freeze-thaw
testing, are summarised in the present paper. Five-year test results on
compressive strength, carbonation, sulphate resistance, chloride
penetration and rebar corrosion are also presented. The results indicate
that the performance of cements containing 5% limestone is, overall,
indistinguishable from that of OPC without additions, vindicating the
decision to permit such additions under British Standards. The
performance of cements containing 25% limestone is akin to what would be
expected from a 'cement' with only 75% cementitious material and
recommendations adopted in the recent BS for Portland limestone cement,
including the need to increase cement contents to maintain concrete
grade, appear to be fully justified.
Keywords: Carbonation, chloride penetration, concrete durability,
freeze-thaw, limestone fillers, permeability, rebar corrosion, sulphate
resistance.

1 Introduction

In 1986 a joint Building Research Establishment (BRE)/British Cement
Association (BCA) Working Party agreed a programme of research to
investigate the effect on cement and concrete properties of the addition
of calcareous fillers to ordinary and rapid-hardening Portland cements.
The work programme was divided between BRE and the UK cement
manufacturers and work commenced in the summer of 1987. Cements with
calcareous additions of 5% and 25% (approximately) by mass were studied.
These addition levels were chosen because (i) the European Pre-Standard
for cement, ENV 197-1[1] and its earlier drafts which were available at

Euro-Cements: Impact of ENV 197 on Concrete Construction. Edited by R.K. Dhir and
M.R. Jones. Published in 1994 by E & FN Spon, 2–6 Boundary Row, London SE1 8HN.
ISBN: 0 419 19980 2.

the time that the research programme was established, permit additions of up to 5% of minor additional constituents, including limestone, to all cement types; and (ii) the earlier drafts of ENV 197-1 included a limestone-filler cement with a maximum limestone content of 20%, although at the time of designing the programme it was unclear whether this maximum value would be 20 or 25%, the latter being chosen for this work in order to represent the possible extreme situation.

The situation has changed somewhat since the inception of this work. ENV 197-1 was published in 1992 and now contains two types of Portland limestone cement, permitted to contain (i) 6 - 20% limestone (Type IIA-L) or (ii) 21 - 35% limestone (Type IIB-L) of defined purity. Since in this work the levels of addition were only approximate, relevance of the results to both of the above types has been assumed.

The work programme included the following elements:-

. characterisation of chemical and physical properties of cements (chemical analysis, density, fineness);
. cement paste properties (setting time, soundness, heat evolution);
. effects on fresh concrete (water demand, air content, bleeding);
. compressive strength development of concrete;
. concrete durability (freeze-thaw resistance, carbonation, sulphate resistance, oxygen permeability, sorptivity and protection of steel reinforcement).

Concrete durability tests were carried out on mixes designed to equal cement content and workability, the latter being measured by slump and controlled by varying the water/cement ratio for different cements. Most work was carried out on a mix with a cement content of 300 kg/m^3 and a nominal water/cement ratio of 0.60 (designated mix C in the programme). However, subsidiary tests on mixes with cement contents and nominal water/cement ratios of 250/0.80 (mix A) and 350/0.50 (mix E) were also carried out for selected cements.

For the main test programme, five sources of Portland cement were used and to each was added a nominal 5% or 25% of limestone. In addition, two pfa cements containing a nominal 30% pfa were included in the programme for comparative purposes. The cements were prepared by individual cement manufacturers and the method of preparation, ie by intergrinding or blending the components, depended upon the particular circumstances at the works preparing the cement. In general, cements with 5% limestone addition were prepared by blending OPC and ground limestone or by grinding a mixture of clinker, gypsum and limestone to a slightly higher fineness than OPC. In contrast, and in order to minimise early strength reductions, cements with 25% limestone were usually prepared by blending rapid-hardening Portland cement (RHPC) with limestone or by intergrinding clinker, gypsum and limestone to a significantly higher fineness than is usual for OPC. In addition to this main programme, individual cement manufacturers also tested materials of particular interest to themselves.

The results of the test programme, including all short-term data and durability tests up to two years, were reported in a series of papers presented at a public seminar held at BRE on 28 November 1989. Each presentation dealt with a different topic and the full set of papers has recently been published as a BRE report[2].

The data presented in the seminar papers made a significant contribution to the drafting of a British Standard for Portland limestone cement, with a maximum limestone content of 20%, published in 1992[3].

Five-year durability tests at BRE have now been completed and the results are presented in this paper, together with a summary of the short-term data on fresh concrete properties, oxygen permeability and freeze-thaw tests.

2 Experimental

A complete synopsis of the test programme, chemical analyses of materials and a full list of cement formulations have previously been given[2]. However, to assist interpretation of the present paper, formulations of cements tested at BRE are given again in Table 1. It was previously noted that the limestone filler used with cement series E was deliberately chosen as an example of a limestone which would not be permitted by ENV 197-1 due to its high clay content. It should also be noted that cements G5 and H5 were inadvertently made by blending 5% limestone with RHPC rather than OPC. This was corrected by producing cements G5X and H5X but it was decided to retain G5 and H5 in the test programme.

Table 1. Formulation of cements

Cement code	Base cement	Addition	Prep Method*
DO	OPC	-	-
D5R	OPC	5% raw meal	I
DOX	OPC#	-	-
D5L	OPC#	5% limestone	B
D25	OPC#	25% limestone	B
EO	OPC	-	-
E5	OPC	5% limestone	I
E25	OPC	25% limestone	I
FFB	OPC	30% pfa	B
FO	OPC	-	-
F5L	OPC	5% limestone	B
F5R	OPC	5% raw meal	B
F25	RHPC	25% limestone	B
FGO	OPCΔ	-	-
FFA	OPC	28% pfa	I
GO	OPC	-	-
G5X	OPC	5% limestone	B
G25	RHPC	25% limestone	B
G5	RHPC	5% limestone	B
HO	OPC	-	-
H5X	OPC	5% limestone	B
H25	RHPC	25% limestone	B
H5	RHPC	5% limestone	B

* B = Blended   I = Interground
# second sample of OPC DO
Δ coarse ground OPC

As noted above, most of the durability tests were carried out on concrete mix C (300 kg/m^3; w/c ~0.60), but certain tests were also carried out on mix A (250 kg/m^3; w/c ~0.80) and mix E (350 kg/m^3; w/c ~0.50).

The tests carried out on the various mixes by BRE were as follows:-

Mix A: Compressive strength (air-stored and water-stored) up to one year
Carbonation

Mix C: Compressive strength (air-stored and water-stored) up to five years
Carbonation
Freeze-thaw resistance (without air entrainment)
Oxygen permeability
Sulphate resistance
Chloride penetration and corrosion of rebars in marine-exposed specimens
Corrosion of rebars in externally-exposed (but sheltered) specimens

Mix E: Compressive strength (air-stored and water-stored) up to one year
Carbonation
Freeze-thaw resistance (with and without air entrainment)

Work on mix C concretes was carried out with the complete range of cements but work on mixes A and E was carried out on the F series of cements only (see Table 1), together with pfa cement FFB, for which the base OPC was different from the remainder of the F series. In addition, freeze-thaw testing on mix E with air entrainment was also carried out on all the cements containing 25% limestone.

Early-age data on fresh concrete properties, compressive strengths, permeability and freeze-thaw tests have already been reported[2], but they are summarised below for completeness. Two-year durability data on carbonation, sulphate resistance, chloride penetration and rebar corrosion have also been reported previously[2] and the following paragraphs describe the continuation of these tests to an age of five years.

2.1 Concrete mixes

The nominal mix proportions of mixes A, C and E are given in Table 2. As noted above, w/c ratios were varied in order to meet target slump values of 60 - 70 mm. Thames Valley aggregates (coarse and fine) were used throughout and aggregate properties are given in Table 3. Values of

Table 2. Nominal concrete mix proportions

Mix	Cement (kg/m3)	Aggregates (kg/m3)			Fines (%)
		20-10mm	10-5mm	5mm down	
A	250	729	365	826	43
C	300	738	369	738	40
E	350	740	370	710	39

Table 3. Properties of Thames Valley gravel aggregates

BS sieve size	Percentage by mass passing		
	20-10mm	10-5mm	5mm down
20mm	100	-	-
10mm	10	100	-
5mm	0.3	9	100
2.36mm	-	0.5	87
1.18mm	-	-	74
600μm	-	-	58
300μm	-	-	22
150μm	-	-	3.8
75μm	-	-	0.6

Other properties	20-10mm	10-5mm	5mm down
Clay/silt/fine dust content (%)	-	-	0.4
Relative density OD basis	2.52	2.43	2.58
Relative density SSD basis	2.56	2.51	2.61
Apparent relative density	2.61	2.63	2.66
Water absorption (%)	1.4	3.1	1.1
Bulk density (OD) compacted (kg/m3)	1500	1420	1740
Bulk density (OD) uncompacted (kg/m3)	1400	1370	1660
10% fines value (kN)	240	-	-

OD = Oven dry   SSD = Saturated surface dry

total w/c ratios, wet concrete density and workability data are given together with compressive strengths in Table 4 for mix C and Table 5 for mixes A and E.

2.2 Concrete water demand
Concrete water demand data have previously been discussed in detail[2]. For the equal slump mix C concretes prepared at BRE, a mean increase of 0.01 in total w/c ratio was observed for concretes made with cements containing 5% limestone additions, with a further increase of 0.01 between the 5% and 25% limestone cements. This analysis excludes data on cement E25 for which a significantly higher w/c ratio, thought to be associated with the high clay content of limestone E[2], was observed.

2.3 Compressive strength tests
At an age of five years, compressive strength tests were carried out only on water-stored 100 mm cubes for mix C concretes. Three replicate specimens were used for each test and results, together with all earlier compressive strength results, are given in Table 4. For completeness, earlier compressive strength data on mixes A and E for the F series cements are given in Table 5, together with data on air entrained concretes based on mix E.

2.4 Oxygen permeability tests
Oxygen permeability data have previously been discussed in detail[2]. For the mix C concretes cast at BRE, after demoulding at one day concrete cylinders (300 mm x 150 mm diameter) were either stored in water at 20°C or in air at 20°C and 65% relative humidity. At an age of 28 days, three

Table 4. Fresh concrete properties and compressive strengths (mix C concretes)

Cement	Total w/c	Density (kg/m3)	Slump (mm)	CF	Compressive strengths (MN/m2)													
					Air stored						Water stored						
					1d	3d	7d	28d	90d	1y	3d	7d	28d	90d	1y	2y	5y
DO	0.64	2380	65	0.91	9.0	18.1	23.6	32.2	35.8	33.4	18.9	24.4	40.3	50.8	56.1	58.6	62.8
D5R	0.66	2370	50	0.92	10.2	20.3	24.9	32.2	32.5	33.2	21.5	27.8	38.4	45.3	49.6	53.9	56.2
DOX	0.63	2360	65	0.93	8.0	19.0	25.6	31.9	31.4	33.3	19.7	30.2	43.5	49.6	54.2	55.7	61.5
D5L	0.62	2360	60	0.93	7.9	17.6	22.6	27.1	28.6	31.0	18.4	24.3	35.2	40.5	47.5	49.8	53.0
D25	0.65	2340	65	0.95	5.5	12.2	15.2	19.9	20.3	20.9	12.6	17.1	23.2	26.4	29.9	31.5	33.8
EO	0.63	2360	70	0.93	12.3	22.3	29.1	37.3	36.3	36.6	23.6	33.7	45.3	51.6	55.3	58.4	61.1
E5	0.63	2370	70	0.93	9.7	22.3	31.7	37.6	37.9	37.1	23.9	35.1	46.5	50.7	54.9	56.0	59.6
E25	0.69	2340	50	0.93	6.3	15.0	19.4	23.6	23.5	21.6	14.6	20.7	26.2	29.7	32.8	34.9	37.2
FFB	0.59	2380	70	0.93	8.1	17.0	22.5	27.8	27.4	29.2	19.2	28.5	39.3	49.0	58.5	64.8	65.1
FO	0.62	2360	60	0.92	10.7	23.5	31.3	37.2	38.8	41.1	23.2	32.2	47.5	53.2	58.9	57.4	62.8
F5L	0.63	2350	60	0.94	10.9	23.6	30.6	35.4	37.6	35.5	22.5	31.1	44.6	51.3	55.5	57.0	58.7
F5R	0.63	2370	55	0.93	10.3	20.8	28.4	36.7	36.2	36.2	20.8	30.8	43.6	50.4	54.7	57.9	60.0
F25	0.64	2340	65	0.95	8.8	17.7	23.9	29.8	30.9	29.8	18.3	23.9	33.1	36.4	39.4	41.2	43.0
FGO	0.63	2380	80	0.94	6.8	16.5	23.5	32.8	33.4	31.2	16.7	28.9	42.3	48.7	50.8	55.9	57.7
FFA	0.56	2390	50	0.92	7.2	16.7	23.2	29.6	31.2	31.5	18.3	27.1	41.8	55.5	65.0	69.9	68.8
GO	0.64	2350	70	0.95	10.0	24.4	30.0	35.1	37.1	34.7	24.2	35.0	44.2	45.4	49.6	53.2	55.0
G5X	0.64	2350	65	0.93	9.2	22.3	31.0	38.7	40.3	38.1	24.2	36.3	45.6	48.9	51.8	53.3	57.0
G25	0.65	2350	70	0.95	9.3	20.5	26.1	29.1	30.3	29.4	21.9	28.1	34.1	35.9	37.7	40.8	42.4
G5	0.64	2350	60	0.94	12.6	27.6	33.8	40.6	39.0	38.1	29.4	38.2	47.8	51.4	51.5	54.4	53.7
HO	0.63	2370	65	0.92	10.6	21.2	30.0	38.3	37.4	35.7	24.7	35.5	48.8	53.3	54.4	56.3	60.3
H5X	0.64	2360	80	0.96	9.4	21.4	29.5	33.9	35.2	31.9	21.4	33.9	44.1	48.0	50.8	52.8	57.0
H25	0.65	2350	80	0.95	9.2	16.8	22.2	25.9	26.3	24.5	17.0	24.0	30.3	31.5	34.6	35.7	37.8
H5	0.63	2370	60	0.93	14.7	26.7	35.6	40.5	40.4	36.1	29.3	37.6	46.3	49.4	51.6	54.8	57.5

Table 5. Fresh concrete properties and compressive strengths (mix A and mix E concretes)

Cement	Total w/c	Slump (mm)	Compressive strength (MN/m2)					
			Air stored			Water stored		
			1d	28d	1y	28d	1y	
FO	0.78	45	6.0	23.7	25.9	30.8	39.4	
F5L	0.79	70	6.7	24.4	25.7	26.9	35.0	
F5R	0.78	70	6.7	24.0	25.4	27.2	35.7	
F25	0.80	90	5.2	17.8	17.7	18.8	24.2	mix A
FGO	0.79	70	4.4	19.1	21.9	26.5	35.6	
FFA	0.72	70	4.5	20.0	22.5	21.7	44.3	
FFB	0.72	60	4.5	20.8	22.1	23.9	41.6	
FO	0.51	40	20.3	50.9	51.7	56.2	67.8	
F5L	0.52	60	16.7	45.7	49.6	53.7	66.1	
F5R	0.51	40	17.1	45.6	49.3	53.0	67.7	
F25	0.54	70	13.0	33.8	37.0	40.9	49.4	mix E
FGO	0.52	65	12.3	38.8	43.6	50.7	63.9	
FFA	0.49	90	10.9	34.9	40.6	46.2	72.3	
FFB	0.50	85	11.7	35.6	39.4	46.9	68.7	

	AEA dose (ml / kg cement)	% Air	28 day strength (MN/m2)	
FO	1.1	6.1	39.6	
F5L	1.1	6.0	38.2	
F5R	1.1	5.9	36.2	
F25	1.4	5.6	30.3	
FGO	0.8	6.6	36.3	
FFA	2.0	6.2	33.7	
FFB	2.5	5.5	29.7	mix E plus air
D25	1.3	6.3	21.3	
E25	2.1	6.4	23.4	
G25	1.3	5.5	27.3	
H25	1.3	5.9	28.5	

50 mm thick slices were sawn from the top of each cylinder and these slices were then conditioned in air at 20°C and 65% rh until tested at an age of 100 days. The test method employed was that described by Lawrence[4]. After testing, the specimens were returned to air storage and repeat tests were carried out an an age of 400 days. Oxygen permeability tests at 28 days on oven-dried samples were also carried out by one of the participating cement industry laboratories and these results have also been discussed previously[2].

2.5 Freeze-thaw tests

Freeze-thaw tests were carried out at BRE using a procedure adapted from the method given in BS 5075[5], whilst tests in participating cement industry laboratories employed the method given in ASTM C-666[6]. The procedure employed at BRE consisted of cycling concrete prisms (76 x 76 x 305 mm) between -15°C and +16°C on a daily basis, deterioration being monitored by length change and weight loss. Specimens were water-cured for 14 days before commencing the tests and were freeze-thaw cycled under water throughout the test. Tests were carried out on mix C concretes, mix E concretes (F series plus pfa cements only) and mix E concretes with air entrainment (F series, pfa and 25% limestone cements). Three replicate specimens were used for each test. The results have previously been discussed in detail [2].

2.6 Carbonation tests

Carbonation tests were carried out on 75 x 75 x 200 mm prisms at an age of five years by taking a slice approximately 30 mm thick using a rock splitter and then spraying the freshly broken face of the slice with phenolphthalein indicator. Tests were carried out on mix C concretes which had been moist cured for 1 or 3 days prior to exposure indoors at 20°C and 65% RH or outdoors but sheltered from direct rainfall. Tests were also carried out on mix A and mix E concretes. For these specimens, only a 1 day cure was used. Duplicate specimens were used for each test and the five-year results are given in Table 6. Earlier carbonation measurements were made at ages of 28 and 91 days and 1 and 2 years and were fully reported previously[2].

Additional carbonation tests were carried out when 100 x 100 x 300 mm reinforced prisms were broken open to examine the condition of the reinforcing bars (see Section 2.9 below). These specimens were again mix C concretes which were either well cured (28 days in water) or poorly cured (1 day in moist air) before exposure in the outdoor sheltered environment. Measurements were made by breaking off a thin slice at each end of each prism and spraying the freshly broken face of the main body of the prism with phenolphthalein indicator. Thus, both ends of each prism were measured, and duplicate prisms were used for each test. Results are also given in Table 6. Although more difficult to measure than the unreinforced prisms because of the difficulty in attaining a flat surface when reinforcing bars were protruding, a reasonably good correspondence was noted between the data from the poorly cured reinforced prisms and the poorly cured (ie 1 day moist air) unreinforced prisms stored in the same outdoor environment (columns 3 and 9 in Table 6).

2.7 Sulphate resistance tests

Sulphate resistance tests were carried out on 100 mm cubes (mix C concretes) cured for 28 days in water and then stored in sodium sulphate (1.5% SO_3; solution I) or magnesium sulphate (0.35 SO_3; solution C and 1.5% SO_3; solution E) at 20°C with the solutions being changed every three months. Specimens (three replicate) were tested by measurement of wear rating and compressive strength (not a true compressive strength due to the reduced surface area of deteriorated specimens). Wear rating was determined by measuring the extent of loss of concrete from cube corners along the diagonals of the trowelled and opposite faces, so that all eight corners were measured. These values were then summed for the set of three cubes tested at each age and then divided by six to give a quantity termed the wear rating per face. It should be noted that in the earlier results reported in reference 2, measurements of loss of material from deteriorated specimens were termed 'corrosion assessment' rather than wear rating. Both sets of values are average values per face but the change in nomenclature has been made to distinguish the values from corrosion assessment measurements reported by Harrison[7] which are values per corner and furthermore only apply to the trowelled faces of specimens. Measured compressive strengths of five-year sulphate-stored specimens are given, together with corresponding one and two year data previously reported[2] in Table 7. Values of compressive strengths as a

Table 6. Five year carbonation test results

Cement	Five year carbonation depths (mm)								Reinforced prisms	
	Unreinforced prisms								Mix C	
	Mix A		Mix C				Mix E			
	Curing / storage condition									
	1	2	1	2	3	4	1	2	1	5
DO			8.0	20.5	5.0	13.0			11.5	2.0
D5R			9.0	18.5	6.5	13.0			10.5	4.5
DOX			10.0	19.0	7.5	12.0			7.5	5.5
D5L			9.5	19.0	8.0	14.0			9.0	5.0
D25			17.0	26.5	15.5	21.5			14.5	12.0
EO			9.0	22.0	4.0	12.5			11.5	1.5
E5			6.5	18.0	4.5	12.5			8.0	2.5
E25			13.5	28.5	10.5	20.0			16.0	11.5
FFB	20.0	29.0	12.0	21.5	8.0	15.0	10.0	16.0	13.5	6.5
FO	14.5	23.5	11.0	19.0	6.0	12.0	5.5	12.0	6.5	1.5
F5L	15.5	26.0	11.0	19.0	7.5	12.0	6.0	12.0	9.5	2.5
F5R	15.0	24.0	11.0	19.0	7.0	12.5	5.5	12.5	10.0	3.0
F25	25.0	f.c	14.5	22.0	10.0	17.0	9.5	17.5	14.5	8.0
FGO	20.5	32.5	13.0	20.5	7.5	14.5	10.5	17.5	14.0	2.5
FFA	22.5	f.c.	13.5	21.5	9.0	15.0	9.5	17.5	13.0	6.0
GO			7.0	15.0	5.0	10.5			9.0	1.5
G5X			9.0	14.5	5.5	9.5			9.0	3.5
G25			15.0	20.5	10.0	15.0			12.5	8.5
G5			8.0	14.5	4.0	9.0			6.5	2.0
HO			9.0	21.0	4.0	11.5			11.0	1.5
H5X			10.5	21.0	5.5	12.5			13.5	5.5
H25			15.0	26.0	12.5	18.5			15.5	10.0
H5			7.0	17.0	3.5	12.0			9.0	4.5

Curing/storage :   1=1day / outdoor ; 2=1 day / indoor ; 3=3 days / outdoor ;
4=3 days / indoor ; 5=28 days / outdoor
f.c.=fully carbonated

percentage of the corresponding water-stored compressive strengths ('percentage strength retained') and wear ratings are given in Table 8.

2.8 Chloride penetration and rebar corrosion in marine-exposed specimens
Chloride penetration measurements were made on 100 x 100 x 300 mm reinforced prisms (mix C concretes) recovered from the tidal zone of the BRE marine exposure site at Shoeburyness in Essex. Specimens were water cured for a minimum period of 28 days before exposure, the exact period depending upon the logistics of arranging site visits. The maximum curing period received by any specimens was 52 days - any possible systematic influence of variation in curing period upon chloride penetration has been considered and rejected.

Table 7. Compressive strengths of sulphate-stored cubes

	Compressive strength (MN/m2)											
	1 year				2 years				5 years			
	Water	Solution			Water	Solution			Water	Solution		
Cement		I	C	E		I	C	E		I	C	E
DO	56.1	55.7	56.7	51.6	58.6	60.6	58.7	42.2	62.8	58.3	55.6	28.5
D5R	49.6	51.7	50.6	49.7	53.9	55.4	53.3	44.9	56.2	50.5	55.5	29.5
DOX	54.2	54.7	54.2	52.0	55.7	57.4	56.9	52.2	61.5	52.2	56.0	35.1
D5L	47.5	48.0	47.6	45.8	49.8	50.6	51.9	49.9	53.0	48.2	49.7	36.2
D25	29.9	32.1	31.0	29.1	31.5	33.8	33.2	31.5	33.8	31.5	30.8	22.2
EO	55.3	56.0	56.9	44.4	58.4	58.0	56.4	39.4	61.1	47.2	56.8	26.0
E5	54.9	55.0	54.7	47.4	56.0	54.3	58.7	37.7	59.6	42.3	53.3	16.2
E25	32.8	33.1	34.3	29.8	34.9	36.6	36.1	25.5	37.2	34.7	36.2	9.5
FFB	58.5	57.2	55.9	48.3	64.8	60.7	63.2	44.5	65.1	60.6	60.3	34.9
FO	58.9	59.2	55.8	51.7	57.4	57.4	56.8	47.9	62.8	55.2	40.5	39.0
F5L	55.5	55.3	55.9	46.6	57.0	55.7	58.3	31.8	58.7	47.3	55.0	0.0
F5R	54.7	55.1	54.4	48.0	57.9	56.6	57.4	34.3	60.0	44.8	51.7	10.7
F25	39.4	38.9	37.6	31.6	41.2	40.3	36.7	32.0	43.0	26.2	8.7	3.8
FGO	50.8	51.2	53.5	43.7	55.9	46.1	55.9	27.6	57.7	0.0	53.8	17.7
FFA	65.0	66.0	65.6	56.6	69.9	69.5	73.1	42.6	68.8	68.8	69.0	28.0
GO	49.6	38.2	43.9	25.9	53.2	15.7	33.6	10.9	55.0	0.0	0.0	0.0
G5X	51.8	28.2	42.8	34.1	53.3	0.0	19.2	14.6	57.0	0.0	0.0	0.0
G25	37.7	22.5	23.7	13.2	40.8	3.7	7.2	0.0	42.4	0.0	0.0	0.0
G5	51.5	42.1	49.6	26.1	54.4	20.4	31.6	9.9	53.7	0.0	0.0	0.0
HO	54.4	44.4	53.6	35.7	56.3	24.4	45.6	19.2	60.3	0.0	19.0	0.0
H5X	50.8	44.7	51.5	47.0	52.8	33.3	45.2	33.2	57.0	0.0	0.0	0.0
H25	34.6	34.0	33.3	29.6	35.7	33.5	29.9	20.1	37.8	16.0	0.0	0.0
H5	51.6	50.8	52.7	51.2	54.8	50.6	55.6	48.3	57.5	32.0	43.5	17.7

Table 8. Results of sulphate resistance tests in solutions I, C and E

Cement	Percentage strength retained									Wear rating								
	1 year			2 years			5 years			1 year			2 years			5 years		
	I	C	E	I	C	E	I	C	E	I	C	E	I	C	E	I	C	E
DO	99	101	92	103	100	72	93	89	45	4	3	11	4	2	21	5	3	49
D5R	104	102	100	103	99	83	90	99	52	3	4	6	2	4	22	5	4	50
DOX	101	100	96	103	102	94	85	91	57	0	0	3	2	3	4	3	5	63
D5L	101	100	96	102	104	100	91	94	68	5	2	2	4	3	3	6	6	38
D25	107	104	97	107	105	100	93	91	66	5	4	11	4	4	22	5	8	51
EO	101	103	80	99	97	67	77	93	43	0	0	19	3	4	21	7	5	29
E5	100	100	86	97	105	67	71	89	27	3	3	22	6	4	26	24	8	59
E25	101	105	91	105	103	73	93	86	26	3	3	17	3	5	25	4	5	59
FFB	98	96	83	94	98	69	93	93	54	0	0	12	7	3	22	5	4	39
FO	101	95	88	100	99	83	88	64	62	0	0	11	6	6	18	12	28	31
F5L	100	101	84	98	102	56	81	94	0	0	0	16	4	6	28	14	28	163
F5R	101	99	88	98	99	59	75	86	18	0	0	15	4	6	32	29	17	132
F25	99	95	80	98	89	78	61	20	9	1	19	17	11	35	31	43	176	190
FGO	101	105	86	82	100	49	0	93	30	8	2	12	34	7	32	141	32	134
FFA	102	101	87	99	105	61	100	100	41	0	0	15	4	4	16	3	10	47
GO	77	89	52	30	63	20	0	0	0	55	23	55	162	77	204	282	282	282
G5X	57	86	69	0	36	27	0	0	0	91	38	62	282	144	185	282	282	282
G25	60	63	35	9	18	0	0	0	0	88	77	107	257	197	282	282	282	282
G5	82	96	51	38	58	18	0	0	0	57	24	61	126	84	183	282	282	282
HO	82	99	66	43	81	34	0	32	0	25	12	33	94	33	83	282	107	260
H5X	88	101	93	63	86	63	0	0	0	21	12	22	78	27	62	268	214	240
H25	98	96	86	94	84	56	43	0	0	4	24	35	7	42	88	54	220	270
H5	98	102	99	92	101	88	56	76	31	1	1	7	10	8	24	77	38	73

Concrete powder samples were obtained at 5 mm depth intervals by drilling with a rotary hammer-drill, the surface 1 mm being discarded. Drillings were taken from all four side faces of each specimen and combined. These samples were analysed by X-ray fluorescence for chloride and calcium contents which, with a knowledge of the CaO content of the original cements, enabled chloride concentrations by weight of cement to be determined. Values obtained, each representing the mean of duplicate specimens, are given in Table 9.

Table 9. Chloride concentrations (wt % of cement) at various depths for marine exposed prisms

Cement	Depth interval (mm)					
	1\6	6\11	11\16	16\21	21\26	26\31
DO	3.03	2.61	2.27	1.93	1.87	1.66
D5R	2.49	2.10	1.63	1.56	1.30	1.23
DOX	6.00	4.72	4.25	3.93	3.82	3.59
D5L	1.36	1.15	1.07	1.04	1.00	0.92
D25	3.09	2.41	2.55	2.77	2.70	2.52
EO	3.60	2.70	2.35	2.31	2.06	2.02
E5	3.94	3.51	3.36	2.60	2.98	2.79
E25	3.86	3.17	2.88	2.71	2.57	2.80
FFB	3.43	2.74	2.13	1.48	0.86	0.49
FO	5.04	4.25	3.63	3.03	2.96	2.98
F5L	2.69	2.11	2.02	1.92	1.68	1.57
F5R	2.47	2.15	1.88	1.66	1.54	1.34
F25	4.00	3.63	3.39	3.39	3.10	2.73
FGO	4.88	4.06	3.28	2.91	2.81	2.58
FFA	2.83	2.14	1.48	0.86	0.42	0.15
GO	4.99	4.04	3.64	3.89	4.10	3.83
G5X	4.55	4.14	3.78	3.47	3.34	2.98
G25	5.02	4.56	4.00	3.59	3.50	3.24
G5	7.34	6.47	5.24	5.02	4.50	3.90
HO	5.20	4.15	3.75	3.25	3.14	3.20
H5X	5.42	4.48	4.01	3.47	3.12	3.01
H25	5.44	4.91	4.04	4.02	3.94	4.09
H5	6.12	4.56	4.43	4.24	3.96	3.83

Subsequent to drilling, specimens were broken open and the reinforcing bars removed. Adhering concrete was removed manually before the bars were cleaned in a 50% (by volume) solution of hydrochloric acid containing 1% hexamine as inhibitor to prevent acid attack on the metal. This solution cleans the bars of remaining concrete and all corrosion products. The bars were then washed, dried and weighed to enable weight loss due to corrosion to be determined by comparison with the original weights of the bars.

2.9 Carbonation and rebar corrosion in outdoor exposed specimens

As noted in Section 2.6 above, further 100 x 100 x 300 mm reinforced prisms (mix C concretes) cured for 1 or 28 days were placed on the BRE sheltered outdoor exposure site. Carbonation measurements are described in Section 2.6 and results given in Table 6. Specimens were then broken open and the rebars retrieved, cleaned and weighed as described in 2.8 above. It had previously been noted that rebars extracted from the poorly cured specimens at two years showed no signs of corrosion and so the cleaning and weighing operations were not carried out at two years. For the same reason, the corresponding well cured specimens were not tested at two years.

3 Results and discussion

3.1 Compressive strength

Strength data up to an age of one year from all participating laboratories were comprehensively analysed earlier[2]. Five-year water-stored strengths from BRE tests reported in Tables 4 and 5 indicate slightly lower values for the cements containing 5% additions compared with their OPC controls, and substantially lower values for the 25% limestone cements. The degree of strength reduction is dependent upon the particular limestone filler but it is noteworthy that the best performance is consistently observed with the filler used in the G series cements.

The effect of poor curing on the various cement types is illustrated in Figure 1. As the limestone filler content increases the relative proportion of water-stored strength attained under air storage conditions also increases, indicating a reducing sensitivity to poor curing with increasing limestone content. The apparently low results from the pfa concretes are due mainly to the continuing pozzolanic reaction under favourable water storage conditions which resulted in the highest water-stored strengths for the pfa cement concretes.

It is of interest to compare the long term strength gains of concretes containing the various cement types from the strength data reported in Table 4. For the two pfa cements FFA and FFB, the mean percentage strength gain between 28 days and 5 years is 65%. In contrast, the mean percentage strength gains for cements with 0, 5, and 25% limestone are 36, 32 and 33% respectively. The high percentage strength gain for the pfa cements is again the result of the continuing pozzolanic reaction

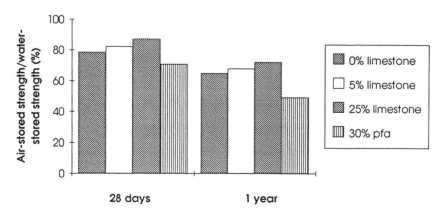

Fig.1 Air-stored strength as percentage of water-stored strength (mix C concretes)

under the favourable water storage conditions, but the similarity between the figures for the other cement types indicates little difference in the proportionate strength gain beyond 28 days for cements with or without limestone additions.

3.2 Oxygen permeability
Oxygen permeability data have previously been discussed in detail[2]. Figure 2 illustrates mean 100-day oxygen permeability values, for air-stored and water-stored specimens, for the various cement types. Data for the coarse-ground cement FGO have been omitted since this cement gave rise to extremely high permeability values. It is clear that, on average, reductions in permeability are obtained with increasing levels of limestone addition. Lowest permeability values were obtained with the pfa cements. However, differences due to cement type were relatively small compared with differences due to curing conditions. Permeability data obtained at 400 days showed a close correlation with the 100-day data[2], the 400 day values being systematically higher due to the continuing drying of specimens between the two test ages.

3.3 Freeze-thaw
Freeze-thaw data were also discussed in detail in the earlier report[2]. In Figure 3, mean percentage expansions after 20 cycles for the different cement types are shown for mix C (300 kg/m^3 cement content), mix E (350 kg/m^3 cement content) and mix E with air entrainment. Expansions for the latter are also shown after 100 cycles. This Figure illustrates that, without air entrainment, the performance of the concretes containing limestone-filler cements decreased with increasing limestone content. The pfa cements also performed relatively poorly.

The significance of these results has already been discussed in detail[2] and, in particular it was recognised that the freeze-thaw test employed is very damaging to all concretes without air entrainment and may indeed result in the destruction of some concretes which nevertheless perform satisfactorily in practice. It is possible, however, to make some observations based upon existing knowledge of the performance of

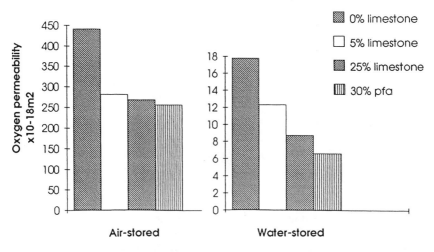

Fig.2 Mean oxygen permeability data for the different cement types

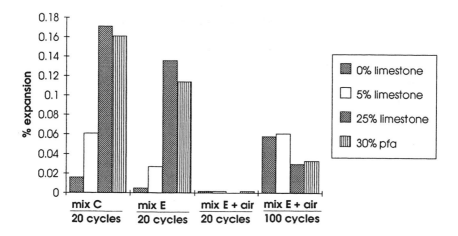

Fig.3 Mean freeze-thaw expansion data for the different cement types

familiar cements in practice. For example, the test data showed that, in the same concrete mix, OPCs from different sources gave rise to a wide range of performance which also encompassed most of the cements containing 5% limestone. The cements with 25% limestone clearly gave an inferior performance but, overall, they were comparable with pfa cements which have been used successfully in practice.

Returning to Figure 3, it can be seen that a small overall improvement was obtained in going from mix C (300 kg/m^3 cement content) to mix E (350 kg/m^3 cement content) with the ranking order of the various cement types remaining unchanged. However, a dramatic improvement was obtained, as may have been expected, with the addition of 6% entrained air. All concretes gave very low expansions after 20 cycles and, even after 100 cycles, expansions were still relatively low with the 25% limestone and pfa cements faring best. It was noted from weight loss data, however, that some of the 25% limestone filler cements tended to show a greater degree of surface scaling. BS 7583 [3] advises that this research programme has shown that Portland limestone cement may be used in conditions of freezing and thawing provided that air entrainment is used and the relevant recommendations of BS 5328 : Part 1 [8] are observed.

3.4 Carbonation
All five-year carbonation data are given in Table 6. Correlations between carbonation depth and 28-day strength have previously been noted[2]. Figure 4 illustrates the relationship between five-year carbonation depth and 28-day water-stored strength. Similarly good correlations were obtained for 1-day cured specimens and between carbonation depth and air-stored strength. This illustrates that, for given curing and exposure conditions, there is a single relationship between carbonation depth and 28-day strength, whether water-stored or air-stored, for all cement types tested.

In Figure 5, the effects of curing and storage conditions on five-year carbonation depths are shown for the F series cements with concrete mix C (300 kg/m^3). On average, extending the curing period from one to three days produced a reduction of 34% in the five-year carbonation depth.

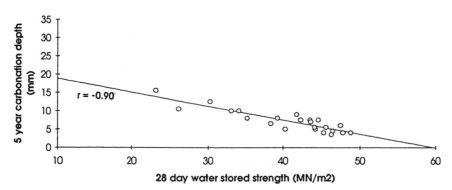

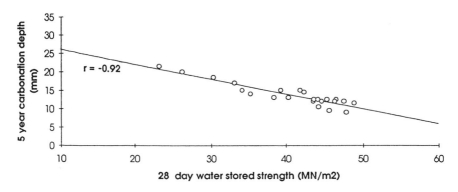

Fig.4 Relationship between five year carbonation depth and 28 day strength

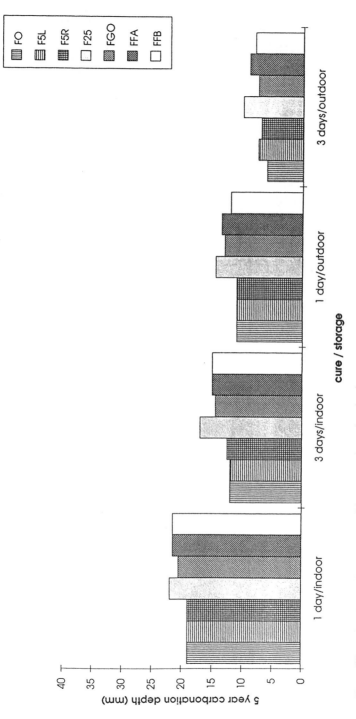

Fig.5 Effect of curing and storage conditions on carbonation depth

Storage in external sheltered conditions rather than internally produced reductions in carbonation depth of 40 and 44% for the 1-day and 3-day cured specimens respectively.

The effect of cement content (or, more correctly, w/c ratio) on carbonation is shown in Figure 6. This figure relates only to 1-day cured specimens since the 3-day cured specimens were tested at only one cement content (mix C). Increasing the cement content from 250 kg/m^3 to 300 kg/m^3 to 350 kg/m^3 produced mean percentage reductions in carbonation depth of 30% and 27% for internally stored specimens and 34% and 35% for externally stored specimens.

3.5 Sulphate resistance
3.5.1 Dependence upon C_3A content
The percentage strength retained and wear rating data given in Table 8 clearly show a dependence of sulphate resistance on the C_3A content of the parent cement. The C_3A contents of the OPCs used in this programme were as follows:-

DO 7.1%, DOX 5.3%, EO 8.6%, FO 8.5%, GO 13.1% and HO 10.3%

Concretes made with the G series cements, with the highest C_3A content of 13.1%, had all completely disintegrated at five years and most of the H series concretes (parent OPC contained 10.3% C_3A) had also completely or partially disintegrated. An exception to this was concrete made with cement H5 (RHPC blended with 5% limestone) which showed a markedly lower degree of attack in all three solutions. In contrast, all concretes made with the D and E series of cement (C_3A contents 7.1%, 5.3% and 8.6% for DO, DOX and EO respectively) performed very well in all three solutions.

The performance of the F series concretes, in which the parent OPC FO had a C_3A content of 8.5%, was generally intermediate between the extremes of the poor G and H series and the good D and E series.

The dependence of sulphate resistance on the C_3A content of the cement is shown for the OPCs in Figure 7. In this Figure, the parameter chosen to represent sulphate resistance is the percentage strength retained after 2 years in solution E. This is because the two-year data offers a wider range of performance than the five-year data and GO and HO could not be distinguished at five years, both having completely disintegrated. Solution E was chosen for this illustration simply because the widest range of performances at two years was observed in this solution.

For the OPCs tested in this programme there clearly exists a strong relationship between sulphate resistance and C_3A content.

3.5.2 Effect of 25% limestone additions
In Figures 8-10, percentage strength retained in solutions I, C and E respectively is plotted at 1, 2 and 5 years for each of the OPCs and the corresponding cements containing 25% limestone. There is no consistent difference in the performances of the OPCs and the 25% limestone cements. In general, the performance of the 25% limestone cements relative to their parent OPCs was best in sodium sulphate solution (I) and poorest in magnesium sulphate solutions (C and E). For cements F and G, the incorporation of 25% limestone produced a poorer performance in all solutions, whilst for cements E and H the addition of 25% limestone improved the performance in solution I but had variable effects in solutions C and E.

Overall, the effect of 25% limestone addition was to extend the range of performances obtained from the OPCs with a wide range of C_3A contents,

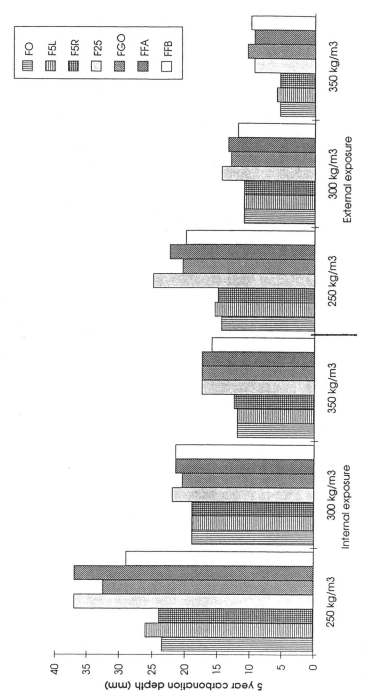

Fig.6 Effect of cement content on carbonation depth

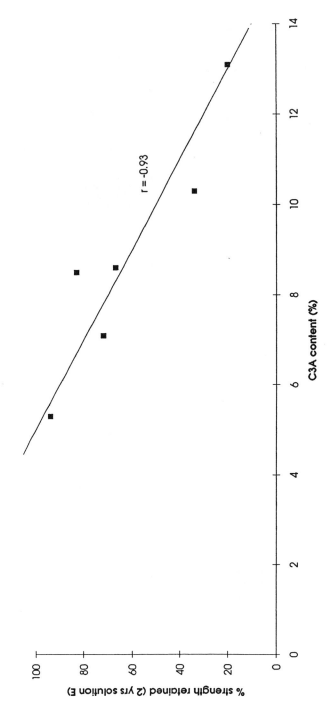

Fig.7 Dependence of sulphate resistance upon C3A content of OPCs

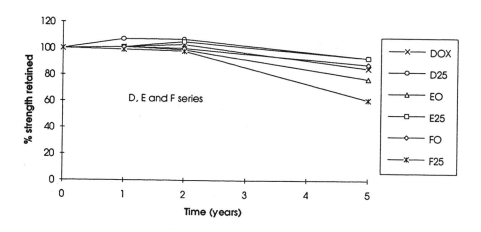

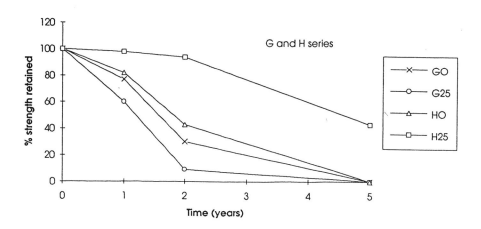

Fig.8 Percentage strength retained with time (0% and 25% limestone cements) in solution I

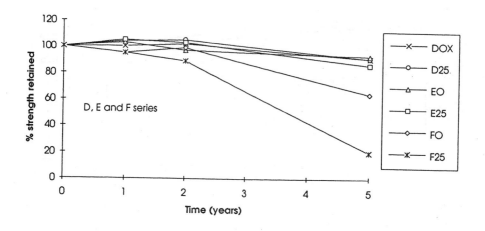

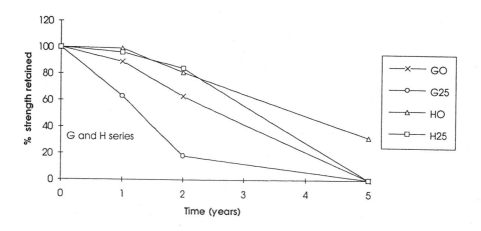

Fig.9 Percentage strength retained with time (0% and 25% limestone cements) in solution C

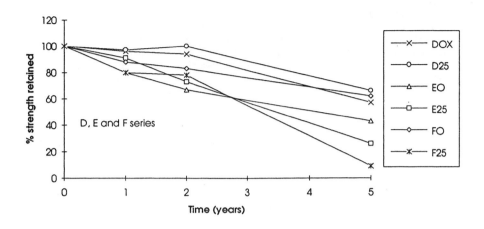

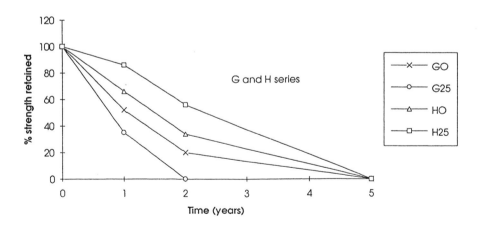

Fig.10 Percentage strength retained with time (0% and 25% limestone cements) in solution E

the OPC with the lowest C_3A content (DOX) being improved and the rate of deterioration of the highest C_3A OPC (GO) being increased.

3.5.3 Effect of 5% limestone additions

Percentage strength retained values at 1, 2 and 5 years are plotted for all OPCs and the corresponding cements with 5% limestone additions in Figures 11-13, relating to solutions I, C and E respectively.

There is little evidence of any systematic effect of 5% addition. For cements DO, DOX and EO, the addition of 5% limestone had minimal effect. The range of performance was wider with cements FO, GO and HO and their 5% limestone counterparts but with no consistent improvement or worsening of performance. For example, for the F series cements, 5% additions worsened performance in solutions I and E but improved performance in solution C. In the H series, the performance of H5 (RHPC + 5% limestone) was consistently better than the equivalent cement made with OPC (H5X) and the OPC control (HO). One possible explanation for this latter observation is the higher SO_3 content of cement H5 (3.1%) compared with H5X (2.4%) and HO (2.5%). This could result in greater consumption of C_3A to form ettringite during the setting and hardening process, leaving less of the vulnerable aluminates and aluminate hydrates available for reaction with sulphate from external sources. This difference in SO_3 level between these cements is greater than between corresponding cements in the other series.

Returning to the F series cements, it is noted above that 5% additions produced a poorer performance in solutions I and E and this is particularly noticeable in solution E with both F5L (5% limestone) and F5R (5% cement raw meal). There are, however, no obvious differences in the chemical composition [2] of cements FO, F5L and F5R to suggest a reason for this and since both 5% limestone and 5% raw meal produce a poorer performance, the explanation is unlikely to be with the nature of the particular addition. Indeed, Figure 7 suggests that the differences may arise from a better than expected performance from the OPC FO and it is concluded that 5% additions are unlikely to have any systematic effect on sulphate resistance (but see Section 3.5.5 below).

3.5.4 Performance of pfa cements

The two pfa cements included in this programme (FFA and FFB) both gave an excellent performance in solution I and solution C. Their behaviour in solution E was less good although FFB fared better than OPC DO (7.1% C_3A) and the performance of FFA was comparable with DO. These findings are consistent with earlier BRE observations on pfa-containing concretes and with the recommendations of BRE Digest 363[9] which permits the use of pfa cements in Class 4 sulphate conditions as long as the concentration of magnesium ions in the groundwater or soil extract is below a value of 1 g/l.

3.5.5 Thaumasite formation

There is recent evidence that a form of sulphate attack may occur, especially in very wet and cold conditions, on concretes containing finely divided calcium carbonate but which would normally be expected to be sulphate resistant. In these cases the usual form of attack by reaction of sulphate with calcium aluminates to form ettringite is supplemented or replaced by reactions between sulphates, calcium silicate hydrate and a source of carbonate to form the mineral thaumasite.

In the light of this evidence the concretes in the current work were examined by qualitative X-ray diffraction after 3.5 - 4 years storage in

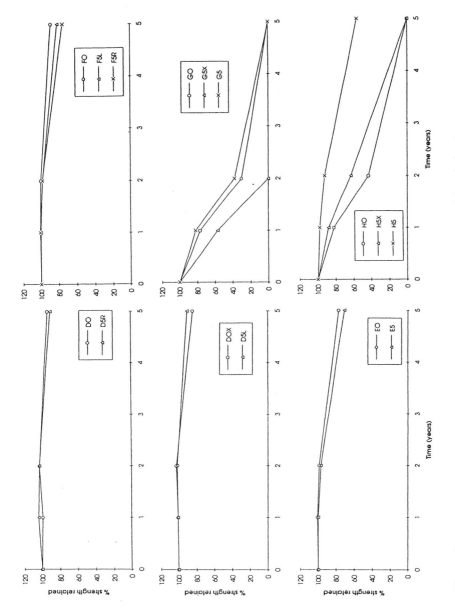

Fig. 11 Percentage strength retained with time (0% and 5% limestone cements) in solution I

Fig.12 Percentage strength retained with time (0% and 5% limestone cements) in solution C

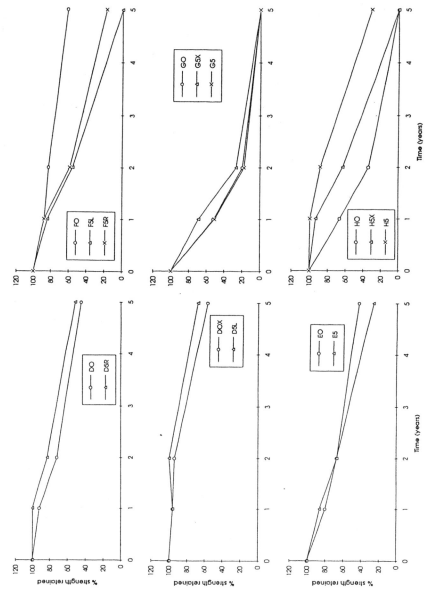

Fig.13 Percentage strength retained with time (0% and 5% limestone cements) in solution E

all three sulphate solutions, to try to detect the presence of thaumasite. Samples of reaction products were taken from specimens which showed signs of sulphate attack and in most cases the presence of thaumasite was detected, especially in the magnesium sulphate solutions. The occurrence of thaumasite was most frequent with the G series of cements which had suffered the greatest degree of attack, followed by the H series, F series and E series. No thaumasite was detected with the D series cements which had suffered very little attack. Ettringite and gypsum were also found in a number of specimens. The occurrence of thaumasite thus matched the degree of attack (and therefore, as discussed above, the C_3A content of the cements) suggesting that thaumasite formation is not independent of ettringite formation but that reaction sequences involving formation of both minerals are involved. There was no obvious dependence of thaumasite formation on the level of limestone filler in the cements, it being detected in the 5% and 25% limestone filled cements alike. Indeed, traces of thaumasite were also found in some of the OPCs suggesting that the source of carbonate was either calcareous material in the Thames Valley gravel aggregates or cross-contamination from the corresponding 5% filler cements which were stored within the same sulphate solution-containing tank. Overall, the indications are that thaumasite may indeed form in limestone filled cements even at 20°C, although it is known that lower temperatures favour its formation.

Further BRE work is continuing to attempt to further elucidate reaction mechanisms through a test programme to screen a range of limestone-filled cement mortars in sulphate solutions at lower temperatures. Preliminary results of this work have indicated a relationship between rate of deterioration and limestone content especially at temperatures in the range 5°-15°C. In view of these results and taking into account the worse performance of the G25 cement compared with the corresponding high C_3A OPC (G0), BRE has advised that it would be prudent to restrict, for the present time, the use of limestone filled cements to Class 1 sulphate conditions. This recommendation has been adopted in the British Standard, BS 7583, but debate on this issue is continuing.

3.6 Chloride penetration in marine-exposed specimens

The chloride penetration data given in Table 9 have been averaged for each cement type and plotted in Figure 14 together with corresponding two-year data. Although there are considerable differences between individual cements, these mean values reveal only relatively small systematic differences between cements with 0%, 5% and 25% limestone, the 5% cements being slightly better and the 25% cements somewhat worse than OPC. The poorer performance of the 25% limestone cements may be related to their lower ability to bind chlorides due to their lower content of cementitious material and/or the greater total porosity of these cements [2] compared with cements with 0% or 5% limestone. Indeed, Moukwa [10] observed greater chloride penetration into mortar containing 20% limestone compared with a reference OPC mortar and related this effect to the greater volume of macropores (radius >0.03 μm) at the surface of the limestone mortar.

One of the most striking features of these data is the excellent performance of the pfa cements. Chloride levels at all depths have increased between two and five years by significant amounts for all except the two pfa cements. For these two cements not only are the chloride levels at depth (> 20 mm) very much lower than for all other

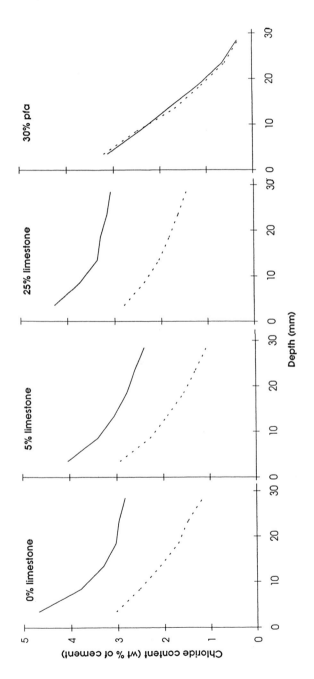

Fig.14 Mean chloride penetration profiles for the different cement types

cements but, significantly, little or no increase has been observed beyond two years. This confirms the previously observed[11] ability of pfa cement concretes to significantly reduce chloride penetration compared with similar grade, or in this case similar cement content, concretes made with OPC, and now shows that pfa cement concretes are also more effective than limestone cement concretes in this respect. The effect has been attributed to the more refined pore structure, leading to lower permeability, and greater chloride-binding capacity of the hydrates in concrete containing pfa. The continuing long-term pozzolanic reaction in seawater, producing greater quantities of hydrated phases and leading to high long-term strengths, is also likely to be an important factor[2].

3.7 Corrosion of rebars in marine-exposed specimens
Mean percentage weight losses of rebars at 10 and 20 mm cover are plotted against chloride concentration at the location of the rebar in Figure 15. The chloride concentration in the 11 - 16 mm depth interval was taken as the value relevant to the 10 mm cover bar and that in the 21-26 mm interval for the 20 mm cover bar. A good single correlation exists indicating that the degree of corrosion for a given chloride level is independent of cement type. There was some suggestion from the two-year data that the corrosion in cements with 25% limestone may be higher than with other cement types at a given chloride level but this suggestion does not seem to be substantiated by the five-year data, although the two points off the regression line showing high rebar weight loss at 4% chloride do in fact relate to cements G25 and H25. Other data for the cements with 25% limestone, however, are not distinguishable from those for other cement types.

3.8 Rebar corrosion in outdoor/sheltered exposed specimens
Percentage weight losses of rebars extracted from prisms which were poorly-cured (exposed on demoulding at 1 day) or well cured (28 days in water) before storage in outdoor sheltered conditions were measured as for the marine-exposed specimens.

No significant corrosion was observed on any of the 20 mm cover bars whether from poorly cured or well cured concrete, a mean weight loss of about 0.1% being measured for these bars, which can therefore be attributed to processing weight loss. The exceptions to this generalisation are for cements G0, G25, H0 and H25 (well cured specimens only) for which weight losses of the order of 0.25% were recorded. However, no significant corrosion was observed on the 20 mm cover bars from these specimens so it is possible that higher processing losses were incurred with these specimens, perhaps due to over-long immersion time in the cleaning solution.

The weight loss data on the 10 mm cover bars from the poorly cured specimens ranged from 0.08 to 0.49% and suggested, as would be expected, a relationship with carbonation depth. This relationship is shown plotted in Figure 16 and a good correlation was obtained.

The 10 mm cover rebars extracted from the well cured specimens showed varying degrees of corrosion, notably associated with the cements with 25% limestone. This again is related to the higher carbonation depths for these specimens which ranged from 8.6 mm (G25) to 11.3 mm (E25). The higher carbonation depths of the 25% limestone cement concretes, and to some extent the pfa concretes, have been discussed in relation to the lower strengths of these concretes in Section 3.4 above.

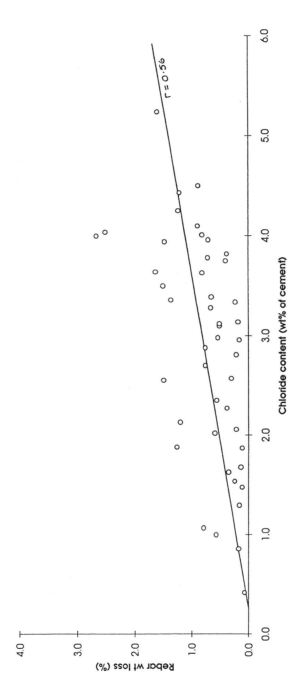

Fig.15 Relationship between rebar weight loss and chloride content at the location of the bar

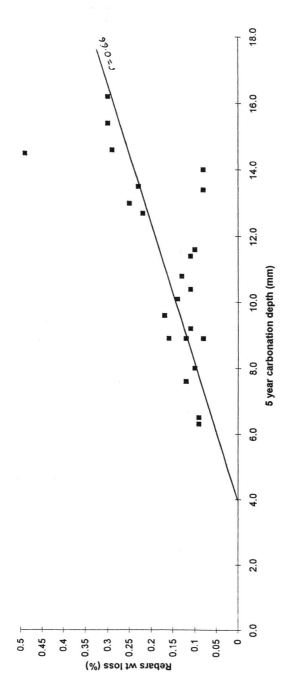

Fig.16 Relationship between rebar weight loss and five year carbonation depth (outdoor exposed specimens)

3.9 General
The overall performance of cements with 5% limestone additions has not been consistently different from that of the parent OPCs. When revising the main British Standards for cements in 1991 in order to introduce a number of the concepts from ENV 197-1, the relevant BSI committee took the decision to permit, for the first time, additions of up to 5% of materials such as pfa, ground granulated blastfurnace slag (ggbs) and limestone to all cement types. The current work appears to vindicate the decision to allow such additions of limestone.

The performance of concretes containing cements with 25% additions of limestone has been consistent with what would be expected from 'cements' containing only about 75% of cementitious material. Thus, lower strengths, increased carbonation depths and, to a degree, increased chloride penetration levels, are to be expected unless cement contents of concrete are increased appropriately. The recently published new BS for Portland limestone cement, BS 7583, recognises this fact and recommends accordingly: 'The substantial research programme under the auspices of the Building Research Establishment (BRE) on the 32.5 strength class of this cement has indicated that it can be used for a wide range of applications in concretes designed for the same concrete cube strength, when they are likely to have similar performance to concrete made with cement complying with BS 12. Thus, concrete made with this cement in accordance with the designed mixes described in BS 5328: Part 1 may be considered to be potentially as durable as that made with Portland cement conforming to BS 12, provided that it achieves the same grade as a concrete made with the Portland cement. However, in prescribed or standard mixes, as described in BS 5328: Part 1, the use of any cement of the 32.5 standard strength class will lead to concrete of lower compressive strength compared with cements of a higher strength class. In consequence, in order to maintain 28-day strength, carbonation resistance and durability, the cement content should be increased; this increase is approximately 10% for standard mixes ST1 to ST4 but for Portland limestone cement may need to be greater for ST5. The use of this cement is therefore not recommended for standard mix ST5'.

The above advice would appear to be vindicated by the results of the current research programme. However the good performance of the two pfa cements in respect of sulphate resistance and chloride penetration should be noted. Whilst the maintenance of concrete grade referred to above is likely to improve the carbonation resistance of concrete made with 32.5 class limestone cements to equal that of concrete made with 42.5 class OPC, it is unlikely to improve resistance to sulphates and chloride penetration to match that of pfa concrete since these depend not so much on 28-day strength but on the chemistry of the system and the potential for long-term pozzolanic reaction and strength gain in pfa concrete under favourable conditions.

4. Conclusions

4.1 Five-year water-stored compressive strengths of cements with 5% limestone addition are slightly lower than their corresponding OPC controls, whilst cements with 25% addition have substantially lower strengths. There appears to be a reducing sensitivity to poor curing with increasing limestone content. Pfa cements give high strengths and also show high percentage strength gains between 28 days and 5 years due to the pozzolanic reaction. Percentage strength gains for cements with 0, 5 and 25% limestone additions were all modest but similar to one another.

4.2 Oxygen permeability data indicate reduced permeability with increased limestone content but the pfa concretes had the lowest permeabilities. Differences due to cement type, however, were relatively small compared with differences produced by dry and moist curing conditions.

4.3 All non-air-entrained concretes deteriorated in the freeze-thaw tests, with those containing 25% limestone and pfa cements deteriorating the most rapidly. The introduction of air entrainment significantly reduced expansion and produced a good performance from all cement types, although some of the concretes containing cements with 25% limestone continued to lose weight due to surface scaling at a faster rate than their 0% and 5% counterparts.

4.4 Five-year carbonation depths correlate well with 28-day compressive strengths whether air or water stored. Increasing the curing period from 1 to 3 days or the cement content by 50 kg/m^3 each produced a reduction in carbonation depth of 30 - 35%.

4.5 Sulphate resistance showed a clear dependence upon the C_3A content of the parent OPC. Additions of 5% or 25% limestone produced no consistent effect, sometimes producing an improvement and sometimes a worsening. In general, the performance of the 25% limestone cements in relation to the OPC controls was better in sodium sulphate than in magnesium sulphate solution. The detection of thaumasite in many of the limestone-filled cements and the worsening of the performance of the OPC with the highest C_3A content when 25% limestone was added has led to the inclusion in the British Standard for such cements of BRE's recommendation that limestone filled cements should not be used beyond Class 1 sulphate conditions. Good sulphate resistance was obtained from the pfa concretes, especially in sodium sulphate and the weaker magnesium sulphate solution.

4.6 Pfa concretes performed well in marine conditions, restricting the penetration of chloride at depth and showing virtually no increase in chloride concentration levels between 2 and 5 years. In contrast, OPCs, and especially 25% limestone cements, permit a more even distribution of chlorides through the concrete and show substantial increases in chloride levels between 2 and 5 years.

4.7 Corrosion of rebars in marine-exposed specimens was related to the chloride concentration at the location of the rebar and showed no clear dependence upon cement type.

4.8 Corrosion of rebars in externally-stored (sheltered) specimens showed a strong correlation with carbonation depths which, in turn, can be related to 28-day strengths.

4.9 The overall performances of concretes containing cements with 5% additions of limestone were not significantly or consistently different from their corresponding parent OPC concretes. The performance of concrete containing cements with 25% limestone additions was generally consistent with a concrete with a proportionately lower cementitious content. Cement contents should therefore be increased appropriately to maintain concrete grade if equivalent durability to OPC concrete is required from concretes containing these cements.

5 Acknowledgements

The work described was originally part of a joint BRE/BCA Working Party programme and the author would like to thank other members of the Working Party for providing the cements and for their contributions to the work. Support for carrying out the long-term durability tests was received from the Construction Sponsorship Directorate of the Department of the Environment. The author is indebted to Mr M R Nelson for carrying out the experimental work and Mr M A Halliwell for his assistance with data processing.

6 References

1. European Prestandard ENV 197-1(1992). Cement - Composition, specifications and conformity criteria - Part 1: Common cements. European Committee for Standardisation, Brussels.
2. Building Research Establishment (1993). Performance of limestone-filled cements. Proceedings of a seminar of the BRE/BCA/Cement Industry Working Party held at the Building Research Establishment, Garston, on 28 November 1989. BRE, Garston, UK. Report BR 245.
3. British Standards Institution (1992). Specification for Portland limestone cement. BSI, London. BS 7583.
4. Lawrence, C.D. (1986). Measurements of permeability. Proceedings of the Eighth International Congress on the Chemistry of Cement, Rio de Janeiro, Brazil, Vol V, pp 29-34.
5. British Standards Institution (1982). Concrete admixtures. Part 2. Specification for air-entraining admixtures. BSI, London. BS 5075 : Part 2.
6. American Society for Testing and Materials (1984). Standard test method for resistance of concrete to rapid freezing and thawing. ASTM, Philadelphia, USA. C666-84.
7. Harrison, W.H. (1992). Sulphate resistance of buried concrete. Building Research Establishment, Garston, UK. Report BR 164.
8. British Standards Institution (1991). Concrete. Part 1. Guide to specifying concrete. BSI, London. BS 5328 : Part 1.
9. Building Research Establishment (1991). Sulphate and acid resistance of concrete in the ground. BRE, Garston, UK. Digest 363.
10. Moukwa, M. (1989). Penetration of chloride ions from seawater into mortars under different exposure conditions. Cement and Concrete Research, Vol. 19, No. 6, pp 894-904.
11. Thomas, M.D.A. (1991). Marine performance of pfa concrete. Magazine of Concrete Research, Vol 43, No 156, pp 171-185.

PERFORMANCE IN CARBONATING AND CHLORIDE-BEARING EXPOSURES

M R JONES
Lecturer, Concrete Technology Unit
University of Dundee, UK

Abstract

Perhaps the most significant implication of the adoption of ENV 197 will be the onus that will be placed on the engineer to ensure that the optimum binder is specified in severe exposures which contain chlorides. ENV 197 offers considerable scope for tailoring concrete to resist carbonating and chloride-containing environments. However, there is a lack of authoritative information on many of the CEM cements with additions and the effect of fillers on their durability is simply not known at this juncture. It is shown that all the CEM cements containing additions currently available in the UK, i.e. fly ash, granulated blastfurnace slag and silica fume can greatly improve resistance to chloride ingress when compared to a Type I portland cement. The position with regard to carbonation is less clear since depending on the quantity of the addition used in the cement and the grade of concrete produced, the rate of carbonation may be greater or lower than an equivalent grade Type I cement concrete. This raises the question of how concrete made with such cements will perform when both carbonation and chloride attack occur. It is clear that the challenge to further Euro-standards is to address how to assist engineers to specify ENV 197 CEM cements for severe environments.

Keywords: Carbonation, Chloride Ingress, Fly Ash, Granulated Blastfurnace Slag, Silica Fume.

1 Introduction

1.1 The 'Chloride' Problem

Specifying concrete for the severe exposure conditions of the northern European winter climate has always been a difficult problem and particularly where the environment contains chlorides. The record so far has not been good. A large majority of the UK highway bridgestock suffer from 'chloride' damage[1] and the repair cost for this class of structure alone may run into tens of billions of pounds over the next 25 years. In the UK, at least, the major specifying authorities have not tackled the problem of chloride ingress through the use

Euro-Cements: Impact of ENV 197 on Concrete Construction. Edited by R.K. Dhir and M.R. Jones. Published in 1994 by E & FN Spon, 2–6 Boundary Row, London SE1 8HN. ISBN: 0 419 19980 2.

of blended cements but through the application of penetrating surface coatings. It would appear, therefore, that the use of cement additions has yet to be fully accepted into UK practice as the sole method by which to protect concrete.

1.2 The 'Carbonation' Problem

The other major durability problem is carbonation. Arguably it is not as acute as that of chloride damage, since it rarely leads to catastrophic failure, however, carbonation affects a much wider range of structures. Changes in cement composition allowed under ENV 197[2] need careful analysis to ensure that the traditional relationship between cover depth requirements and water/cement ratio are equally applicable to high pozzolanic content cements.

Most engineers would agree that current UK codes of practice, ie BS 8110[3] and BS 8007[4], are generally adequate in their treatment of cover for exposures where carbonation is the dominant durability problem. There is an economical balance between cover and concrete grade. The main problem seems to come from the minimum cover requirement not being achieved. In all the structural investigations carried out by the Author into cases of surface spalling of reinforced sections, the problem was traced to a lack of cover, typically this was as low as 5mm and was rarely more than 20mm to links. The real problem does not directly lie with the cement type but with failings in the construction process.

1.3 Euro-Cements, Euro-Standards and Codes of Practice

The formulation of these codes can be traced back to the 1970's when on a practical basis the only cement available was OPC to BS 12[5]. Even then BS 8110 recognises that the durability of even OPC concrete varies considerably. The situation in ENV 197 with currently 80 CEM cements being introduced none of which are correspond to what was a 'traditional' OPC of this time engineers will have to be vigilant such that the current poor image of concrete durability does not get any worse.

It should be noted that ENV 197 does not directly make any reference to the environment and gives no guidance on which cements may be more applicable. Other European standards will address these issues, particularly ENV 206[6] which will eventually replace BS 5328[7]. The recent update of BS 5328 has aligned itself closely with ENV 206 to provide a smooth transition into use in the UK. However, it should be recognised that the long-term objective of the European standards is to introduce performance-based specifications for durability. This will overcome many of the problems of the performance of unfamiliar cements to carbonation and chloride ingress. The formulation and acceptance of such specifications is, however, a long way off.

The real question that engineers are posing is simple; does a grade 40 concrete containing Type I cement (Portland) gives the same durability as an equivalent concrete containing for example a Type II/A-D cement (Portland Silica Fume) or a Type III/C (Blastfurnace Cement with up to 95% slag addition) and whether the presence of a 5 % limestone filler has any effect on this performance. Unfortunately, this question cannot be answered simply. While certain cements may provide a high degree of resistance to one form of attack, they may be vulnerable to others, for example durable to chloride but having low freeze/thaw resistance.

1.4 Assessing the Potential Durability CEM Cements with Additions

This paper is concerned with the durability of concrete made with cements that are currently available in the UK, as follows:

Type I	*Portland cement*	
Type II/A-V	*Portland Fly Ash cement*	*(fly ash content 6-20% by mass)*
Type II/B-V	*Portland Fly Ash cement*	*(fly ash content 21-35% by mass)*
Type II/A-S	*Portland Slag cement*	*(slag content 6-20% by mass)*
Type II/B-S	*Portland Slag cement*	*(slag content 21-35% by mass)*
Type III/A	*Blastfurnace cement*	*(slag content 36-65% by mass)*
Type III/B	*Blastfurnave cement*	*(slag content 66-80% by mass)*
Type III/C	*Blastfurnace cement*	*(slag content 81-95% by mass))*
Type II/A-D	*Portland Silica Fume cement*	*(silica fume content 6-10% by mass)*

It has not been possible to establish what the effect of limestone filler is on the results reported but it may be possible to infer the results from Dr Matthews' paper reported in these Proceedings. The portland cement grade used throughout corresponds to 42.5N to BS 12 (1992) and again it has not been possible to identify whether similar durability performance would be achieved with the higher grade of 52.5 (the 32.5 grade is not available in the UK and, in any case, is likely only to be manufactured as a Type II CEM cement).

2 Effect of Fly Ash on Chloride Ingress

Although originally used to reduce heat of hydration, it was noted as far back as the 1930's that fly ash had the potential of improving the durability of concrete. In the main this was thought to be due simply to improvement in the concrete microstructure produced by the pozzolanic reaction[8].

Over the last 20 years, however, fly ash has increasingly been specified for concrete exposed to chloride-bearing environments. A great deal of research work has been carried, both at Dundee University[9-12] and elsewhere, to provide guidelines for the specification of fly ash concrete for very severe exposures.

2.1 Effect of Fly Ash Content

The coefficient of chloride diffusion (D) measurements obtained for the concretes with two different fly ash replacement levels are given in Figure 1. The results indicate that there was an order of magnitude reduction in D value across the range of grades considered for all concretes. It was also clear that inclusion of fly ash even at low levels lead to a substantial reduction in D.

Across the range of grades, reductions of approximately 3 to 4 times compared to the control were seen with fly ash 15%, with similar order reductions between fly ash concretes with a further 15% addition. The results also indicate that at grade 25, the high fly ash content concrete had a slightly lower D value than portland cement concrete at grade 70, although in both cases low D values, suggesting good chloride resistance in these concretes, were obtained.

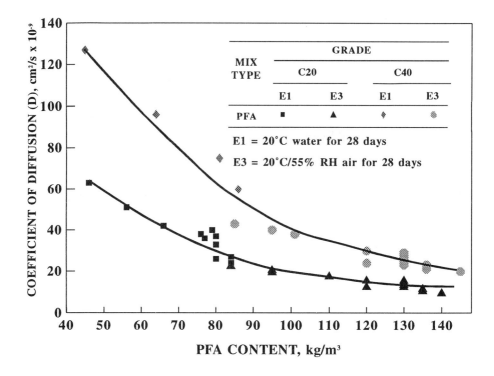

Figure 1.   Effect of fly ash on content on chloride ingress.

2.2 Effect of Curing/Exposure Environment

The effect of different curing conditions on D of strength grade 40 concrete, with a 25% fly ash content, is shown in Figure 2. In line with the results seen previously, the portland cement control concrete had substantially higher D values than the fly ash concrete.

It is clear that 28 days water curing will always produce the lowest D values for both portland cement and fly ash concretes and that the highest D values will be obtained under the air curing condition.

Practically, the results for limited moist curing are more significant. For both portland and fly ash concretes the D value is increased by around 100%. More importantly, assuming that a D below 10×10^{-9} cm^2/s is necessary to provide a 'high' degree of resistance to chloride ingress, then this could not be achieved even with a C40 concrete given typical curing practice, even with the presence of fly ash.

It is also interesting to note that the curing membrane (wax based) was not particularly effective and only equal to around 3 days water curing.

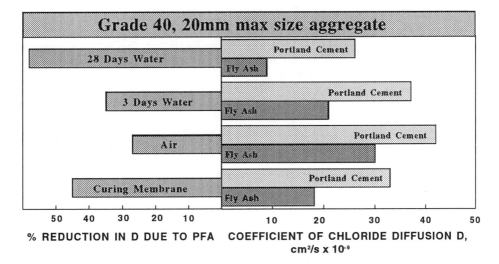

Figure 2.   Effect of curing on chloride ingress into fly ash concrete.

2.3 Effect of Exposure Temperature

The effect on chloride diffusion of a range of exposure temperatures on fly ash concrete are compared with portland cement concrete in Figure 3.

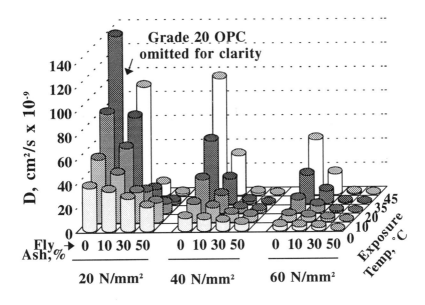

Figure 3.   Effect of exposure temperature on chloride ingress into fly ash concrete.

This Figure shows that temperature indeed plays an important role in the diffusion of chlorides into concrete. This is perhaps obvious from thermodynamic principles since an increase in temperature will lead to an increase in ionic diffusivity but, in fact, the opposite is true for fly ash concrete. Chloride diffusion reduces to almost negligible levels at high temperatures with the fly ash concretes.

The reasons for this are not fully clear but it would appear that acceleration of the pozzolanic reaction due to the thermal energy results in the production of additional products which can bind chlorides. This also underlines the fact that the fly ash reaction products are far more efficient at binding chloride than those produced by portland cement hydration.

2.6 Effect of Fly Ash Quality

One of the key concerns of UK specifiers is what the effect of broadening the range of fly ash qualities will be on concrete durability under ENV 197. As noted in Professor Dhir's paper, ash with a fineness of up to 40% by mass retained on a 45μm sieve will be allowed compared with 12.5% under the current BS 3892 Part 1.

Table 1 shows the D values measured for 12 different fly ashes with fineness from 1.6% to 23.0% retained on a 45 μm, sieve for a C40 concrete. It can be seen that on a practical basis, there is no real difference between the D values and this supports the hypothesis that it is the quantity of fly ash, rather than quality, that is important to resist chloride ingress.

Table 1. Effect of fly ash quality on the coefficient of ash quality.

*COEFFICIENT OF CHLORIDE DIFFUSION, $cm^2 \times 10^{-9}$	MAIN FLY ASH CHARACTERISTICS		
	Al_2O_3 Content, kg/m^3	Glass Content, kg/m^3	Fineness, %
10.3	46.5	109.6	4.0
10.1	46.4	103.1	6.7
12.2	55.4	82.1	1.6
11.4	53.4	77.5	12.8
10.7	54.2	80.0	7.1
11.5	44.6	97.8	11.8
15.0	52.1	70.9	20.1
12.6	55.1	81.0	3.1
12.1	54.6	75.4	5.7
14.0	53.4	73.3	16.5
13.0	45.6	104.3	7.0
15.9	52.4	72.5	23.0

* C40 concrete, standard cured.

2.5 Effect on Corrosion

Figure 4 shows that the benefits of fly ash in terms of reduced chloride ingress are also noted even when corrosion is initiated. This is not surprising considering that one of the controlling factors for corrosion is the recharge of chloride ions to the anodic area. If this is restricted, as is the case with the low chloride diffusivity of fly ash concrete, then corrosion activity is similarly reduced.

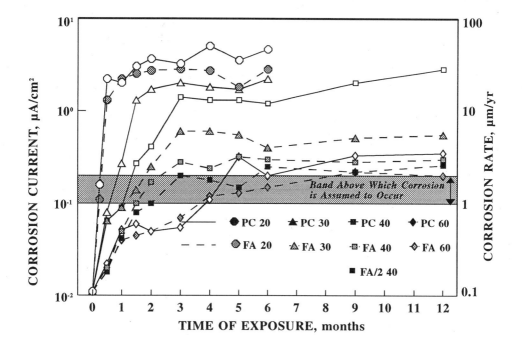

Figure 4.   Effect of fly ash on chloride induced corrosion.

2.6 Implications for Specifiers

The inclusion of fly ash in concrete has a beneficial effect on the chloride resistance of concrete. This is of significance to engineers designing structures to be located in chloride containing environments and attempts have been made to practically rationalise this.

As noted above, the impact fly ash has on the chloride resistance of concrete depends largely on the quantity of fly ash added.   Even small additions lead to significant improvements, but the inclusion of larger quantities of fly ash can offer additional benefits.

The results of further work at Dundee University indicate that the inclusion of 45% fly ash in concrete substantially improves chloride resistance and that for practical purposes a binder content of approximately 350 kg/m^3 and water/binder ratio of 0.45 at this level will provide a concrete of very high chloride resistance.

By way of example Tables 2 and 3 have been developed. Table 2 illustrates the different strength grade/fly ash content combinations required to achieve D in a particular range. This is extended in Table 3, where for a particular set of exposure conditions, critical chloride level and cover the time to corrosion initiation was estimated[13]. This reinforces the significant advantages that can be achieved through the use of fly ash, in particular at high levels.

Table 2. Minimum strength grade requirements to achieve particular chloride resistance.

COEFF. OF CHLORIDE DIFFUSION, $cm^2/s \times 10^{-9}$	MINIMUM GRADE REQUIRED			
	Fly Ash Content, %			
	0	15	30	45
D < 20	40	25	25	25
10 < D < 10	50	35	25	25
5 < D < 10	60	40	35	25
5 < D	70	50	35	25

Table 3. Time to corrosion for different fly ash content/grade combinations.

STRENGTH GRADE N/mm^2	TIME TO CORROSION INITIATION, years			
	Fly Ash Content, %			
	0	15	30	45
35	15	35	55	70
50	25	60	90	>100
60	35	90	>100	>100
70	45	>100	>100	>100

Cover 50 mm
Critical chloride level 0.2% Cl by weight cement (water-soluble)
External exposure concentration 0.3M

3 Effect of Fly Ash on Carbonation

Carbonation is a continuous process by which atmospheric CO_2 enters the cover zone due to a concentration difference and diffuses inwards[14]. The result of this is that the pore fluids become neutralised by carbonic acid. In itself, this has no practical effect on the concrete fabric but the passivity of normal steel reinforcement is no longer maintained and corrosion will ensue, provided there is sufficient moisture to support it. The latter point is important since, generally, there will not be sufficient moisture indoors for significant corrosion to occur, even though higher CO_2 concentrations and lower cover depths mean that the conditions for carbonation-induced corrosion are present inside most structures.

Like all pozzolanas, fly ash has a complex effect on concrete, not only on its microstructure but also the chemistry of the pore fluids. The former effects are beneficial since the permeation properties are improved and this results in less CO_2 being able to penetrate fly ash concrete. On the other hand, the pozzolanic reaction consume calcium hydroxide, thereby reducing the alkalinity of concrete and affecting the resistance to carbonation.

3.1 Effect of Fly Ash Content
Figure 5 shows that fly ash contents of up to 30% have only a marginal effect on the rate of carbonation of typical structural concretes. Not surprisingly, given the interaction of fly ash with the concrete microstructure and pore fluid chemistry, the lowest grade (C35) of concrete with the highest fly ash content produced the deepest level of carbonation, indicated with the phenolpthelien test[15].

The lower depth of carbonation of the higher grade fly ash concrete is probably due to the improvement in concrete microstructure outweighing the depletion of pore fluid alkalinity. In any case, at these grades it would be expected that alkalinity was near its peak level and the effect of consumption of calcium hydroxide would be minimal.

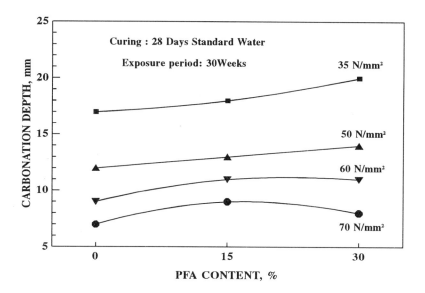

Figure 5.   Effect of fly ash on carbonation rate in concrete.

4 Effect of Granulated Blastfurnace Slag on Chloride Ingress

Like fly ash, one of the key advantages of specifying Type II and III granulated blastfurnace slag (GBS) cements is its ability to increase the resistance of concrete to chloride ingress[16-17]. The following summarises recent research carried out at Dundee University into the performance of GBS concrete in chloride containing environments.

4.1 Effect of Granulated Blastfurnace Content

Figure 6 shows chloride ingress rates into a wide range of GBS concretes. It can be seen that even small quantities of GBS have marked effects on the coefficient of chloride diffusion (D) and that virtually any grade of concrete can be manufactured to give a high degree of chloride resistance.

To obtain a D value below 10×10^{-9} cm^2/sec, it is necessary to select GBS content in accordance with grade. As the grade increases, the quantity of GBS required decreases, reflecting the improved microstructure with less reliance on GBS providing additional sites for chloride binding.

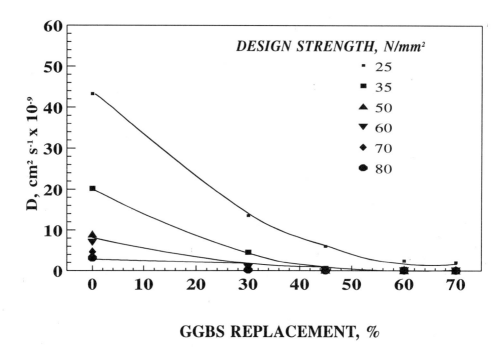

Figure 6.   Effect of GBS content on chloride diffusion into concrete

4.2 Effect of Curing/Exposure Environment

As was noted with the fly ash concrete, curing has an equally important role with GBS concretes, as given in Table 4 for a C50 concrete with a Type III/A cement (45% GBS content). It should be noted that even a poorly cured GBS concrete has a lower D value than an equivalent strength, fully water-cured, Type I portland cement concrete.

However, GBS concrete is not immune from poor curing practice and with 3 days water curing the D value is increased by 50%. Portland cement concrete is more sensitive to curing, since it relies almost exclusively on resisting chloride ingress through the physical barrier of the cover concrete. Consequently, with only 3 days water curing, D for the portland cement concrete increased by 2 times.

Again as far as chloride ingress is concerned, membrane curing was not found to be particularly effective and, similarly to fly ash concrete, was only equal to about 3 days water curing. However, the membraned-cured GBS concrete still retained a high degree of resistance to chloride ingress.

Table 4. Effect of curing on chloride ingress into GBS concrete.

CONCRETE TYPE*		CURING PERIOD, Days					
	Membrane	Water Air+	28 0	14 14	7 21	3 25	1 27
D, Portland Cement Concrete, cm²/s x 10⁻⁹							
	11.5		9.0	10.9	13.0	18.0	22.5
D, 45% GBS Concrete, cm²/s x 10⁻⁹							
	4.0		1	1.6	3.2	4.6	5.4
D, 45% GBS Concrete wrt Portland Cement Concrete, %							
	35		11	15	25	25	26
D wrt 28 Day Water-Cured wrt Portland Cement Control, %							
Portland Cement	128		100	120	145	200	250
45% Slag	44		1	18	36	51	60

*Grade 50 concrete.
+Air curing at 20°C, 65% RH.

4.3 Effect of Exposure Temperature

Figure 7 shows the effect of winter temperatures on the ingress of chlorides into 28 day water cured, C50 grade GBS and portland cement concrete. Sub-zero temperatures were obtained by adding ethylene glycol to the chloride solution to prevent it from freezing.

In this case, temperature appears to have only a minor effect on chloride diffusion. In contrast to fly ash, GBS concrete behaves in exactly the same way as portland cement concrete. As the temperature decreases so does chloride diffusion and from 20°C to -10°C the value of D reduces by 33% for the portland cement concrete and becomes virtually unmeasurable using a conventional chloride diffusion test for the GBS concrete.

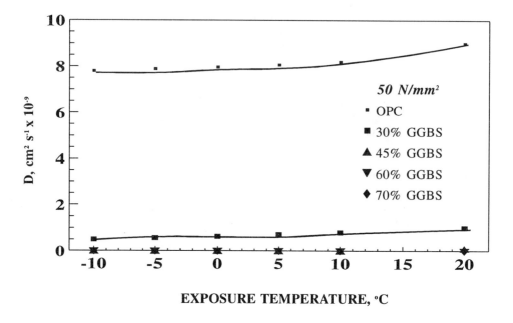

Figure 7.   Effect of winter exposure temperatures on chloride ingress into GBS concrete.

5 Effect Of Granulated Blastfurnace Slag On Carbonation

5.1 Effect of GBS Content

The carbonation depths of two high quality (C50 and C60) concretes with various quantities of GBS after 30 weeks exposure to an accelerated carbonation exposure are shown in Table 4. The exposure atmosphere consisted of recycled air with a partial pressure of CO_2 of 4% at 50% RH. The various test specimens were cured in water for 28 days prior to exposure.

It is immediately apparent from Table 5 that GBS concretes carbonate considerably faster than the equivalent portland cement concretes, even with a 30% GBS content. Even allowing 28 days water curing, the resulting carbonation rate is between 25 and 130% higher in the GBS concrete.

The reason for this is not clear since there is no apparent mechanism by which the rate of carbonation should be higher in GBS concrete than equivalent portland cement concrete. As has already been noted for chloride ingress, GBS generally improves the concrete microstructure and is not as pozzolanic as fly ash, so is unlikely to produce a significant depression of the pore fluid alkalinity. Yet for the same content in concrete, GBS produces a much higher rate of carbonation than fly ash and even at very high strengths, with high GBS contents, concrete may be vulnerable to premature deterioration through corrosion where cover depths are inadequate[18].

Table 5. Carbonation of concrete with different quantities of GBS addition[19].

DESIGN STRENGTH, N/mm^2		CARBONATION EXPOSURE TIME, weeks			
		5	10	20	30
Portland	50	14	20	28	34
Cement	60	10	14	21	25
GBS 30%	50	18	26	35	43
	60	14	19	27	33
GBS 45%	50	21	28	41	48
	60	17	22	32	39
GBS 60%	50	24	33	47	57
	60	20	27	39	48
GBS 70%	50	30	41	59	78
	60	26	36	52	64

* not measurable, greater than 100 mm.

5.2 Effect of Curing/Exposure Environment

Figure 8 compares the depth of carbonation of GBS and portland cement concrete after 30 weeks accelerated exposure. The same trend of lower resistance to carbonation is noted across the range of environments.

Of interest is the very poor durability performance noted in the cool (10°C) environment. Since this is the average exposure temperature in the UK, it would appear that GBS concrete is particularly vulnerable.

The reason why carbonation increases as temperature decreases is not clear, since it would normally be expected that a diffusion-based phenomena should obey thermo-dynamic laws and the gaseous flux reduce with temperature. It would, therefore, appear that carbonation in GBS concrete is strongly affected by reaction and is not a simple diffusion process.

5.3 Influence of Design Strength

Table 6 compares how grade influences carbonation. In these tests standard water-cured concrete strengths up to 80 N/mm^2 were again exposed to accelerated carbonation and, in addition, the period of curing was extended to 6 months prior to testing to ensure that a mature microstructure had been formed.

Again the same trend is noted, even with the longer curing period. Since GBS concrete has a long history of use worldwide with no reported carbonation problems in the literature this does beg the question of the efficacy of accelerated testing and the comparison of like with like. However, until further studies are carried out, it is important to recognise the potential rapid carbonation rate of GBS concrete.

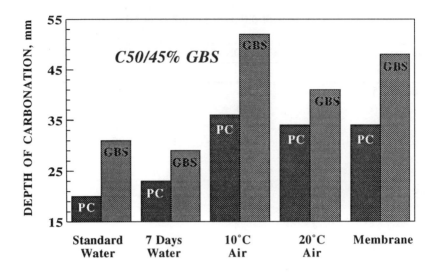

Figure 8.   Effect of curing on the carbonation resistance of GBS concrete[19].

Table 6.   Comparison of carbonation depths of portland cement and slag concrete at different grades.

CONCRETE MIX	MEAN CARBONATION DEPTH, mm							
	Exposure Time, weeks							
Design Strength N/mm²	28 DAY CURING				180 DAY CURING			
	5	10	20	30	5	10	20	30
Portland Cement								
25	19	27	38	45	16	22	30	35
35	10	16	25	33	8	12	18	20
50	8	14	16	19	6	7	10	12
60	4	6	8	10	0	0	2	3
70	0	3	4	5	0	0	1	2
80	0	0	0	0	0	0	0	1
GBS 45%								
25	28	37	49	58	20	28	40	45
35	17	24	34	54	12	16	24	28
50	14	19	24	29	8	12	16	19
60	6	8	12	15	2	5	6	7
70	2	5	7	9	0	2	4	5
80	1	2	3	4	0	0	2	4

6. Effect of Silica Fume on Chloride Ingress

Silica fume has not been widely used in the UK, probably for no other reasons than it is considered expensive, there is only a minor production capacity and it is generally associated with high strength concrete (the economics of producing high strength concrete through the use of silica fume are probably similar to producing it by water/cement control).

The Department of Transport was the first major body to recognise the use of silica fume and a special concrete mix is allowed in the latest version of the Specification for Highway Works. Steetley and subsequently Tarmac Topmix have pioneered the more general use of silica fume in the UK and, therefore, the material has been exclusively used as a mixer blend.

In addition, silica fume is used as an addition to the total portland cement content and not as a replacement. To the Author's knowledge there are currently no UK suppliers of Type II/A-D cement, ie a silica fume addition of 6-10%.

6.1 Effect of Silica Fume Content

A number of studies[21-23] have shown that a 10% by mass silica fume content provides the optimum resistance to chloride ingress. Reductions in depth of penetration of concentrated chloride solutions into concrete of grade 50 of the order of 65% are widely quoted.

Figure 9 compares the chloride concentrations at various depths of concrete with a water/cement + silica fume ratio of 0.5 with silica fume contents of 5 to 15% after 6 month exposure to 1.9 weight percent chloride solution[21]. This shows that there are advantages to resisting chloride ingress by increasing the silica fume content above 10% but as outlined below, this results in significantly increased carbonation rates. This corresponds to a coefficient of chloride diffusion of around 20×10^{-9} cm^2/s.

It should be noted that there is strong evidence to suggest that it may be more effective to use a ternary blend cement with fly ash rather than increase the silica fume above 10%. For example, a 10% ternary blend with fly ash would result in a D value of the above mix reducing to 3×10^{-9} cm^2/s.

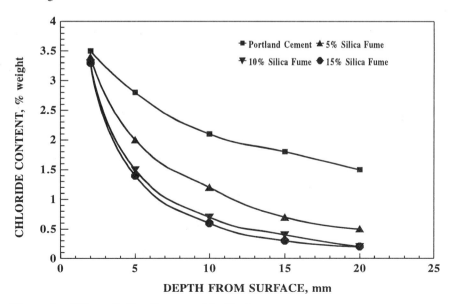

Figure 9.   Effect of silica fume on chloride ingress

7. Effect of Silica Fume on Carbonation

Figure 10 shows the depths of carbonation against square root time of the silica fume concretes with up to 30% by weight silica fume over 20 weeks of accelerated carbonation. The results are what might be expected with a highly pozzolanic addition and the depths of carbonation of the 20% and 30% silica fume concrete are indeed very much higher than the portland cement concrete.

The 10% silica fume concrete, on the other hand, carbonates only marginally faster than the portland cement concrete[21]. Although towards the end of the exposure period non-linearity does appear occur. This suggests that silica fume concrete may carbonate at a broadly similar rate to portland cement concrete after short exposure periods but may go on to carbonate faster after longer periods. The durbility record of existing structures with silica fume concrete will, therefore, also have to be reviewed before a final assessment can be made.

Based on the current evidence it would appear that the limit of 10% by mass set in ENV 197 for Type II/A-D silica fume cement is a reasonable choice, achieving a high resistance to chloride ingress with only a marginal increase in carbonation rate.

Given these results for silica fume concrete, this does still throw into question why the GBS concrete was found to carbonate so quickly.

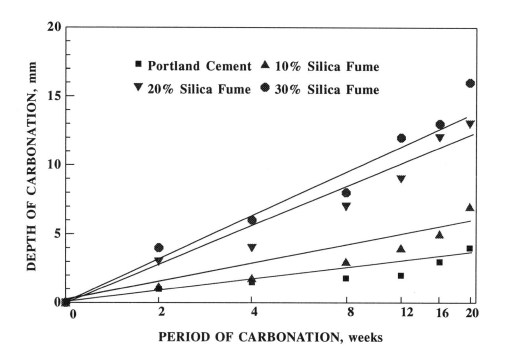

Figure 10.   Effect of silica fume on the carbonation rate of concrete.

8 Summary

It is clear that there is wide variation in durability performance of the various CEM cements with additions inthe carbonating and chloride-bearing exposures. Table 7 compares this performance for the main Type I, II and III CEM cements with fly ash, granulated blastfurnace slag and silica fume additions.

The chloride resistance of concrete can be substantially improved with the use of Type II fly ash cement over Type I portland cement. It was clear that this was controlled principally by the fly ash quantity. It would appear that a fly ash content of at least 35% is necessary to provide a high degree of resistance to chloride ingress. This indicates that a Type II/B-V at the highest fly ash content should be specified. With increasing fly ash levels the effects of poor curing on chloride resistance become less significant. Indeed, at the 45% fly ash level only minor differences between water and air-curing occur.

Fly ash also reduces the rate of corrosion once initiated since the low diffusion rate of chlorides restricts the rate at which they can be replenished to the site of corrosion.

Water-cured concrete of 50 N/mm^2 design strength or more with at least 45% granulated blastfurnace slag has a D below 5 x 10^{-9} cm^2/sec and is a suitable alternative to fly ash. Increasing the period of water-curing prior to exposure decreases the coefficient of chloride diffusion of concrete. The largest reduction occurs with high GBS replacement levels. For any given curing condition or concrete strength the coefficient of chloride diffusion tends to zero as the GBS content is increased. Decreasing the temperature of exposure to chloride solution reduces the D of GBS concrete. The coefficient of chloride diffusion of GBS

Table 7. Comparison of performance of CEM cement concretes in carbonating and chloride-containing exposures.

ENV 197 DESIGNATION	CEMENT TYPE	ADDITION CONTENT	DURABILITY	
			Carbonation	Chloride-Bearing
Type I	Portland	Nil	Good	Poor
Type II/A-V	Portland Fly Ash	6-20%	Moderate	Good
Type II/B-V	Portland Fly Ash	21-35%	Moderate	Excellent
Type IIA-S	Portland Slag	6-20%	Poor	Very Good
Type II/B-S	Portland Slag	21-35%	Very Poor	Excellent
Type II/A-D	Portland Silica Fume	6-10%	Moderate	Good
Type III/A	Blastfurnace	36-65%	Do Not Use	Excellent
Type III/B	Blastfurnace	66-80%	Do Not Use	Excellent
Type III/C	Blastfurnace	81-95%	Do Not Use	Unknown

concrete has been shown to be dependent upon initial curing, GBS replacement level, design strength and exposure temperature.

The carbonation of concrete is a complex function of design strength of concrete, cement content, GBS content, period of water-curing and duration of exposure to carbon dioxide. The carbonation rate of concrete increases with GBS content and decreases with both increasing design strength and duration of moist curing. Increasing the period of water-curing lowers the depth of carbonation. In contrast, increasing the period of air-curing increases the depth of carbonation. All concrete carbonates to a greater extent when cured at 10°C than when cured at 20°C in air, but this is particularly so with GBS concrete.

Silica fume although a familiar material is specified as an addition in ENV 197 and therefore replaces portland cement. Type II/A-D cement appears to be an effective binder for reducing chloride ingress and has only a marginal increase in carbonation despite being a very active pozzolana.

Although little information exists on the use of ternary additions and what would be allowed in ENV 197 is limited, Type II/A & B-N Portland Pozzolanic and Type V/A & B Composite cement, there appear to be major advantages for such cements. It should be possible by careful selection to develop a cement where different binder combinations offset any weakness they may have to particular aspects of durability. This may be the only way in which a concrete could be produced which was resistant to the very severe environments such as the highway or marine exposure, where multiple attack mechanisms occur either concurrently or cyclically.

References

1.   WALLBANK, E. J.   The performance of concrete in Bridges: A survey of 200 highway bridges. Department of Transport, April 1989, 96 pp.

2.   EUROPEAN STANDARDS COMMITTEE.   Specification of portland cement. ENV 197, Part 1. 1991.

3.   BRITISH STANDARDS INSTITUTION. Code of practice for the structural concrete. BS 8110. London. 1985.

4.   BRITISH STANDARDS INSTITUTION. Code of practice for design of concrete structures for retaining aqueous liquids. BS 8007. London. 1987.

5.   BRITISH STANDARD INSTITUTION. Specification for Portland Cements. BS 12, 1989.

6.   EUROPEAN STANDARDS COMMITTEE. Specification of concrete. ENV 206, 1991.

7.   DHIR, R.K., JONES, M.R. and McCARTHY, M.J. PFA Concrete : Chloride - induced reinforcement corrosion (In press). Magazine of Concrete Research.

7.   BRITISH STANDARD INSTITUTION. Specification for concrete including ready mixed concrete. BS 5328.

8.   DHIR, R.K. AND BYARS, E.A. PFA concrete : near surface absorption properties. Magazine of Concrete Research, Vol 43, No 157, December 1991, pp 219-232.

9.   DHIR, R.K. and BYARS, E.A. PFA concrete : Chloride diffusion rates. Magazine of Concrete Research, Vol 45, No 162, 1993, pp 1 - 9.

10.   DHIR, R.K., JONES, M.R. and ELGHALY, A.E.   PFA Concrete : Exposure temperature effects on chloride diffusion. Cement and Concrete Research, Vol 23, No 5, 1993, pp 1105-1114.

11.   DHIR, R.K., JONES, M.R. and SENEVIRATNE, A.M.G. Diffusion of chlorides into concrete : Influence of PFA quality. Cement and Concrete Research, Vol 21, 1992, pp 1092 - 1102.

12.   DHIR, R.K., JONES, M.R., AHMED, H.E.H. and SENEVIRATNE, A.M.G. Rapid estimation of chloride diffusion coefficient in concrete. Magazine of Concrete Research, Vol.42, No.152, September 1990, pp. 177-185.

13.   DHIR, R.K., JONES, M.R. and AHMED, H.E.H. Concrete durability : Estimation of chloride concentration during design life. Magazine of Concrete Research, Vol 20, 1990, pp 579 - 590.

14.   DHIR, R.K., JONES, M.R. and MUNDAY, J.G.L. A practical approach to studying carbonation of concrete. Journal of Concrete, Vol 19, 1985, pp 32-34.

15.   ROBERTS, M.H. . Carbonation of concrete made woth dense natural aggregate. Building Research Establishment Information Paper 6/81. Garston. 1981.

16.   ROY, D.M. Hydration, microstructure and chloride diffusion of slag-cement pastes and mortars. Proceeding Third International Conference on the Use of Fly Ash, Granulated Blastfurnace Slag, Silica Fume and Other Mineral By-Products in Concrete. Ed V M Malhotra. Trondheim. 1989. pp 1265-1281.

17.   COOK, D.J., HINCZAK, M., JEDY, M. and CAO, H.T. The behaviour of slag cement concretes in marine environment - chloride ion penetration. Proceeding Third International Conference on the Use of Fly Ash, Granulated Blastfurnace Slag, Silica Fume and Other Mineral By-Products in Concrete. Ed V M Malhotra. Trondheim. 1989. pp 1467-1483.

18.   OSBOURNE, G.J. Carbonation and permeability of blastfurnace slag cement concretes from field structures. Proceeding Third International Conference on the Use of Fly Ash, Granulated Blastfurnace Slag, Silica Fume and Other Mineral By-Products in Concrete. Ed V M Malhotra. Trondheim. 1989. pp 1209-1237.

19.   DHIR, R.K. GGBS Concrete: Chloride diffusion rate. Concrete Technology Unit. Report RKD/GRC/6-7. University of Dundee. 1994.

20.   DHIR, R.K. GGBS Concrete: Carbonation rate. Concrete Technology Unit. Report RKD/GRC/5. University of Dundee. 1994.

21.   YAMATO, T., SOEDA, M and EMOTO, Y. Chemical resistance of concrete containing condensed silica fume. Proceeding Third International Conference on the Use of Fly Ash, Granulated Blastfurnace Slag, Silica Fume and Other Mineral By-Products in Concrete. Ed V M Malhotra. Trondheim. 1989. pp 897-913.

22.   MARUSIN, S.L. Influence of length of moist curing time on weight change behaviour and chloride ion permeability of concrete containing silica fume. Proceeding Third International Conference on the Use of Fly Ash, Granulated Blastfurnace Slag, Silica Fume and Other Mineral By-Products in Concrete. Ed V M Malhotra. Trondheim. 1989. pp 929-944.

23.   BILODEAU, A. and CARETTE, G.G. Resistance of condensed silica fume concrete to the combined action of freezing and thawing cycling and de-icing salts. Proceeding Third International Conference on the Use of Fly Ash, Granulated Blastfurnace Slag, Silica Fume and Other Mineral By-Products in Concrete. Ed V M Malhotra. Trondheim. 1989. pp 945-969.

THE DURABILITY OF SRPC/GGBS CONCRETES IN AGGRESSIVE SULPHATE, ACIDIC AND MARINE ENVIRONMENTS

G J OSBORNE
Head, Concrete Durability Section
Building Research Establishment, UK

Abstract

This paper summarises the results of studies carried out at the Building Research Establishment on the performance and long-term durability of concrete specimens after 5 years of storage in aggressive sulphate, marine and soft acid water environments. The concretes assessed were of a similar mix design and contained combinations of the same ground granulated blastfurnace slag (GGBS) with three Portland cements of varying tricalcium aluminate (C_3A) contents. Of particular interest were the data obtained using blends of slag and sulphate resisting Portland cement (SRPC) and comparisons were made with the data from concretes containing the same slag with two Ordinary Portland Cements (OPC).

The performance and long term durability of the different concretes, were generally very good. There was little physical evidence of degradation, although there were some slight differences in behaviour concerning sulphate attack and frost resistance. Overall, the results confirmed earlier findings which led to the recommendations, for the effective and proper use in concrete of Portland and blended cements containing granulated blastfurnace slag, published in earlier BRE Information Papers and Digests and set out in British Standard Specifications and Codes of Practice.

These data are of direct relevance to the UK readymix concrete industry practice of blending all cementitious components at the concrete mixer. The UK practice of "mixer-blends" is different from that used across most of the rest of Europe where slag and fly ash - containing cements tend to be interground or blended, prior to adding to the aggregates at the concrete mixer. Changes in performance of concretes which might be attributed to differences in European concrete mix practice need to be researched. This has become more necessary as cements, unfamiliar to the UK users, are imported and CEN standards normalisation becomes a reality.

Keywords: Durability, performance, Portland Cements, SRPC, granulated blastfurnace slag, concrete, curing regime, aggressive environments, sulphates, freezing and thawing, standards, specifications.

Euro-Cements: Impact of ENV 197 on Concrete Construction. Edited by R.K. Dhir and M.R. Jones. Published in 1994 by E & FN Spon, 2–6 Boundary Row, London SE1 8HN. ISBN: 0 419 19980 2.

1 Introduction

This paper is the culmination of more than 5 years of studies carried out on the durability of cement replacement materials, and deals with the final series of concrete mixes, mainly containing SRPC and SRPC/GGBS blends of cement. Earlier results from the main series of over 20 concretes tested at 2 years for sulphate resistance[1] and then at 5 years for the same property[2], followed by a paper on the mechanisms and protection afforded by GGBS[3] and on the performance of Portland and blastfurnace slag cement concretes in marine environments[4] have provided a suite of papers. All these previous results together with data from site structures were summarised in a BRE Information Paper which compared the properties and performance of slag cement concretes with those of conventional Portland cement concretes of similar mix design[5]. A number of recommendations were made for the effective and proper use of cementitious blastfurnace slag in concrete from the results of these studies which with similar work carried out using pulverised fuel ash in concrete[6-8] have provided important input to BRE Digest 363[9], British Standards Specifications[10-11] and to Codes of Practice[12-13].

2 Experimental

The detailed test procedures and experimental data from a comprehensive study to determine the resistance, of more than twenty Portland and blastfurnace slag cement concretes, to physical and chemical attack following storage for 5 years in a number of aggressive environments, has been reported previously[1-5]. However for this particular study attention is focused on those concretes containing an SRPC and blends of this cement with a GGBS which was itself typical of present day UK production, as these concretes were hitherto untested at 5 years. The performance of 100 mm concrete cubes was assessed in terms of their visual appearance, attack ratings and retention of compressive strength and the results compared with similar data obtained for two OPC's and their blends using the same GGBS.

2.1 Materials
The cementitious materials used in this study were three Portland cements containing low, medium and high tricalcium aluminate (C_3A) contents and a GGBS which originated from Frodingham Cement Co. The SRPC, medium C_3A OPC and the GGBS were considered to be representative of modern cements and slags available in the UK today. The other OPC contained a very high tricalcium aluminate (C_3A) content, a type not likely to be found in the UK or elsewhere in Europe at the present time, but known to be vulnerable to sulphate attack. The chemical analyses and main physical data of the cements and slag are given in Table 1. The two OPC's have similar physical properties but C_3A contents ranged from 8.6 to 14.1%. The low C_3A (0.6%) SRPC was more finely ground (425 m^2/kg) than the two OPC's and the GGBS which were in the range 340-360 m^2/kg.

2.2 Concrete mixtures
Concretes were prepared to appropriate mix proportions which originally satisfied (a) the minimum requirements of BS 5328, Part 1, 1990[10] for the "Guide to specifying concrete", when placed in exposure conditions classified as most severe and (b) the requirements for concrete exposed

Table 1. Chemical analyses data of Portland cements and
         blastfurnace slag

Portland Cements				Slag**
Oxide	SRPC 853	OPC 850	OPC 814	M364
SiO_2	20.55	20.29	19.70	36.67
Al_2O_3	3.30	5.27	6.93	11.48
Fe_2O_3	4.84	3.09	2.54	0.70
CaO	65.30	65.18	65.08	39.39
MgO	0.48	0.90	1.14	7.77
K_2O	0.34	0.48	1.11	0.82
Na_2O	0.12	0.21	0.20	0.43
TiO_2	0.17	0.25	0.31	0.56
P_2O_5	0.15	0.19	0.26	0.02
Cr_2O_3	0.15			
Mn_2O_3	0.05	0.03	0.14	0.76
BaO	0.01	0.19		0.08
SrO	0.15	0.03	0.14	0.07
SO_3	2.03	2.72	2.22	1.29*
LOI at 100°C	1.65	1.35	0.83	
V_2O_5				0.02
Cl				0.05
Free CaO	–	2.39	1.74	–
Density (kg/m^3)	3185	3125	3185	–
Fineness (m2/kg)	425	340	360	~350
C_3A (Bogue)	0.57	8.8	14.1	–
TOTAL	99.29	100.18	100.46	100.77

* As total S   ** ground granulated blastfurnace slag

to sulphate and acid attack in classes 3-5 conditions of sulphate in BRE Digest 363[9]. It should be stressed that the Portland and slag cement concretes were proportioned to provide equal cement content and workability rather than equal 28 day strength.

The specimens were made in BRE's concrete laboratory at 20°C using dried Thames Valley coarse aggregates and fine sand with the appropriate Portland cements and ground glassy slag additions blended at the concrete mixer. The basic concrete mixture proportioning is given in Table 2 with the mean values of the fresh concrete properties, including cement content, wet density and slump. A more detailed description of these properties is given in Table 3.

All the concretes had similar workabilities with compacting factors in the range 0.92-0.97 and slumps of 65-100 mm. There were no significant differences in the fresh concrete properties, other than the marginal water reduction produced by the use of the ground slag with SRPC. This may be partly due to the effect of the more finely ground SRPC which thereby contributed to the slightly enhanced wet density and cement contents of the SRPC concretes. The concretes were vibrated into 100 mm cube moulds and stored for 24 hours below a cover of damp hessian and

Table 2   Concrete mixture proportions and wet concrete properties
(mean values)

Concrete Mixture Proportions					Fresh Concrete Properties		
Thames Valley Aggregates		'Cement'		'Water'			—
20-10 mm (67%)	10-5 mm (33%)	<5 mm	(Slag+PC)	Total W/C (free W/C)	Cement Content (kg/m^3)	Wet Density (kg/m^3)	Slump (mm)
2.91	1.75	1.0		0.5 (0.45)	380	2340	75

Table 3 Wet concrete properties of individual mixtures

Mixtures				Wet Concrete Properties				
	SRPC 853	GGBS (%)	Slump (mm)	VB Time (secs)	Compact-ing Factor	Cement Content (kg/m^3)	Wet Density (kg/m^3)	Water TOTAL Cement
GS 11	100	0	65	3.0	0.95	384	2363	0.49
SR 22	60	40	90	2.0	0.92	386	2368	0.48
SR 21	40	60	75	2.5	0.93	384	2355	0.48
SR 20	30	70	75	3.0	0.93	382	2346	0.48
	OPC 850							
SR 1	100	0	95	1.5	0.93	379	2344	0.526
SR 18	40	60	75	2.0	0.94	381	2345	0.50
	OPC 814							
SR 5	100	0	75	2.5	0.96	380	2347	0.52
SR 16	40	60	100	1.0	0.97	378	2326	0.50
SR 17	30	70	100	N.D.	0.95	382	2351	0.50

polythene sheet to maintain an initial curing condition close to 100%
relative humidity. The total number of cubes cast per batch of concrete
was 78. The concrete cubes were then demoulded, numbered and most were
pre-cured in water at 20°C for a further 27 days prior to placing
randomly in the different storage environments for periods of time up to
5 years. The pre-curing and storage regimes are given in Table 4 and
have been reported previously[1,2,4]. Thus, in some of the sulphate tank
tests, air curing of cubes for 27 days or no further pre-curing, beyond
the first 24 hours in the moulds, was also used to simulate probable site
curing conditions for precast and in-situ concrete practice.

Table 4 Pre-curing and 5 year storage regime

Curing regime after demoulding at 24 hours	Storage Environment for 5 years					
	Water at 20°C	Sulphate Solution		Marine Zone		Soft Acid Water
		Sodium (1.5% SO$_3$)	Magnesium (1.5% SO$_3$)	Tidal	Full Immersion	
Water at 20°C	Control	Solution I	Solution E			
Water at 20°C for 27 days (W 27d)	√	√	√	√	√	√
Air at 20°C and 65% RH for 27 days (A 28d)			√			
No further pre-curing (A 1d)			√			

3 Aggressive storage environments

The 3 main severe storage environments were:

i)   Strong sodium and magnesium sulphate solutions containing the equivalent of 1.5% SO$_3$, which represents Class 5 conditions of sulphate as classified by BRE Digest 363[9].

ii) The BRE marine exposure site, tidal and full immersion zones, situated at Shoeburyness[4], 4 miles east of Southend on the Thames estuary.

iii) The BRE soft acid-water site at Butterley reservoir in South West Yorkshire[8].

3.1 Sulphate tank test
The sulphate resistance of the 100 mm concrete cubes was measured according to the method established at BRE following procedures described by Steele and Harrison[14]. Cubes stored in tanks of sodium and magnesium sulphate solutions containing the equivalent of 1.5% SO$_3$ by weight, (designated Solutions I and E), and in water as control. The normal pre-cure for the BRE tank test is 27 days in water at 20°C after demoulding at 24 hours. This provides a severe form of test, a deliberate choice as the test was intended as a relatively short-term performance test (2-3 years) for appraising and comparing concretes containing different cements to determine whether the concretes were

generally sulphate resistant or not. The comparative assessment involves the visual appearance (photographs), measurement of the sulphate "attack" rating and compressive strength retention in comparison with that of water-stored control specimens at the same age, when the mean results for 3 cubes at each age are taken. The detailed procedures have been previously reported[1,2,4].

3.2 Marine and soft acid water site tests

The 100 mm concrete cubes were collected in batches of 3 after 1, 2 and 5 years from the various storage environments and their performance determined by means of a series of experimental techniques; these included assessments of physical appearance, chemical and frost attack ratings, retained compressive strength and the extent of chloride ingress[4]. This paper only gives the five year results for SRPC and SRPC/GGBS concretes and those comparative data for the two PC's where the same GGBS has been used. Table 5 gives the chemical analysis of the seawater at Shoeburyness and all the durability data is presented in Table 6.

Table 5   Chemical analysis of sea-water at Shoeburyness

Ions Analysed	Amount Present (%)	(g/l)	Atlantic Sea-water (g/l)*
SO_4^{2-}	0.26	2.60	3.54
$Cl-$	1.82	18.20	17.83
Ca^{2+}	0.04	0.40	0.41
Mg^{2+}	0.12	1.20	1.50
Na+	0.97	9.74	9.95
K+	0.04	0.40	0.33

* Lea, 1970 (4)

4   Results and discussion

The use of 100 mm concrete cubes as a research facility for durability studies has sometimes been criticised as not providing realistic data as the specimens are quite small compared with concrete of larger dimensions in real structures. However, the outer 50-100 mm of reinforced concrete is that which protects the steel reinforcement and it may not behave too differently from the concrete cubes used in the present studies. The main objective of this type of study is to obtain a comparative assessment of a range of concretes with similar mix proportions following storage in the different aggressive, environments.

4.1 Performance and durability

The 5-year durability data for 100 mm concrete cubes, following their storage in, (i) water at 20°C (as controls), (ii) strong sodium and magnesium sulphate solutions and (iii) both seawater and acid water environments, are given in Table 6. The performance of the concrete specimens was determined by assessing the physical appearance in terms of the "attack rating" per cube face and the compressive strength or percentage strength retained in comparison with the water-stored control specimens, as in earlier studies[1,2,4].

Table 6. Durability Data for 100mm Concrete Cubes Following 5 Years in Aggressive Environments

Mix No of Concrete	Cement Composition		Compressive Strength (Load at failure) MPa								
	Portland Cement (%)	GGBS (%)	Water control		Sulphate Solutions				Marine zones		Soft Acid Water
			28d	5y	(W27d) Na2SO4 (.1.5%)	(W27d) MgSO4 (1.5%)	(A.1d)	(A28d)	Tidal	Full Imm.	
	SRPC 853 (0.3% C3A)	M 364 (A = 11.5%)									
GS 11	100	0	53.5	71.0	55.5	57.5	ND	ND	57.0	45.0	43.0
SR 22	60	40	53.5	75.5	50.0	39.0	40.5	ND	50.0	52.0	46.0
SR 21	40	60	47.5	72.0	51.0	24.5	37.0	ND	55.5	51.0	44.5
SR20	30	70	42.0	60.0	50.5	17.5	14.0	ND	51.0	52.5	40.5
	OPC 850 (8.8% C3A)										
SR1	100	0	53.0	75.5	51.0	28.0	31.0	49.5	60.5	63.0	ND
SR18	40	60	44.5	68.5	38.0	18.0	44.0	ND	57.0	56.0	37.5
	OPC 814 (14.1% C3A)										
SR 5	100	0	51.5	69.0	NM	NM	6.0	47.5	50.0	40.0	ND
SR 16	40	60	39.5	67.0	46.5	15..5	44.0	53.5	57.0	60.0	53.5
SR 17	30	70	41.0	60.0	42.0	19.5	15•0	54.0	53.0	54.0	54.0

Mix No of Concrete	Strength Retained (%)							Attack Rating (mm)						
	Sulphates				Marine		Acid	Sulphates				Marine		Acid
	Na (W27d)	Mg (W27d)	Mg (A1d)	Mg (A27d)	Tidal	F.I.	SAW	Na (W27d)	Mg (W27d)	Mg (A1d)	Mg (A27d)	Tidal	F.I.	SAW
GS 11	78	81	ND	ND	80	63	61	19	6	ND	ND	<4	<4	ND
SR 22	66	52	54	ND	66	69	61	32	34	37	ND	18	26	<4
SR 21	71	34	51	ND	77	69	62	49	78	67	ND	16	21	<4
SR20	84	29	23	ND	85	88	68	30	80	92	ND	15	15	<4
SR1	98	37	41	66	80	83	ND	35	74	16	32	4	4	ND
SR18	55	26	64	ND	83	82	55	81	87	34	ND	21	22	11
SR 5	NM	NM	8	69	72	58	ND	>200	216	229	38	10	51	ND
SR 16	69	23	66	80	85	90	80	62	99	55	<4	21*	17	<4
SR 17	64	30	23	82	80	82	82	64	89	95	<4	30*	20	<4

ND = Not Determined   NM = Not Measurable   * = Frost damage

4.2 Compressive strength of water-stored controls

The 28 day data showed that all water stored (control) concretes were of C40 grade with the SRPC and two OPC concretes having higher early strength than the slag cement concretes. At 5 years all strength data were in the range 66-75.5 MPa, with the exception of the concrete containing 30% SRPC and 70% slag. All control concretes have exhibited good, sustained strength development and would be classified as high strength concretes.

4.3 Resistance to sulphate attack

Previous studies[1-3] showed that the sulphate resistance of Portland and blastfurnace slag cement concretes is dependent upon the following physical and chemical criteria: curing regime, cement type (C_3A content of OPC and alumina content of slag) and the storage solution.

Curing regime   The early curing of concrete (ie in the first few weeks after manufacture) was again shown to be the most significant factor influencing sulphate resistance of concrete[5]. The effectiveness of a limited degree of air curing prior to storing the concrete cubes in strong sodium and magnesium sulphate solutions was clearly demonstrated, as in previous studies[1]. Curing for 27 days in air at 20°C and 65% RH, (and to a lesser extent by placing specimens in sulphates several hours after demoulding at 24 hours), ensured that the concrete specimens had good sulphate resistance. This was evidenced by the excellent physical appearance, strength retention and low attack ratings for the two OPC concretes and their slag cement counterparts, which had <u>not</u> been water cured. The beneficial effect is thought to be primarily due to the formation of a carbonated outer layer leading to pore blocking and refinement of the pore structure[3,5], combined with the enhanced strength developed due to an effective reduction in w/c ratio near the concrete surface. However the SRPC concretes, (with and without GGBS addition), were not pre-cured in air, as plain SRPC concrete is widely acknowledged as being highly sulphate resisting whatever pre-curing condition it may have been subjected to[9]. The practical significance of the benefits of a limited amount of air-curing in enchancing the sulphate resistance of concrete is discussed in a BRE report of long-term studies of sulphate resistance of buried concrete[15-16].

Cement type   The main chemical factors that influenced the sulphate resistance of Portland and blastfurnace slag cements were again shown to be the C_3A content of the Portland cement and the alumina level of the slag[5,9]. Previous work[1-3] had shown that low C_3A, SRPC concretes were highly resistant to attack, as were combinations of the medium and high C_3A OPC's with low alumina slags. Sulphate attack was greatest when both the C_3A content of the Portland cement and the alumina level of the slag were high. The level of replacement of OPC by slag was also important with 70% and 80% proving most beneficial, particularly for high C_3A OPC's, when substantial reductions in sulphate ion ingress and improved resistance to attack were realised[1,5]. The results in Table 6 provide further evidence for the above findings and Figure 3 demonstrates the good correlation between percentage strength retained and concrete attack rating for all specimens after 5 years storage in aggressive sulphate solutions.

The SRPC concrete was highly resistant, the medium C_3A OPC concrete was moderately resistant and the high C_3A concrete had very poor resistance when pre-cured in water to obtain its designed strength, prior to immersion in strong sulphate solutions. The addition of slag was shown to be either a benefit (with high C_3A OPC, especially in sodium sulphate solution), have little or no effect at 60% level in both solutions (with medium C_3A OPC), or to be an actual disbenefit, (as with SRPC in magnesium sulphate solution). These effects are illustrated graphically in Figures 1 and 2.

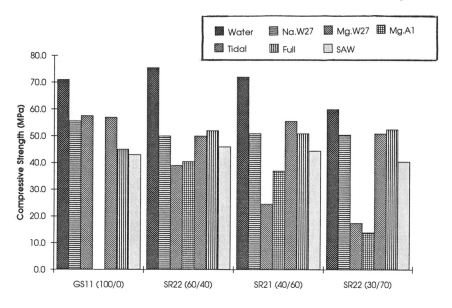

Figure 1. Compressive Strength (load at failure) for 100mm Concrete
Cubes Containing SRPC / GGBS Blends Stored for 5 Years
in Aggressive Environments [() = % SRPC / % GGBS]

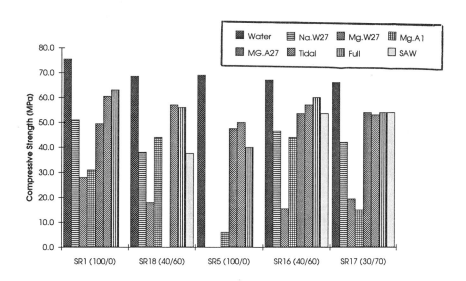

Figure 2. Compressive Strength (load at failure) for 100mm Concrete
Cubes Containing Portland Cement / GGBS Blends Stored
for 5 years in Aggressive Environments [() = % PC / % GGBS]

Storage solution   the results described above are in line with previous findings that magnesium sulphate was generally a more aggressive agent than the equivalent strength sodium sulphate solution.   There also appears to be an increased sensitivity of slag cements, (and cements containing pulverised fuel ash)[6], to strong magnesium sulphate solution.   This has led to the additional precaution being introduced of limiting water-soluble magnesium when these cements are used in sulphate classes 4 and 5 in BRE Digest 363[9] and to advocating the use of SRPC in these circumstances.   The results from this study confirm the advisability of this requirement.

BRE Digest 363   Whilst the beneficial effect of slag (GGBS) is recognised in BRE Digest 363, which advocates the use of a minimum of 70% slag as replacement for OPC in severe sulphate conditions Classes 4 and 5, there are caveats on the alumina content of the slag and C_3A level of the OPC.

The Digest recommends that "for sulphate resistance purposes, slags with an alumina content of over 14% should be used only with Portland cements with low to moderate C_3A content (typically less than 10%)".   The present data again lends support to this recommendation, where SRPC concretes, with and without slag, and the concrete containing high C_3A OPC with 70% slag, have all exhibited good sulphate resistance in strong sodium sulphate solution, whilst the plain SRPC concrete alone demonstrated its good resistance to attack in magnesium sulphate solution (see Table 6 and Figure 3).

4.4 Acid-water resistance

The performance of SRPC and SRPC/GGBS concretes was moderately good after 5 years of storage in the soft acid moorland waters at the Butterley reservoir in South Yorkshire. This water has a pH around 4.0, but with

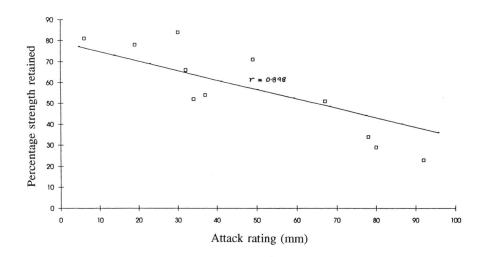

Figure 3   Percentage Strength Retained vs Attack Rating for 100mm concrete cubes after storage in Sulphate Solutions for 5 years

little dissolved carbon dioxide. Concrete strengths of 40-46 MPa, (strength-retentions of 61-68% with only gradual erosion of concrete surfaces) indicated that these good quality concretes have performed fairly well. This supports the views or expectation that, in general, the quality of concrete is of greater importance than the type of cement used in such aggressive conditions[6,8]. It is noteworthy that the best acid resistance was obtained with those concretes containing the high C_3A OPC blended with 60 to 70% of the medium alumina-slag, when concrete strengths of about 54 MPa and strength retentions of 80%, with hardly any wear, were achieved after 5 years of exposure. This is in line with the contention suggested by earlier studies[5] that marginal benefits are achieved by using higher levels of slag as replacement for OPC.

4.5 Resistance to seawater attack
The data in Table 6 showed that in general terms all of the Portland and blastfurnace slag cement concretes had good resistance to seawater attack after 5 years of exposure in tidal and full immersion zones at BRE's marine exposure site at Shoeburyness[4]. However the SRPC and high C_3A OPC concretes in the full immersion zone had somewhat higher strength losses and some of the slag cement concretes had suffered superficial surface frost damage in the form of "pop-outs" and spalling, characteristic of freeze-thaw attack. The use of air entrainment should prevent this happening[5].

4.5.1 Chloride ingress and protection of rebar
The results of the chloride ion ingress at different depths are given in Table 7 and the trends compared for the three Portland cement concretes in Figure 4. These data were previously reported and discussed[4,5] in relation to the reductions achieved with slag cement concretes, where, at depths of 21 mm there was less than 0.5% chloride by weight of cement, compared with more than 2% for the SRPC concrete at a depth of 31 mm[4]. These high levels of chloride ingress in the SRPC concrete, in both tidal and full immersion seawater zones, provide an environment in which the rebar would be more vulnerable to corrosion. These findings are consistent with BS 6349[13] recommendations for a minimum C_3A level of 4% for maritime structures, and BS 8110[12] which advocates the use of higher cover (an extra 10 mm) for SRPC concrete in very severe or extreme exposure conditions.

5 Conclusions

1. Plain SRPC concretes made with gravel aggregates and sand were highly sulphate resistant in both strong sodium and magnesium sulphate solutions and can be fully recommended for use in Classes 4 and 5 classification of sulphate in BRE Digest 363[9]. The addition of slag in SRPC concretes was found to be acceptable in strong sodium sulphate, of slight benefit in seawater but a disbenefit in strong magnesium sulphate solution.

2. The use of 70% slag of medium alumina content (11.5% Al_2O_3) as replacement for Portland cement is of benefit in accordance with Digest 363[9], BS 8110 : Part 1 : 1985[12] or BS 5328 : Part 1 : 1990[10], where chemical resistance to sulphates, chlorides and seawater is required. The need for the caveats, in BRE Digest 363[9], for limiting the use of slag in higher concentration magnesium

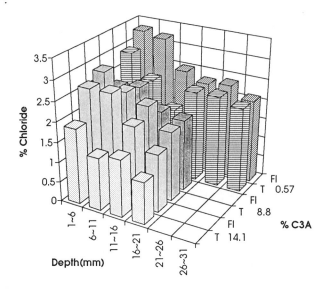

Figure 4   Chloride ingress vs C3A level in cement for 100mm concrete cubes following approx.
5 years storage in seawater (OPC 814 = 14.1% OPC 850 = 8.8% SRPC 853 = 0.57%)

Table 7   Ingress of chloride for 100 mm Portland cement concrete cubes
following approximately 5 years storage in seawater

				Chloride as % Cement		
Mix No	Portland Cement	C_3A (%)	Storage Time (Yr)	Depth (mm)	Tidal Zone	Full Immersion Zone
GS11	SRPC 853	0.57	5.1	1- 6	2.92	3.30
				6-11	2.34	3.20
				11-16	1.70	2.48
				16-21	2.27	2.28
				21-26	2.28	2.35
				26-31	2.12	2.08
SR1	OPC 850	8.8	4.8	1- 6	2.83	2.25
				6-11	2.46	2.37
				11-16	2.25	1.88
				16-21	1.74	1.79
SR5	OPC 814	14.1	4.6	1- 6	1.89	2.64
				6-11	1.32	2.65
				11-16	1.44	1.98
				16-21	1.05	1.45

sulphate solutions and of maintaining slag alumina levels of below 14%, other than with Portland cements of C_3A contents of typically less than 10%, is again indicated.

3. In situations where superficial spalling, in for example the tidal zone, is aesthetically unacceptable, air entrainment may be used as a means of preventing frost attack.

6 Future work

It is important to note that the slag cement concretes assessed in these BRE studies were "mixer-blends", to simulate current UK practice of blending cementitious materials at the concrete mixer. The UK readymix concrete industry has for many years stored Portland cements, ground granulated slags and pulverised fuel ashes in separate silos in order to provide customers with a range of concrete mixes where the different cementitious components can be blended at the mixer as required or specified. This practice is different from that used across most of the rest of Europe where slag and fly ash-containing cements tend to be prepared as a composite, interground cement for direct addition to the aggregates at the concrete mixer. The properties and performance of "blended cement" concretes produced in the UK could therefore differ in some respects from those "interground cement" concretes produced on the Continent. Certainly the cement industry, when commenting on the guidance in BRE Digest 363 has claimed superior properties for interground cements. Basic differences in concrete practice and the cementitious materials used in the UK and abroad should provide important evidence for those working towards the unification of standards for cements and concretes within CEN Working Groups[17,18]. These data could help to explain why 65% replacement levels of granulated blastfurnace slag interground with cement clinker is deemed a sufficient level of slag to produce sulphate resisting cements in most other European countries. There is an urgent need for industry and government research to determine any changes in performance which might be attributed to differences in European concrete mix practice. This has become necessary as more cements, unfamiliar to the UK users, are imported and harmonised CEN standards become a reality. Work could be carried out at BRE with sponsorship from both industry and the Construction Directorate of DOE within the collaborative research scheme recently advocated. Another option worthy of consideration is a possible Brite-Euram Research Contract.

7 Acknowledgements

The Work described has been carried out as part of the research programme of the Building Research Establishment of the Department of the Environment and this paper is published by permission of the Chief Executive. The author thanks Mrs J L Hardcastle for carrying out the experimental studies.

8 References

1. Osborne, G.J. "The effectiveness of a carbonated outer layer to concrete in the prevention of sulphate attack". Proceedings of the International Conference on The Protection of Concrete, Dundee, September 1990, pp 74-79.

2. Osborne, G.J. "The sulphate resistance of Portland and blastfurnace slag cement concretes". Proceedings of Second CANMET/ACI International Conference on the Durability of Concrete, Montreal, August 1991. Volume II, SP 126-56, pp 1047-1071.

3. Osborne, G.J. "Sulphate attack on Concrete. Mechanisms. Protection afforded by GGBS. Design recommendations in BRE Digest 363". Proceedings of National Seminar on "The use of GGBS in concrete construction". University of Dundee, September 1992, pp 31-44.

4. Osborne, G.J. "The performance of Portland and blastfurnace slag cement concretes in marine environments". Proceedings of the Fourth International Conference on Fly Ash, Silica Fume, Slag and Natural Pozzolans in Concretes, Istanbul, May 1992, Vol 2, SP132-70, pp1303-1323. (paper also presented at CANMET/ACI International Symposium on Advances in Concrete Technology, Toronto, September/October, 1992.

5. Osborne, G.J. "Durability of blastfurnace slag cement concretes". Building Research Establishment Information Paper, IP 6/92. BRE Garston 1992.

6. Matthews, J.D. "Pulverised-fuel ash - its use in concrete, Part 2 : Influences on durability". Building Research Establishment Information Paper IP 12/87. Garston, BRE, 1987.

7. Thomas, M.D.A. "Marine performance of PFA concrete". Magazine of Concrete Research, 1991, 43, No 156, September, pp 171-185.

8. Matthews, J.D. "The resistance of PFA concrete to acid groundwaters", Proceedings of the Ninth International Congress on the Chemistry of Cement, New Delhi, India, November 1992, Vol V, pp 355-362.

9. Building Research Establishment. "Sulphate and acid resistance of concrete in the ground". BRE Digest 363, Garston, BRE, 1991.

10. BS 5328 : Part 1: 1990. "Concrete. Part 1. "Guide to specifying concrete". British Standards Institution, London.

11. BS 6699 : 1986. "Specification for ground granulated blastfurnace slag for use with Portland Cement". British Standards Institution, London.

12. BS 8110 : Part 1 : 1985. "Structural use of concrete Part 1. Code of Practice for design and construction". British Standards Institution, London.

13. BS 6349 : Part 1 : 1984. "Code of Practice for maritime structures, Part 1, General criteria". British Standards Institution, London.

14. Steele, B.R. and Harrison, W.H. "Immersion tests on the sulphate resistance of concrete". Proceedings of a RILEM International Symposium on Durability of Concrete, Prague, 1969. Prague Academia, 1969, Preliminary report, Part II, C163-C186.

15. Harrison, W.H. "Sulphate resistance of buried concrete". Building Research Establishment Report, Garston, BRE, 1992.

16. Harrison, W.H. and Osborne, G.J. "Sulphate resistance of slag cement concretes excavated after 15 years from a site at Northwick Park, London". Ibid ref [3]. pp 45-52.

17. European Committee for Standardisation, "Concrete - Performance, production, placing and compliance criteria". ENV 206, Brussels, 1990.

18. European Committee for Standardisation, "Cement - Composition, specifications and conformity criteria - Part 1 : Common cements". ENV197-1, Brussels, 1992.

CONFORMITY CRITERIA FOR COMMON EUROPEAN CEMENTS

P BROOKBANKS
Quality Controller, Technical Services Department
Rugby Cement, UK

Abstract
The conformity criteria to be adopted within Part 1 (common cements) of the eventual European standard for cement, are principally statistical and require compliance to be continuously assessed on the basis of spot samples taken at the point of release from the factory (autocontrol testing). Assessment of the major properties is by variables, whilst other properties are normally assessed by attributes. Limit value conformity criteria also apply to most properties. Acceptance inspection at delivery is not addressed.

Clause 9 (conformity criteria) of the European prestandard ENV 197-1: 1992, has been revised by Working Group 13 of CEN Technical Committee TC51 (cement), in line with the development of the prestandard for evaluation of conformity. This paper, therefore, refers to the revised clause 9, incorporated in the draft standard prEN 197-1 of January 1994.

The conformity criteria are discussed and principal differences from existing UK practice are summarised.
Keywords: Attributes, autocontrol, conformity criteria, limit values, probability of acceptance, variables.

1 Introduction

Continuous assessment of cement conformity, using statistical methods, was introduced to the UK with the 1991 revision of the British Standards for cement [1]. Annex A - "Conformity Criteria" of those standards, was based on clause 10 of the June 1989 draft of the European prestandard for specification of cements [2].

This draft prestandard was developed as Part 1 of the eventual EN 197 and was approved by the CEN Technical Committee TC 51, in 1992 as the prestandard ENV 197-1: 1992 [3]. In this document, conformity criteria had become clause 9.

Euro-Cements: Impact of ENV 197 on Concrete Construction. Edited by R.K. Dhir and M.R. Jones. Published in 1994 by E & FN Spon, 2–6 Boundary Row, London SE1 8HN. ISBN: 0 419 19980 2.

CEN/TC 51 had set up a Working Group (WG13) in 1991 to consider assessment of conformity for cements. This group has produced a draft certification scheme for European cements, designed to meet the anticipated requirements for attestation of conformity under the EC Construction Products Directive [4]. This scheme document has now become ENV 197-2:1994 "Cement-conformity evaluation"[5], and is discussed in paper number 7 of this seminar. It was apparent that clause 9 of ENV 197-1: 1992 required revision to simplify it and remove redundant terminology, and at the May 1992 meeting of CEN/TC51, it was agreed that this task should also be given to WG13.

Clause 9 of ENV 197-1 has, therefore, been revised in parallel with the development of ENV 197-2 and is complimentary to it. The revision of clause 9 has been approved by CEN/TC51 Working Group 6 and forms part of the draft standard prEN 197-1: 1994 [6].

The existing clause 9 in ENV 197-1: 1992 is superseded and will not form part of the eventual EN 197-1. This paper will, therefore, in addressing cement conformity criteria, refer specifically to the revised clause 9 in prEN 197-1: 1994. Sub clauses and table numbers of that document are referenced as appropriate.

The revision has attempted to minimise on the use of statistical terminology and reference has been deleted to a number of terms, including: "Operating Characteristic Curves" and "Producers' Risk". A notable change, is the removal of the terms: "defect" and "major defect"; we now refer to test results that are outside of characteristic or limit value conformity criteria, respectively.

2 Autocontrol testing

Autocontrol is defined in prEN 197-1 as "continuous quality control of the cement, carried out by the producer". The word "control", is used here in the European context, in that we are considering a system of statistically based continuous quality inspection. To assess compliance of cement with the requirements of the standard, the manufacturer must use test data derived from testing by relevant EN 196 [7] methods, spot samples taken at the point of release from the factory. The spot samples shall be as defined in EN 196 part 7; ie. each sample shall be taken at one time and place, although it may consist of one or more consecutive increments. The autocontrol properties and required minimum test frequencies are given in table 1.

The series of autocontrol test results to be statistically evaluated is obtained over a length of time known as the "control period". In ENV 197-1, this period was optional between 6 and 12 months. The revised clause 9 in prEN 197-1, however, now makes no stipulation in this respect, although if conformity is to be attested in accordance with ENV 197-2, then the requirements of that document fix the control period at 12 months.

It should be noted, that, the manufacturer is free to test for all properties at more than the minimum frequency, if he considers it advantageous to do so. For chloride content, loss on ignition and insoluble residue, the minimum test frequency may be reduced (from 2 per week to 1 per month), provided that test results are not exceeding 50% of the characteristic value.

Table 1. Minimum testing frequencies and statistical assessment procedure
(Table 6. of prEN 197-1: 1994)

Property	Number of samples	Statistical assessment by	
		Variables[1]	Attributes
Strength	2 per week	X	
Initial setting time	2 per week	X	
Sulfate content	2 per week[2]		X
Soundness	1 per week		X
Chloride content	2 per week[2)3)]		X
Loss on ignition	2 per week[2)3)]		X
Insoluble residue	2 per week[2)3)]		X
Pozzolanicity	2 per month		X

1) If the data are not normally distributed then the method of assessment may be
decided on a case by case basis

2) If the number of samples is at least 2 per week the assessment may be made by
variables

3) When none of the results exceed 50 % of the characteristic value the frequency
may be reduced to 1 per month

3 Conformity criteria (prEN 197-1: 1994 cl 9.2)

3.1 General
The revised clause 9 in pr EN 197-1, uses two types of conformity criteria:

1. statistical conformity criteria
   - conceptually appropriate to a mass produced material - ie. assessment is against
   characteristic values associated with an acceptable percentage of non-conforming
   test results.
2. limit values
   - contrary to the statistical concept but accepted in principle because customers
   want, in addition to a statistical evaluation, some absolute limiting value for
   important properties - ie. a percentage of test results may be outside of the
   characteristic value but for each of those results, the deviation from that value is
   limited.

3.2 Statistical conformity criteria (prEN 197-1: 1994 cl 9.2.2)

3.2.1 Principles
The statistical conformity criteria are based on three elements:-

1. Characteristic values for requirements in respect of mechanical, physical and chemical properties that are measured on autocontrol samples, as specified in clause 7 of the standard.
2. An acceptable overall percentage [P_k] of test results not meeting the characteristic value for each property, as shown in table 2. This percentage is set at 10% for all properties other than strength lower limits, for which it is 5%.
3. The allowable probability of acceptance [CR] more usually known as the consumer's risk and set at 5% (see table 2). That is to say, there is a 5% risk that non-conforming cement may be accepted by a given sampling plan. Conformity assessment by a procedure based on a finite number of measurements can only produce an approximate value for the proportion of results outside of characteristic values. The bigger the sample, the better the approximation. The selected probability of acceptance CR, controls the degree of approximation by the sampling plan.

3.2.2 Means of assessment

Two methods are included, depending on the importance of the property and the frequency of sampling adopted:-

1. by variables
2. by attributes

Generally, when considering whether to adopt a variables or an attributes scheme, the greater elaboration of the variables method has to be weighed against the worth of the increased knowledge gained.

Assessment by variables involves calculations, based on the sample mean and standard deviation of each relevant property but gives an indication of how good the product is together with earlier warning of quality changes. This method may be less easy to understand to begin with, in particular, it may be difficult to accept that a series of test results may be deemed non-conforming when no individual result is outside of the characteristic value (see 3.2.2.1).

Table 2. Required values P_k and CR
        (Table 7. of prEN 197-1: 1994)

	Mechanical requirements		
	2 (or 7) and 28 day strength (Lower limit)	28 day strength (Upper limit)	Physical and chemical requirements
Acceptable overall percentage of test results P_k outside the characteristic value	5 %	10 %	
Allowable probability of acceptance CR		5 %	

Assessment by attributes is the simpler of the two procedures and merely involves counting the total number of test results in a series, that are outside of the characteristic value and checking against the number that would be expected from probability theory for a given sample size. This method is frequently used for products where it is convenient to assess numbers of imperfections by simple physical inspection. In the case of cement, of course, chemical and physical tests measurements are still required (see 3.2.2.2).

A variables scheme becomes less attractive as the required number of measurements increases, as each property has to be considered separately. It is often advantageous to apply "attributes" to the majority of the properties and "variables" to one or two of the more important requirements. This is the approach that is followed in clause 9, with assessment by variables being adopted for compressive strength and initial setting time, whilst assessment by attributes is the normal approach for other properties. Autocontrol properties and their methods of assessment are given in table 1. It should be noted, that, for properties other than strength and setting time, assessment by variables is also permitted, with the exception of soundness and pozzolanicity, providing that the test frequency is increased to a minimum of 2 samples per week. The manufacturer thus, has an option to increase his inspection efficiency if he considers the advantages to outweigh the cost of increased testing. The method of assessment for strength and, in particular, setting time, may also be decided on a case by case basis, when the data are not normally distributed.

3.2.2.1 Assessment by variables (prEN 197-1: 1994 cl 9.2.2 a))
This method assumes that the test results to be assessed are normally distributed. In principle, the overall percentage P_k of autocontrol test results that are outside of the characteristic value is estimated from the totality of test results obtained on samples taken during the control period. For practical purposes, an acceptability constant k_A is used instead of P_k. k_A represents a limiting number of standard deviations of the sample test results inside of the characteristic value. To assess conformity, therefore, a "margin" of k_A standard deviations must be added to, or subtracted from the mean of the test results (upper or lower limits). Provided that the mean $\pm$ margin is not outside of the characteristic value, then, for a given probability (CR), the acceptable percentage of test results outside of the characteristic value will not have been exceeded . This acceptable percentage is set at 10% for all properties other than lower strength limits, where it is 5% (see table 2).

As we are sampling and the true population mean is not known, the applicable values of k_A have to be calculated from the "non-central t" distribution. Discussion of the theory involved is outside the scope of this paper and for further information, the reader is referred to the Resnikoff and Lieberman tables [8], which were produced for sampling inspection by variables in particular. Derivation of the acceptability constant is also given in Annex B.8.1 of ISO 3951:1989 [9].

Sampling plans are given in table 3 which provide values of k_A for P_k = 5% and 10% for a range of sample sizes. In all cases, the values of k_A are valid for 5% probability of acceptance CR of a set of test results not conforming to the requirements (consumers risk as discussed in 3.2.1). It should be noted, that, a sample size of twenty, is generally, the minimum number accepted for assessment by variables.

Table 3. Acceptability constant k_A
          (Table 4. of prEN 197-1: 1994)

Number of test results n	k_A [1]	
	for P_k = 5 %	for P_k = 10 %
	(lower strength property)	(other properties)
20 to 21	2,40	1,93
22 to 23	2,35	1,89
24 to 25	2,31	1,85
26 to 27	2,27	1,82
28 to 29	2,24	1,80
30 to 34	2,22	1,78
35 to 39	2,17	1,73
40 to 44	2,13	1,70
45 to 49	2,09	1,67
50 to 59	2,07	1,65
60 to 69	2,02	1,61
70 to 79	1,99	1,58
80 to 89	1,97	1,56
90 to 99	1,94	1,54
100 to 149	1,93	1,53
150 to 199	1,87	1,48
200 to 299	1,84	1,45
300 to 399	1,80	1,42
> 400	1,78	1,40

Values given in this table are valid for CR = 5 %

1) The value of k_A valid for each value of n may be used instead.

The calculations for lower and upper characteristic limits, respectively, are as follows:-

Lower limits: $\bar{x} - k_A * S \geq L$
Upper limits: $\bar{x} + k_A * S \leq U$

where $\bar{x}$ = arithmetic average of the autocontrol test results obtained on all samples within the control period

S = standard deviation of the autocontrol test results obtained on all samples within the control period

k_A = the acceptability constant

L = the specified lower characteristic value (table 2 and clause 7 of pr EN 197-1)

U = the specified upper characteristic value (table 2 and clause 7 of pr EN 197-1)

EXAMPLE
Conformity assessment of 28 day strength for a cement of strength class 42.5 (upper and lower limit assessment) ie. designation: Portland cement EN 197-1 CEM I 42.5.

No. of samples in control period $= 104$
mean strength $= 56.0 \text{ N/mm}^2$
standard deviation $= 2.0 \text{ N/mm}^2$
from pr EN 197-1 table 2, lower characteristic value $= 42.5 \text{ N/mm}^2$
from pr EN 197-1 table 2, upper characteristic value $= 62.5 \text{ N/mm}^2$

From table 3 k_A for lower characteristic value
$P_k = 5\%$, 104 samples $= 1.93$

k_A for upper characteristic value
$P_k = 10\%$, 104 samples $= 1.53$

Assessment against lower characteristic value is:-
$\bar{x} - k_A * S \geq L$
ie. $56.0 - (1.93 * 2.0) \geq 42.5$
$52.1 \geq 42.5$ therefore conformity is satisfied

Assessment against upper characteristic value is:-
$\bar{x} + k_A * S \leq 62.5$
ie. $56.0 + (1.53 * 2.0) \leq 62.5$
$59.1 \leq 62.5$ therefore conformity is satisfied

The manufacturer may also deduce from these data, that with the sample standard deviation of 2.0 N/mm², his minimum operating level to remain in conformity is given by:-
$L + k_A * S = 42.5 + (1.93 * 2.0) = 46.4 \text{ N/mm}^2$

and his maximum operating level is:-

$U - k_A * S = 62.5 - (1.53 * 2.0) = 59.4 \text{ N/mm}^2$

ie. for a control period containing between 100 and 149 test results with a standard deviation of 2.0 N/mm², conformity in respect of 28 day strength will be satisfied when the mean strength is in the range 46.4 - 59.4 N/mm². To minimise the risk of non-conformity, the manufacturer should, obviously, set his mean strength well within these bounds.
Where assessment indicates that test results are running close to conformity limits and corrective action is required, this type of system forces the manufacturer to make such action progressive. Step changes will, in the short term, be counter-productive, as the increase in apparent standard deviation may cause the product $k_A * S$ to become sufficiently large for conformity to be compromised.
Assessment by variables is best accomplished via a computer programme, which

enables assessment for each relevant property to be made rapidly.   It is also advantageous if the software permits graphical representation of the data; $\bar{x}$ and $\bar{x} \pm k_A * S$ may then be plotted on an on-going basis to assess trends against the relevant characteristic values.

3.2.2.2 Assessment by attributes (prEN 197-1: 1994 cl 9.2.2 b))

As outlined earlier, assessment by attributes is made by counting the number of autocontrol test results that are outside of the characteristic value (C_D) and comparing this number with the estimated number (C_A), that would be expected for the total number of test results within the control period.
    For conformity:- $C_D \leq C_A$

Values of C_A are given in table 4 for ranges of test results up to 109. C_A is calculated from Poissons distribution for a probability of acceptance CR (consumers risk) of 5% and an acceptable overall percentage of test results outside of the characteristic value P_k, of 10%. It will be noted from table 4 that for up to 39 test results, C_A is 0. For conformity in respect of pozzolanicity, therefore, when testing at the minimum frequency of 2 per month, no test failures would be permitted in a control period of 12 months. Pozzolanicity is a good illustration of a property that has to be assessed by attributes as the test only provides a pass/fail result.

EXAMPLE

Conformity assessment of sulfate content for EN 197-1 CEM I 42.5 cement.

sulfate characteristic value	= 3.5%
No. autocontrol results in control period	= 104
No. test results above 3.5%, C_D	= 2
from table 4 for 104 results,	
estimated No. C_A	= 5

For conformity:-
    $C_D \leq C_A$
        $2 < 5$ therefore conformity is satisfied.

Table 4. C_A - Values
              (Table 5. of prEN 197-1: 1994)

Number of test results n	C_A for P_k = 10 %
up to 39	0
40 to 54	1
55 to 69	2
70 to 84	3
85 to 99	4
100 to 109	5

Values given in this table are valid
for CR = 5 %

3.3 Limit value conformity criteria (prEN 197-1: 1994 cl 9.2.3)

As stated in 3.1, the revised clause 9 incorporates limit values that are additional to the statistical conformity criteria, for those properties where such limits are considered appropriate. For conformity to be satisfied, each individual autocontrol test result for the properties concerned, must not fall outside of the relevant limit value. Applicable limit values are given in table 5. This table represents a revision and clarification of the tolerances for major defects, given previously in ENV 197-1 clause 9. It was considered that limit values gave greater clarity to the table than the former tolerances and the term "major defect", was dropped following the revision of ISO 3534 [10].

It should be noted, that, for 28 day upper strength limit, insoluble residue and loss on ignition, where no value of deviation was previously specified, it has been felt appropriate to remove these properties from the table to avoid confusion or misinterpretation.

Table 5. Limit values
        (Table 8. of prEN 197-1: 1994)

Property		Limit values					
		Strength class					
		32,5	32,5R	42,5	42,5R	52,5	52,5R
Strength (N/mm²) lower limit	2 day	-	8,0	8,0	18,0	18,0	28,0
	7 day	14,0	-	-	-	-	-
	28 day	30,0	30,0	40,0	40,0	50,0	50,0
Initial setting time (min) lower limit		45				40	
Soundness (mm) upper limit		10					
Sulfate content % upper limit	CEM I CEM II [1] CEM IV CEM V	4,0			4,5		
	CEM III/A CEM III/B	4,5					
	CEM III/C	5,0					
Chloride content (%) upper limit [2]		0,10					
Pozzolanicity		positive at 15 days					

1) Cement type CEM II/B-T may contain up to 5,0 % SO₃ for all strength classes

2) Cement type CEM III may contain more than 0,10 % chloride but in that case the actual chloride content shall be declared

For soundness, chloride content and pozzolanicity, it was considered that the limit value should be set no higher than the characteristic value (no characteristic value as such for pozzolanicity, but the maximum period for a positive test result pertains). Under these circumstances, TC51/WG6 were asked to consider whether lower characteristic values would be appropriate. At the time of writing, it appears unlikely that any such amendment will be made. The limit values, although not consistent with the statistical approach, provide further reassurance to the consumer by constraining the permitted deviation of individual test results. It should be noted, that clause 9 does not address acceptance inspection at delivery. The recommendation is made, however, that any acceptance inspection of CEM-cement, should use, at least, the limit value conformity criteria given.

4   Cement composition (prEN 197-1: 1994 cl 9.3.2)

It is a requirement of clause 9.3.2, that cement composition shall meet the relevant requirements of table 1 of pr EN 197-1. Production procedures to ensure compliance should be documented.

This clause will also be amended to match ENV 197-2 and specify a requirement for a determination of cement composition to be made at a minimum frequency of once per month, using a suitable method (no EN 196 method at present). For the moment, this is a rather "grey" area and no conformity criteria apply. ENV 197-2 requires compositional testing for all cements, however, for a CEM I cement without additions (nucleus 100% clinker), it is difficult to see the relevance.

5   Cement constituents (prEN 197-1: 1994 cl 9.3.3)

Constituents are required to meet the specifications in clause 5 of prEN 197-1. Procedures to ensure compliance are to be documented; no conformity criteria apply.

6   Differences from existing UK practice represented by prEN 197-1: 1994

The conformity criteria given in Appendix A of the current British Standards for cement are based on clause 10 of the June 1989 draft of the European prestandard. The basic methods of autocontrol assessment by variables and attributes remains unchanged in prEN 197-1, however, there are changes to terminology, test frequencies and limit values. Principal differences are as follows:-

1. Consumers risk now re-titled "allowable probability of acceptance CR".
   Producers risk now not referenced.
2. The terms "defect" and "major defect" have been dropped. We now have only non-conformities in respect of statistical or limit value criteria.

3. Acceptance inspection at delivery is no longer addressed. British Standards for cement currently give tolerances for acceptance inspection based on the major defect values that were given in prENV 197.
4. The control period for autocontrol testing is no longer specified in clause 9. This stipulation is now given in ENV 197-2 and is fixed at 12 months (currently 6 - 12 months).
5. Minimum test frequencies for soundness, chloride, loss on ignition, insoluble residue and pozzolanicity have been amended. The test frequency for soundness has been reduced and the other properties increased but with optional flexibility.
6. Limit value conformity criteria will apply to appropriate autocontrol test results. The current British Standards reject the concept of absolute limits (major defects) within a statistically assessed system. The acceptance limits given in those standards are, however, applied to cements certified under the BSI Kitemark Scheme for Cement. These acceptance limits differ in some respects from the limit values given in prEN 197-1.
7. It should be noted that prEN 197-1 does not cover Sulfate-resisting Portland cement, conformity criteria for which, are currently given in BS 4027:1991.

7   References

1. BS 12:1991   Specification for Portland cement
   BS 146:1991   Specification for Portland blastfurnace cements
   BS 4027:1991 Specification for Sulfate-resisting Portland cement
   BS 4246:1991 Specification for High slag blastfurnace cement
   BS 6588:1991 Specification for Portland pulverized-fuel ash cements
   BS 6610:1991 Specification for Pozzolanic pulverized-fuel ash cement

2. prENV 197: 1989E Cement:Composition, specifications and conformity criteria. Final draft June 1989.
3. ENV 197-1: 1992 Cement-Composition, specifications and conformity criteria - Part 1: Common cements.
4. Construction Products Directive: European Council Directive of 21.12.88 on the approximation of laws, regulations and administrative provisions of the Member States relating to construction products (89/106/EEC).
5. ENV 197-2: 1994 Cement-Conformity evaluation.
6. prEN 197-1: 1994 Cement-composition, specifications and conformity criteria - Part 1: Common cements, First Draft, January 1994.
7. EN 196 Methods of testing cement Parts 1, 2, 3, 4, 5, 6, 7 and 21.
8. Resnikoff, G.J. & Lieberman, G.J.. Tables of the Non-Central t-Distribution. Stanford University Press 1957
9. ISO 3951: 1989 Sampling procedures for inspection by variables.
10. ISO 3534: 1993 Statistics - Vocabulary and symbols.

QUANTIFYING CEMENT CONTENT IN FRESH AND HARDENED CONCRETE

M G TAYLOR
Standards Manager
British Cement Association, UK

Abstract
The compositional complexity of concrete, in the fresh or hardened state, ranges from the 'fairly simple' to the 'extremely complicated', when viewed from an analytical perspective. With the introduction of EN(V) 197, the compositional possibilities for the cement component have multiplied and the implications for analytical procedures in a U.K. and a pan-European context, are considered here.

In addition, the circumstances under which the cement content of concrete, in the fresh and hardened state, may be required to be quantified, are identified.

The main analytical techniques are described, a historical perspective is presented and the relevant documentation is identified and discussed where appropriate.

The establishing of compliance criteria is also discussed and limits are compared for the quantification of cement to the fresh and hardened states.

The applicability of 'RAM type' analysis for fresh concrete and the BS 1881: Part 124, chemical and petrographical, methods for hardened concrete, is explored.

The alternative, principally instrumental, approaches to the well documented and familiar methods are also briefly considered for their applicability.

In conclusion, an opinion is expressed on the likely overall effects that the introduction of the EN(V) 197 specifications will have on the practical value of analysis in the U.K. and on the perceptions of the concrete producer.

Keywords: Cement content, fresh, hardened, analysis, RAM, BS 1881: Part 124, compliance, EN(V) 197, microscopy, petrography.

Euro-Cements: Impact of ENV 197 on Concrete Construction. Edited by R.K. Dhir and M.R. Jones. Published in 1994 by E & FN Spon, 2–6 Boundary Row, London SE1 8HN. ISBN: 0 419 19980 2.

1   Introduction

The decision to determine the cement content of concrete, whether in the fresh state or, particularly, in the hardened state, should be carefully considered. Such determinations are frequently labour intensive, expensive in requirements for capital equipment, sometimes both and ultimately often misunderstood by the engineer.

There ought to be a clearly understood and defined need for quantifying cement content. In the case of the hardened material, all other solutions to a problem should have been discounted before any diagnostic analytical 'tool' is applied. In the case of the analysis of fresh concrete, there is rarely a diagnostic aspect, since the purpose will normally be to deploy an effective pre-placement quality or compliance test.

Philosophically speaking, analysis involves a 'reductionist' (prescriptive) solution to a requirement, which is in contrast to the stated aims of, say, the Construction Products Directive[1] and the perceived 'Euro-culture' of 'holistic' performance testing. However, if the available performance tests tend to generate results to a timescale incompatible with construction activity, reductionist techniques become attractive.

In the U.K. there has developed a 'tradition' wherein analysis of hardened concrete, whether chemical, petrographical or optical, is commissioned, as a last resort, when standard concrete specimens have failed to comply with compressive strength requirements. This tradition eventually led to the drafting of a national testing standard for hardened concrete[2] and created a precedent for the introduction of a BSI draft for development, DD83, for assessing the composition of fresh concrete[3]. If a parallel tradition has arisen in any continental European country, it has not yet found expression in the national documentation. Neither will the tradition find early expression within the framework of harmonised Euronorms, since the CEN (TC 104) programme of work on concrete does not address the analysis of composition. Accordingly, the implications for the analysis of concrete, of the advent of EN 197 type cements, can only be considered within a U.K. context. In practice this would generally indicate a fairly minor perturbation to a recognised system, given that cements manufactured in the U.K. will remain compositionally, by and large, as they were prior to the changes in the documentation. In theory, however, any cement specified in EN 197 could be used in U.K. concrete and the implications for the quantification of cement content, bear exploration.

2 General

2.1 Analysis of fresh concrete
Methods for determining the composition and quality of fresh concrete have existed since at least 1929[4].

The buoyancy method (after Kirkham[5]) was eventually documented in BS 1881 (method now withdrawn from the BS but retained in DD 83) in order to provide a complete, although labour intensive and time-consuming, analysis of fresh concrete. The growing insistence on effective standards of quality control on site, particularly for concretes specified in terms of prescribed mix proportions but also for designed mixes specified by strength, led to the development of more rapid instrumental means of analysis. In the case of concretes specified by strength, reliable, rapid analysis can give an early warning of potential failures as well as giving a means for assessing compliance with any additional prescriptive specification for, say, minimum cement content.

Several organisations devoted considerable time and effort, in the 1960's and 1970's, to developing rapid methods for compliance purposes. Each method has since been redrafted and is now documented in BSI DD83. A chemical method was developed by scientists at the then Greater London Council (GLC)[6]. A physical method (pressure filtration) was developed at Messrs. Sandberg[7]. A physical separation system, using dense organic liquids, was developed at Laing[8] and in 1974 the Cement and Concrete Association (now BCA) published a report[9] describing arguably the most rapid technique; the 'constant volume method of the rapid analysis machine (RAM). The RAM, still commercially available, has been subjected to a very detailed laboratory precision experiment[10], a study into delayed analysis by freezing[11] and field investigations[12].

Work continues in BSI Working Group B/517/1/31 on the task of transforming DD83 into BS 1881: Part 128[13]. The latest draft includes only three distinct methods; the constant volume RAM; the pressure filter method and the 'old BS 1881' buoyancy method. The body of the draft deals with the more general aspects of the analytical methods, whereas, a suite of normative annexes describe, in detail, the operation of each technique and the extensions necessary for the determinations of fly ash (pfa), blastfurnace slag and water contents of fresh concrete.

2.2 Analysis of hardened concrete

Hardened concrete may be analysed for its cement content because there is doubt about its compliance with a specification ('cube' analysis), doubt about its quality in the structure ('core' analysis) or more often because its performance in service has not fulfilled expectations (durability study). Although descriptions of chemical methods of analysis have been available since 1950[14], the seminal guide to analysis (chemical, petrographical and optical) has been provided by Figg and Bowden[15], as a development from earlier work at the Building Research Station (BRE). Since 'Figg and Bowden', two further documents have advanced the science (and art) of hardened analysis. BS 1881: Part 124[16] was published in 1988 (revision of BS 1881: Part 6) and Concrete Society Technical Report (CSTR) No. 32[17] was published in 1989. Taken together, these latter two documents provide the practitioner, specifier and engineer alike, with the most up to date detailed information and guidance for the full compositional analysis of hardened concrete.

3 Range of composition of cements to EN 197

Early forecasts by CEN committee TC51/WG6 indicated that some nine or ten major cement types could be standardised within the EN 197 series. The types which were envisaged are reproduced in table 1.

Table 1.   CEN/TC 51/WG6 - Proposed sub-division of
EN(V) 197 into Parts; @ 1991

Part 1:   Common cement.
  (Final draft 1992)

Part 2:   Sulfate-resisting cement.
  (Third draft 1994)

Part 3:   Low heat cement.

Part 4:   Low effective alkali cement.

Part 5:   White cement.

Part 6:   Leaching resistant cement.

Part 7:   Natural prompt cement.

Part 8:   "Danish Blok-cement".

Part 9:   (Not identified at time of proposal).

Part 10:   Calcium aluminate cement.

In terms of composition (but not necessarily standard strength class), cements within the scope of Parts 2 and 3 will be covered by the twenty-five types already specified in EN(V) 197-1 for common cements[18].

The drafting of EN 197-10 for calcium aluminate cement is well advanced but although its quantification in hardened concrete presents few difficulties to an experienced analyst, it is outside the scope of BS 1881: Part 124 and is regarded as outside the scope of the present paper.

No drafting work has taken place for cements to be specified to Parts 4 to 9 and so they merit no further consideration.

Common cements to Part 1 are essentially Portland types but can contain a wide variety of main and minor constituents. The full range of specified types and their compositions are reproduced in tables 2 and 3.

In fact, of these numerous possible cement types (and sub-types), only six or seven are generally available in any particular CEN Member State. Consequently, identification and quantification of a cement within either the hardened matrix of a concrete or present in the fresh mix is, in national practice, not quite so daunting a task as it might at first seem.

If, however, a sample of hardened concrete presented for analysis could, in principle, contain a cement to any one of the compositions listed in tables 2 and 3, precise identification and quantification would rarely be possible. Conversely, if the

Table 2.   Cement types and composition specified in table 1 of EN(V) 197-1 for common cement.

Note: Table 1 in the EN(V) has been reproduced as tables 2 and 3 for legibility.

Cement type	Designation	Notation	Clinker K	Blastf. slag S	Silica fume D[3]	Pozzolana natural P	Pozzolana industr. Q[4]	Flyash siliceous V	Minor additional constit.[2]
CEM I	Portland cement	CEM I	95-100	-	-	-	-	-	0-5
CEM II	Portland-slag cement	CEM II/A-S	80-94	6-20	-	-	-	-	0-5
		CEM II/B-S	65-79	21-35	-	-	-	-	0-5
	Portland-silica fume cement	CEM II/A-D	90-94	-	6-10	-	-	-	0-5
	Portland-pozzolana cement	CEM II/A-P	80-94	-	-	6-20	-	-	0-5
		CEM II/B-P	65-79	-	-	21-35	-	-	0-5
		CEM II/A-Q	80-94	-	-	-	6-20	-	0-5
		CEM II/B-Q	65-79	-	-	-	21-35	-	0-5
	Portland-fly ash cement	CEM II/A-V	80-94	-	-	-	-	6-20	0-5
		CEM II/B-V	65-79	-	-	-	-	21-35	0-5
		CEM II/A-W	80-94	-	-	-	-	-	0-5
		CEM II/B-W	65-79	-	-	-	-	-	0-5
	Portland-burnt shale cement	CEM II/A-T	80-94	-	-	-	-	-	0-5
		CEM II/B-T	65-79	-	-	-	-	-	0-5
	Portland-limestone cement	CEM II/A-L	80-94	-	-	-	-	-	0-5
		CEM II/B-L	65-79	-	-	-	-	-	0-5
	Portland-composite cement	CEM II/A-M	80-94	←--------------------------------------6-20[5]--------------------→					0-5
		CEM II/B-M	65-79	←-------------------------------------21-35[5]-------------------→					0-5
CEM III	Blastfurnace cement	CEM III/A	35-64	36-65	-	-	-	-	0-5
		CEM III/B	20-34	66-80	-	-	-	-	0-5
		CEM III/C	5-19	81-95	-	-	-	-	0-5
CEM IV	Pozzolanic cement	CEM IV/A	65-89	-	←----------------------11-35----------------------→				0.5
		CEM IV/B	45-64	-	←----------------------36-55----------------------→				0-5
CEM V	Composite cement	CEM V/A	40-64	18-30	-	←---------------18-30--------------→			0-5
		CEM V/B	20-39	31-50	-	←---------------31-50--------------→			0-5

1) The values in the table refer to the sum of the main and minor additional constituents.
2) Minor additional constituents may be filler or may be one or more of the main constituents unless these are included as main constituents in the cement.
3) The proportion of silica fume is limited to 10%.
4) The proportion of non ferrous slag is limited to 15%.
5) The proportion of filler is limited to 5%.

Table 3. Cement types and composition specified in table 1 of EN(V) 197-1 for common cement.

Note: Table 1 in the EN(V) has been reproduced as tables 2 and 3 for legibility.

Cement type	Designation	Notation	Clinker K	Fly ash calcar. W	Burnt shale T	Limestone L	Minor additional constit.
				Main constituents			
CEM I	Portland cement	CEM I	95-100	-	-	-	0-5
CEM II	Portland-slag cement	CEM II/A-S	80-94	-	-	-	0-5
		CEM II/B-S	65-79	-	-	-	0-5
	Portland-silica fume cement	CEM II/A-D	90-94	-	-	-	0-5
	Portland-pozzolana cement	CEM II/A-P	80-94	-	-	-	0-5
		CEM II/B-P	65-79	-	-	-	0-5
		CEM II/A-Q	80-94	-	-	-	0-5
		CEM II/B-Q	65-79	-	-	-	0-5
	Portland-fly ash cement	CEM II/A-V	80-94	-	-	-	0-5
		CEM II/B-V	65-79	-	-	-	0-5
		CEM II/A-W	80-94	6-20	-	-	0-5
		CEM II/B-W	65-79	21-35	-	-	0-5
	Portland-burnt shale cement	CEM II/A-T	80-94	-	6-20	-	0-5
		CEM II/B-T	65-79	-	21-35	-	0-5
	Portland-limestone cement	CEM II/A-L	80-94	-	-	6-20	0-5
		CEM II/B-L	65-79	-	-	21-35	0-5
	Portland-composite cement	CEM II/A-M	80-94	←------------------(see table 2)--------------------→			
		CEM II/B-M	65-79	←------------------(see table 2)--------------------→			
CEM III	Blastfurnace cement	CEM III/A	35-64	-	-	-	0-5
		CEM III/B	20-34	-	-	-	0-5
		CEM III/C	5-19	-	-	-	0-5
CEM IV	Pozzolanic cement	CEM IV/A	65-89	-	-	-	0.5
		CEM IV/B	45-64	-	-	-	0-5
CEM V	Composite cement	CEM V/A	40-64	-	-	-	0-5
		CEM V/B	20-39	-	-	-	0-5

cement type/sub-type had been precisely identified from, say, construction records, then quantification could be reasonably straightforward but equally, could depend critically on the aggregate type(s) present.

In the case of cements combined from their constituents as 'mixer blends', then quantification of the **individual constituents** can range from; 'the difficult' through 'the intractable' to 'the impossible' by either fresh or hardened analysis. However, which category of 'difficulty' is actually involved will depend specifically, in the case of hardened analysis, on factors such as the type and numbers of constituents, their solubility in acid compared to the solubility of the aggregates, and the availability of any or all of the concrete's solid components for control/calibration purposes.

4 Analysis of fresh concrete for cement content using the Rapid Analysis Machine (RAM)

4.1 Principle of the method

A weighed sample of concrete is transferred to the elutriation column of the RAM. Fine material of 250μm or less is raised as a suspension, sub-sampled (approx. 10% of original) and screened through a vibrating 150μm sieve into a conditioning vessel in which the suspension is flocculated. The suspension then settles in a removable 'constant volume vessel' (CVV) which is brought to a constant volume state by the operation of siphons. The CVV is removed from the RAM and weighed. At the time of weighing, the CVV contains the separated fraction of fine material in a flocculated state plus supernatant water to give a reproducible total volume. The mass of flocculated fines weighs typically 120g. It consists of cement, of whichever type used, any additional/replacement materials and silt, clay and fines (passing 150μm) from the aggregates; all in the same proportions, by mass, as contained in the original concrete sample. The mass of cementitious material and fine sand ('silt') in the original suspension is determined by reference to a calibration chart. The chart is previously established from tests on the components of the concrete typical of, **or preferably precisely the same as**, those to be used. The cement content is then determined by making a subtraction, silt correction, for the fines contributed by the aggregate.

4.2 Establishing compliance criteria

Analysis of fresh concrete allows concrete mix proportions, in particular cement content, to be assessed directly for compliance with specified requirements. Such requirements may take the form of minimum (or maximum) contents for designed mixes, minimum contents for designated mixes or specified mix proportions for prescribed and standard mixes to BS 5328: Part 2[19]. However, an assessment will only be deemed to be valid, if reliable and transparent compliance criteria have been appropriately derived and have been widely acknowledged and accepted.

It is extremely unlikely that unique values for limiting criteria for compliance, irrespective of circumstances, would now be acceptable to the concrete producer, even though this was the simplistic position taken in the 1981 publication of BS 5328[20].

Assessment of compliance was given in this earlier version by:

"16.4.2. Where compliance [with minimum or maximum cement contents] is assessed from the results of analysis tests on fresh concrete, the cement content shall not be less than 90% of the specified minimum or more than 110% of the specified maximum."

The 1981 publication of BS 5328 has been superseded, and now Part 4[21] provides the references to testing and assessing compliance of concrete, including the analysis of fresh concrete. In Part 4, sub-clause 3.12 states:

"3.12. Cement content or mix proportions by the analysis of fresh concrete.
Where fresh concrete is to be analysed to determine the mix proportions, cement content or free water/cement ratio, the sampling and testing shall be carried out by a method specified in DD 83 or as otherwise agreed."

Three further identically worded sub-clauses (3.13.3, 3.14.4 and 3.15.2) address compliance, based on the analysis of fresh concrete:

"Where compliance is assessed from the results of one of the analysis tests on the fresh concrete described in DD 83, the compliance limits shall be specified or agreed by the purchaser and producer based on the information given in DD 83."

DD83 includes "Sections four and five" which deal rigorously with the establishment of compliance criteria. 'Section four' addresses the accuracy and precision of the test methods and 'Section five' documents the procedure for assessing compliance. The statistically based compliance rules which emerge are generalised in that they can be applied to any of the five test methods described in the draft for development.

The limits are derivable from two equations; one for assessing compliance against a specified minimum cement content and the other for a specified maximum. Each is only applicable for decisions relating to single batches of concrete.

The equation which is recommended for assessing compliance with a specified <u>minimum</u> is given as:

$$"C_{min.} = S\text{-}B_B + B_{SR+T} + B_{C+M} - k\sqrt{SD^2}_{total}$$
where $C_{min.}$ is the minimum cement content compliance limit"

Compliance may be assumed if the measured cement content is:

"(a) equal to or exceeds the compliance limit".

In the case of a specified <u>maximum</u> cement content, the equation which is recommended is given as:

$$"C_{max.} = S + B_B + B_{SR+T} + B_{C+M} + k\sqrt{SD^2}_{total}$$
where $C_{max.}$ is the maximum cement content compliance limit".

Compliance may be assumed in this case if the measured cement content is:

"b) equal to or less than the compliance limit".

In both cases, the terms identified by the B suffix are estimates of bias (accuracy), whereas the term SD^2_{total} is an estimate of the overall precision, expressed as the total variance; k is the statistical constant 1.96.

Detailed procedures for assessing the bias components and the precision components of the methods are given in DD 83. The procedures in clause 14, 15 and 16 are to be used for production concrete. By carrying out the relevant procedures, data is generated for substitution in the previous equations. If the producer is consulted and involved in this process, then agreement can be reached on the applicability of the calculated limits.

In cases where it is impracticable to carry out the aforementioned procedures, assumed values (given in tables 9 and 10 of DD 83) as estimates of bias and variance, may be used. However, the values are based on limited data and agreement with a producer as to their application may be difficult to obtain.

In the specific case of the Rapid Analysis Machine (RAM), a draft compliance specification for the analysis of fresh concrete, for its cement content, was established in 1979[22]. Compliance limits were given as single values for the following applications:

"7. Compliance limits
(a) Not more than 25 kg/m³ above a specified maximum cement content.
or
(b) Not more than 25 kg/m³ below a specified minimum cement content.
or
(c) Not more than 35 kg/m³ above or below the specified cement content when maximum and minimum limits are required."

These quoted limits were obtained from worst case conditions and accordingly are probably acceptable to a concrete producer. Their operation in practice implies that in the case of an average ready-mixed concrete plant operating with a batching error of 5 kg/m³ (cement), the probability of rejecting good concrete is approximately 3%, in the case of the 25 kg/m³ maximum or minimum limit. The probability will be less than 1% in the case of the ± 35 kg/m³ limit.

If a producer were to consider the former 3% to be unacceptable, it could be reduced to 1% if the average cement content were to be increased by 5 kg/m³.

The draft compliance specification was drawn up from work carried out using BS 12 ordinary Portland cements. The following section explores any implications there may be for accuracy of quantification when cements other than BS 12 types (CEM I's in EN(V) 197-1) have been used.

4.3 Implications of the range of compositions of EN(V) 197-1 cements on accurate quantification using the RAM

Accurate quantification of cement content using the RAM is fundamentally dependent on the calibration procedure in which a linear relationship is obtained between cement content and the mass of the constant volume vessel (CVV), including its contents.

The characteristics of a cement which could affect the slope of the calibration line are density and fineness. These will vary to some extent with composition. The former, simply because the particle density of cement clinker will differ from that of other main constituents and the latter, because the manufacturer will optimise fineness for a particular cement type, strength class and strength sub-class.

In practice, the above considerations will be of academic interest only, if specific calibration lines are set up and used for each cement sub-type. The calibration and test system will then have been normalised for any bias which could have been introduced if calibration had been carried out using a cement of a different sub-type to that in the test samples. If, however, as an example, a CEM I cement were to be used for calibration but a CEM IV/B (pozzolanic) cement had been used in the concrete, the significant difference in their densities would lead to an under-estimate of the cement content.

In practical trials using U.K. manufactured Portland cements (CEM I), it was found that the variations in density and fineness had a very small effect on the test result. However, since that work was carried out even CEM I types can contain up to 5% of a minor additional constituent (mac) and in the absence of experimental evidence to the contrary, it would be prudent always to calibrate the RAM using the cement which is being used in the concrete.

When calibration is carried out correctly, using the appropriate cement type/sub-type and aggregates (silt correction), then the compliance criteria previously established from trials using just Portland cements should be equally applicable to any other manufactured cement to EN(V) 197-1. However, experimental trials are required to establish this, both generally, but particularly for cements which contain extremely fine materials such as condensed silica fume.

5. **Analysis of hardened concrete for cement content using the BS 1881: Part 124 procedures**

5.1 **Principle of the method**
Before carrying out any test, it is essential to obtain an adequate sample for testing, using the procedures outlined in the standard and in CSTR No. 32.

The sample is crushed to obtain a representative sub-sample passing the 150 μm sieve. This sample is then subjected to successive extractions with cold dilute acid and hot dilute alkali solutions to dissolve the soluble constituents of the cement (although some of the aggregate often also dissolves).

The extract is then analysed for its content of both silica and calcium oxide (the two major oxides in a Portland cement).

If the cement source is known, or its type/sub-type is known and a reliable elemental analysis (or cement sample) is available, figures should be obtainable for the calcium oxide and soluble and/or total silica contents of the cement, and so the cement content can be determined from each oxide, by simple proportion, and compared.

If a calcareous aggregate is present, and control samples of the aggregates are not available, only the soluble silica is likely to be of value in calculating the cement content. This may well tend to a loss in accuracy.

It is preferable to analyse control samples of the aggregate alongside the sample under test, and to apply appropriate corrections to the results before calculating the cement content. If control samples of the aggregate are either not available, or reliable control analyses cannot be assumed, then determined cement contents will be erroneously high.

5.2   **Establishing compliance criteria - chemical analysis**

The establishment of generally acceptable compliance criteria for the determination of cement content from the analyses of hardened concrete has, so far, not been seriously attempted.   It is unlikely that the attempt will ever be made, given the potential diversity of concrete composition and analytical circumstance.   In the case of fresh analysis, there are a fairly limited number of bias and precision components which contribute to variability.   Conversely, there are an almost unlimited number of components of variability which could contribute to an analysis of hardened concrete. However, if considerations were to be limited to the analysis of 'well-defined' concretes, then useful indicative limits for compliance, of necessarily limited applicability, could be derived.   In this context, 'well-defined' concretes would be those which contained aggregates which contributed either negligible or small known amounts of soluble calcium/silica to the analysis and which contained manufactured cements of known elemental composition.

Such 'idealised' circumstances could, in fact, prevail where the engineer has requested that hardened analysis be used to aid the accurate diagnosis of a 'cube failure'.   At an elapsed time of 28 days or less, the analyst can obtain, either samples of the concrete's components or accurate information about them.

Even in such idealised cases, assuming that compliance criteria had been sufficiently established, it is very unlikely that they would be acknowledged by all the parties to be robust enough to, alone, determine compliance with, say, a minimum cement content specification.   They may, however, by assessing the cement content, be helpful in establishing the cause of a failure to comply with a compressive strength requirement.

Within the publication, CSTR No. 32, a tentative attempt has been made to determine approximate values for compliance limits, applicable to the idealised situation.   These have evolved from the results of an interlaboratory precision experiment carried out in 1983.   The results obtained from the experiment relate solely to testing variability and have been abstracted and reproduced in table 4.

Table 4.   Precision estimates for testing variability. (Results obtained from CS/SCI inter-laboratory precision experiment in 1983).

Concrete	kg/m³ cement				
	Batched mean	observed mean	r	R	95% cl (4 samples)
Flint gravel	240	240	35	55	± 30
Flint gravel	425	425	45	70	± 40
Limestone	345	340	40	40	± 15

In the table, repeatability r, and reproducibility R, are as defined in BS 5497: Part 1[23] and the 95% confidence limits have been determined from:

$$\frac{1}{\sqrt{2}} \sqrt{\frac{R^2 - r^2 (n - 1)}{n}}$$

for n = 4 test results (equivalent to duplicate tests on 2 No. standard cubes)

It can be seen from a comparison of the figures for batched means and observed means that the methods can be accurate under idealised circumstances but cannot generally match the precision estimates obtained for fresh analysis using the RAM.

In order to obtain useable compliance criteria, a measure of sampling variability is also required. Tentative values, abstracted from CSTR No. 32 are reproduced in table 5. These have been obtained from the results of unpublished work.

Table 5.   Sampling variability - results of unpublished work presented in CSTR No. 32, 1989.

Number of samples	Accuracy of measured cement content (95% confidence limits)
1	± 50 kg/m³
2	± 35 kg/m³
3	± 30 kg/m³
4	± 25 kg/m³

If the confidence limits for sampling and testing variability are combined, using the root-square formula, tentative compliance criteria (expressed as 95% confidence limits) can be obtained. Calculated limits are given in table 6.

Table 6.   Sampling and testing variabilities combined. ('Idealised' situation, appropriate to 4 No. samples (cores) and 2 No. standard cubes).

Concrete	Batched mean	Observed mean	95% confidence limits
		kg/m³ cement	
Flint gravel	240	240	± 40
Flint gravel	425	425	± 50
Limestone	345	340	± 30

Clearly these compliance limits are wide in most cases and must be considered to be too wide to be of value in assessing compliance with a specification. Their magnitude is principally a function of the magnitude of reproducibility R. A statistical analysis of variance has revealed that almost all the between-laboratory variability in the precision experiment arose in the measurement of calcium oxide (% CaO) and soluble silica (% SiO_2) in the concrete samples. These two measurements form the fundamental chemical basis for the quantification of any cement in hardened concrete using BS 1881 procedures.

The participation of testing laboratories in a recognised proficiency testing scheme would help to minimise any bias in the determination of these chemical analytes, effectively reduce the magnitude of R and hence reduce the confidence intervals, seen in table 6, to levels which would have a practicable value.

5.3 Implications of the range of compositions of EN(V) 197-1 cements on accurate quantification, using the BS 1881: Part 124 procedures.

5.3.1 Introduction

The implications for accurate quantification of cement using the simple selective dissolution techniques of BS 1881 are manifold. Unfortunately the ramifications are so wide, given the different analytical circumstances that can prevail in practice, that it would be unwise to try to deal with them all exhaustively. In limiting the discussions to manageable proportions, only the quantification of manufactured cements will be considered, together with the effects on analysis of calcareous and siliceous aggregates.

5.3.2 U.K. situation; known cement type, known aggregates and analysis at age up to 28 days

Although there is a large matrix of cement types/sub-types given in EN(V) 197-1, only six or seven are actually specified and generally available in the U.K.; see the second and fourth columns in table 7 below for the current British Standards and the equivalent 'CEM' notations.

British Standard specifications include cements of type CEM I to CEM IV but not CEM V.

In the case where an elemental analysis of the cement, to the acid-soluble basis, is known and the aggregates are either predominantly siliceous, calcareous or a combination of the two, the effects on potential accuracy of cement type are as given respectively in tables 8, 9 and 10.

The analytical circumstances addressed in tables 8 to 10 should be clearly understood, if the implications are not to be misinterpreted.

Firstly, only quantification of the total cement content is being considered. Determination of the proportions of some of the main constituents (granulated blastfurnace slag, limestone, etc.) may be possible, in some cases, using additional chemical techniques described in BS 1881: Part 124, but in the specific case of fly ash, no simple chemical procedure exists.

Secondly, a knowledge of the **acid-soluble** elemental composition of the cement is required, in particular for the soluble SiO_2 component. The U.K. cement manufacturer's total X-ray analysis will only correspond to this for cements which do not contain fly ash or other siliceous minor additional constituent. In those cases, if soluble SiO_2 is the preferred tracer for cement (i.e. calcareous aggregates are present) then a separate sample of the cement should be analysed for its soluble SiO_2 content by the BS 1881 procedures.

Table 7.   Comparison of British and European cements

Cement designation to EN(V) 197-1	British Standard cement	Cement type to EN(V) 197-1	Notation in ENV (197)-1 CEM....	Clinker content %	Content of other main constituents %
Portland cement	BS 12:1991 BS 4027[+]	I	I	95-100	-
Portland slag cement	BS 146:1991		II/A-S	80-94	6-20
			II/B-S	65-79	21-35
Portland silica fume cement	None		II/A-D	90-94	6-10
Portland pozzolana cement	None		II/A-P	80-94	6-20
			II/B-P	65-79	21-35
			II/A-Q	80-94	6-20
			II/B-Q	65-79	21-35
Portland fly ash cement	BS 6588:1991	II	II/A-V	80-94	6-20
	BS 6588:1991		II/B-V	65-79	21-35
	None		II/A-W	80-94	6-20
			II/B-W	65-79	21-35
Portland burnt shale cement	None		II/A-T	80-94	6-20
			II/B-T	65-79	21-35
Portland limestone cement	BS 7583:1992		II/A-L	80-94	6-20
	None		II/B-L	65-79	21-35
Portland composite cement	None		II/A-M	80-94	6-20
			II/B-M	65-79	21-35
Blastfurnace cement	BS 146:1991*	III	III/A	35-64	36-65
	None*		III/B	20-34	66-80
	None*		III/C	5-19	81-95
Pozzolanic cement	None	IV	IV/A	65-89	11-35
	BS 6610:1991		IV/B	45-64	36-55
Composite cement	None	V	V/A	40-64	36-60
			V/B	20-39	61-80

*   BS 4246: 1991 covers a blastfurnace slag content of 50-85%.

[+]   Cement to BS 4027, sulfate-resisting Portland cement is included here, since it complies with EN(V) 197-1, CEM I, although it will eventually be covered specifically in a future part of EN197.

Table 8.   Effect of cement type on quantification (**siliceous aggregates, coarse and fine**; known acid-soluble elemental composition of cement and age of concrete up to 28 days)

Cement designation	Cement type	Using CaO as preferred tracer for cement		
		Potential accuracy		
		good	medium	poor
Portland cement	CEM I	✓		
	CEM I inc. an mac	✓		
Portland slag cement	CEM II/A-S & II/B-S	✓		
Portland fly ash cement	CEM II/A-V & II/B-V	✓		
Portland limestone cement	CEM II/A-L	✓		
Blastfurnace cement	CEM III/A & III/B	✓		
Pozzolanic cement	CEM IV/B	✓		

Note: Soluble SiO_2 tracer would give results as indicated in table 9.

Table 9.   Effect of cement type on quantification. (**Calcareous aggregates, coarse and fine**; known acid-soluble elemental composition of cement and age of concrete up to 28 days)

Cement designation	Cement type	Using soluble SiO_2 as preferred tracer for cement		
		Potential accuracy		
		good	medium	poor
Portland cement	CEM I	✓		
	CEM I inc. an mac	✓		
Portland slag cement	CEM II/A-S & II/B-S	✓		
Portland fly ash cement	CEM II/A-V & II/B-V		✓	✓
Portland limestone cement	CEM II/A-L	✓		
Blastfurnace cement	CEM III/A & III/B	✓		
Pozzolanic cement	CEM IV/B		✓	✓

Note: CaO tracer would be unsuitable for all types.

Table 10. Effect of cement type on quantification. (**Calcareous coarse plus siliceous fines**; known acid-soluble elemental composition of cement and age of concrete up to 28 days)

Cement designation	Cement type	Using soluble SiO_2 as preferred tracer for cement		
		Potential accuracy		
		good	medium	poor
Portland cement	CEM I	✓		
	CEM inc. an mac	✓		
Portland slag cement	CEM II/A-S & II/B-S	✓		
Portland fly ash cement	CEM II/A-V & II/B-V		✓	✓
Portland limestone cement	CEM II/A-L	✓		
Blastfurnace cement	CEM III/A & III/B	✓		
Pozzolanic cement	CEM IV/B		✓	✓

Note: CaO tracer would be unsuitable for all types.

Thirdly, analysis at an early age (less than 28 days) should ensure that representative aggregate samples are available for analysis and that any pozzolanic reactions, leading to an increase in the apparent soluble SiO_2 content of any pozzolanic constituent, and thereby a discrepancy between the original analysis of the cement and that actually pertaining at the time of the concrete analysis, should be limited.

5.3.3   U.K. situation; cement of unknown type

In some cases where the cement is of an unknown type and no additional information is likely to be available, the analyst may or may not detect the presence of constituents (e.g. slag or fly ash, etc.) other than Portland cement. If he does not test for additional constituents and yet some are present, his analysis will be inaccurate, since he will almost certainly apply an inappropriate Portland cement analysis, by default, in the calculations. If, however, slag were to be detected, the analyst would not know for certain whether he was dealing with a manufactured slag cement or with slag added at the mixer, assuming that he had been able to discount the presence of a slag aggregate. In either case, his only recourse would be to determine the slag content directly by the sulfide measurement in BS 1881 and then apportion the determined CaO and soluble SiO_2 between the slag, Portland cement component and aggregate contributions.

It should be apparent from the foregoing simple example that accuracy of quantification for cement types, which are completely unknown, could vary from good, right through to worthless. Where the actual value of a result lies within that range will depend on the skill and experience of the analyst and the rigour brought to bear. Complete reliance on the procedures of chemical analysis would be a mistake in these circumstances and frequently, a multi-disciplinary effort is required in order to improve the value of the analysis.

5.3.4   Pan-European situation; known cement type (other than those of sub-clause 5.3.2), known aggregates and analysis at age up to 28 days

If it were to be considered that any of the cements specified in EN(V) 197-1 could be present in a sample of hardened concrete in any of the CEN Member States, then clearly the implications could be wider than previously described.

The type of aggregates present (whether siliceous, calcareous or a combination) will determine which tracer species (calcium oxide or soluble SiO_2) can be used for cement quantification. Where both tracer analytes can be used, calcium oxide will nearly always give the more accurate results.

The effects on potential accuracy of analysis for cement types, other than those already considered for the U.K., are as given in table 11. The use of either calcium oxide or soluble SiO_2 as tracer is described.

Table 11.   Effect of manufactured cement type on quantification (cements not specified or generally available in the U.K.)

Cement designation	Cement type	Using CaO tracer[1] Potential accuracy			Using soluble SiO_2 tracer[2] Potential accuracy		
		good	medium	poor	good	medium	poor
Portland silica fume cement	CEM II/A-D	✓			✓[3]		
Portland-pozzolana cement	CEM II/A-P	✓				✓	
	CEM II/B-P	✓				✓	
	CEM II/A-Q	✓				✓	
	CEM II/B-Q	✓				✓	
Portland-burnt shale cement	CEM II/A-T	✓				✓	
	CEM II/B-T	✓				✓	
Portland-composite cement	CEM II/A-M	✓					✓[4]
	CEM II/B-M	✓					✓
Composite cement	CEM V/A	✓				✓	✓
	CEM V/B	✓				✓	✓

Note 1:   The CaO tracer would be used preferentially in cases where the aggregates were predominantly siliceous and contributed little CaO to the analysis.

Note 2:   The soluble SiO_2 tracer would be used of necessity in cases where the aggregate contributed significant amounts of CaO to the analysis.

Note 3:   In the case of Portland-silica fume cement, the total SiO_2 content from the cement analysis should be used in calculations together with the soluble SiO_2 content of the concrete. Silica fume is extremely reactive and although much is originally insoluble in anhydrous cement, all will be solubilised during 28 days hydration in concrete.

Note 4:   In view of the wide range of varyingly soluble siliceous constituents which could be present in Portland composite cements, it will rarely be possible to determine accurately what proportion of the total SiO_2 in the cement will have become solubilised at the time of the concrete analysis.

It can be seen from Table 11 that where CaO can be used as the tracer analyte for a manufactured cement (when aggregates are essentially siliceous, i.e. insoluble) accuracy of cement quantification can be good and of no intrinsic difference to that obtained for a traditional Portland cement. Accordingly, the tentative compliance criteria earlier advanced, would also be applicable.

If instead, the soluble SiO_2 tracer has to be used, problems will occur in light of the 'developing and variable solubility' of the SiO_2 species in pozzolanic/reactive constituents, as hydration proceeds.

5.3.5 · **Pan-European situation; unknown cement type**

In the theoretically conceivable limiting case, where a sample of hardened concrete could contain any one of the cements defined in EN(V) 197-1 at any one of the permissible compositions, as an unknown, then it is highly unlikely that any authoritative value could be put on the results using the procedures of BS 1881 either alone or in tandem with alternatives.

As an example in the simple case where only a CEM I has actually been used, will the analyst ever really be certain that he is just dealing with a CEM I? He could make many diagnostic analyses and so rule out the presence of <u>most</u> constituents but if the aggregate contains calcareous species, he will be in great difficulty in accurately differentiating between that fact or whether a Portland limestone cement had been used. Alternatively, a cement containing silica fume leaves little trace of the silica fume constituent as hydration proceeds, and although a comparison of the ratio of determined CaO to that of soluble SiO_2, with that of a CEM I could reveal a discrepancy, the analyst may well assume the additional SiO_2 is derived from aggregate solubilisation. When the cement is of an unknown type, alternative approaches would be mandatory and even then there would be great uncertainty regarding the value of the results.

6 **Alternative approaches**

6.1 **Analysis of fresh concrete - alternatives**

Although several other analytical procedures exist, none will confer any additional technical benefit on a use of the RAM.

Each of the two remaining procedures in draft BS 1881: Part 128 requires a calibration step for 'silt correction', to correct for fine material from the aggregate passing a 150 µm sieve and each requires a further calibration for either a cement density determination (buoyancy method) or cement solubility (pressure filter method).

In contradistinction to the analysis of hardened concrete where microscopy can act as a complementary technique to chemical analysis, the RAM is self-sufficient. Its capability can be further extended (as can the pressure filter method) to allow for the quantification of some of the constituents of cements (particularly valuable for combinations rather than manufactures), such as blastfurnace slag and fly ash. Full details are given in normative annexes to the draft BS 1881: Part 128.

6.2   Analysis of hardened concrete - alternatives

6.2.1   Cement of a known type

The procedures described in BS 1881: Part 124 for quantification of cement are chemically based (optical microscopy is included only for cement identification) and relatively straightforward. In the majority of circumstances, where a manufactured cement of known type has been used and the concrete is immature, these simple methods should prove to be sufficient.

The few cases for which alternative procedures could confer benefit, would be for those concretes which included any cement type with pozzolanic (industrial or natural) constituents together with calcareous aggregates (see table 9 and 11). In the presence of calcareous aggregates only the soluble SiO_2 'tracer analyte' for cement content would be considered to be appropriate. However, as previously stated, the soluble SiO_2 content of a cement containing a siliceous pozzolana changes, to varying degrees, during hydration. The effect this will have on the accuracy of cement quantification will be to reduce it to the 'medium' or 'poor' categories, earlier identified, dependent on the compositional complexity of the cement type.   In these particular circumstances, analysis of the concrete and its individual solid components to the fused or 'ultimate' state, according to the 'method of last resort', after Figg and Bowden, could be instructive, although laborious. In such a scheme no distinction needs to be made between soluble and insoluble SiO_2, since all the SiO_2 present in the concrete, cement and aggregate is rendered available for analysis by a series of high temperature fusions. The 'melts' can then be analysed by the procedures of classical chemistry for SiO_2 and other analytes, or by a suitably calibrated instrumental technique such as wavelength dispersive X-ray fluorescence spectrometry. It should be noted that the manufacturer's analysis of a cement containing a pozzolanic constituent will already be to the fused/ultimate state and can be used with confidence, making the appropriate adjustment for the 'loss on ignition'.

When alternative procedures have been used to replace or complement the standard methods, it is unlikely that the tentative compliance criteria, previously described, would be acknowledged to be acceptable to the concrete producer, without some modification.

6.2.2   Cement of an unknown type

The prime requirements for an accurate determination of cement content, where the cement is of an unknown type, are the identification of the type/sub-type and a precise elemental analysis within the compositional range permitted for the sub-type.

Set within a national context, identification may be relatively straightforward, depending completely on the actual cement types available. Currently in the U.K., only a limited number of types are either manufactured or imported and these are the compositionally-simple 'non-composite' types (see table 8).   Accordingly, the successful identification of a particular cement type currently used in a concrete in the U.K. will be less intractable than in countries where a range of composite types could have been used. However, if in future a greater range of cements were to be introduced to the U.K., the analytical problems of post-hoc identification could be compounded to the point where an accurate assessment of type and content became impossible.

In any event, the chemical and optical procedures of BS 1881: part 124 could not be relied upon, in isolation, to identify the cement type, and recourse to the techniques of petrography would become mandatory. If circumstances were very favourable and an accurate identification of cement type and sub-type (much more speculative) could be made, it is extremely unlikely that any procedure could discern where, in the narrow compositional range permitted for a sub-type (e.g. CEM II/B-P - natural pozzolana 21-35%), the sub-type lay. The analyst must then 'guestimate' the relative proportion(s) of constituent(s) within the compositional range permitted, derive by calculation the likely elemental analysis of the cement used and use that analysis within the framework of the chemical methods of BS 1881. In many instances the errors will be indeterminate and the results obtained should be regarded as, at best indicative and at worst, worthless; unless it is clear from the entire investigation that the cement is of the fairly easily quantifiable CEM I type.

There may be occasions when electron probe microanalysis (EMPA) on polished specimens (or polished thin sections) or scanning eletron microscopy (SEM) can be used to help to determine the elemental composition of matrix material However, it must be borne in mind that for the more compositionally complex of the cement types, the same (or very similar) elemental analysis could be obtained for completely different cements.   This fact alone would signal caution to the experienced microscopist, petrographer, chemical analyst and presumably, concrete producer.

7 References

1.   Construction Products Directive (Council Directive of 21 December 1988 on the approximation of laws, regulations and administrative provisions of the Member States relating to construction products (89/106/EEC), Official Journal of the European Communities (No L40 of 11.2.1989, pages 12-26).

2.   British Standards Institution. BS 1881: Part 6. *Analysis of hardened concrete.* [Now withdrawn and superseded by BS 1881: Part 124].

3.   British Standards Institution.   DD 83: 1983.   *Draft for Development: Assessment of the composition of fresh concrete.*

4.   Griesenauer, G. J. *A substitute for the compression test of concrete: a method for determining the composition and quality of concrete while in its plastic state.* Engineering News-Record. Vol. 103, No. 22. November 1929, pp 846-847.

5.   Kirkham, R. H. H. *Concrete and Constructional Engineering.* February 1949. pp 54-60.

6.   Kelly, R. T. and Vail, J. W. *Rapid analysis of fresh concrete.* Concrete, Vol. 2, No. 4, April 1968. pp 140-145, May 1968, pp 206-210.

7.   Bavelja, R. *A rapid method for the wet analysis of fresh concrete.* Concrete. Vol. 4, No. 9. September 1970. pp 351-353.

8.   Kenny, R. A. Report No. D.1466. John Laing Research and Development Limited.

9.   Forrester, J. A., Black, P. F. and Lees, T. P. *An apparatus for the rapid analysis of fresh concrete to determine its cement content.* Wexham Springs. Cement and Concrete Association (now British Cement Association). April 1974. pp 15. Technical report 490. (Publication No. 42.490).

10. Dhir, R. K., Munday, G. L. and Ho, N. Y. *Analysis of fresh concrete: determination of cement content by the Rapid Analysis Machine.* Magazine of Concrete Research. Vol. 34, No. 119. June 1982. pp 59-73.

11. Clear, C. A. *Delayed analysis of fresh concrete for cement and water content by freezing.* Magazine of Concrete Research. Vol. 40, No. 145. December 1988.

12. Cooper, I. and Barber, P. *Field investigation of the accuracy of the determination of the cement content of fresh concrete by use of the C&CA Rapid Analysis Machine (RAM).* 1976. pp 19.

13. British Standards Institution. Draft of BS 1881: Part 128. July 1993. Testing concrete. Part 128. *Methods for the analysis of fresh concrete.*

14. Bowden, S. R. and Green, E. H. *The Analysis of Concretes.* National Building Studies Technical Paper (8), 1950, reprinted as Research Paper (8). HMSO, London. (Includes a bibliography of 30 items prior to 1949).

15. Figg, J. W. and Bowden, S. R. *The Analysis of Concretes.* Building Research Station. HMSO. 1971. SBN 11 670294 X.

16. British Standards Institution. BS 1881: 124: 1988. *Methods for analysis of hardened concrete.*

17. Concrete Society Technical Report No. 32. 1989. *Analysis of Hardened Concrete. A guide to tests, procedures and interpretation of results.* Report of a Joint Working Party of the Concrete Society and Society of Chemical Industry. TR.032. ISBN O 946691 22.3.

18. European Committee for Standardisation. prEN 197-1 (PNE version). *Cement -composition, specifications and conformity criteria - Part 1: Common cements.* First Draft. March 1994, CEN/TC51/WG6 rev.

19. British Standards Institution. BS 5328: Part 2: 1991, Concrete. Part 2. *Methods for specifying concrete mixes.*

20. British Standards Institution. BS 5328: 1981. *Methods for specifying concrete, including ready-mixed concrete.* [Now superseded].

21. British Standards Institution. BS 5328: Part 4: 1990. Concrete. Part 4. *Specification for the procedures to be used in sampling, testing and assessing compliance of concrete.*

22. *Hollington, M. R. The development of compliance rules for the analysis of fresh concrete.* RILEM Symposium, Quality Control of Concrete Structures, June 1979, Stockholm, Swedish Cement and Concrete Research Institute, 1979. Vol. 2. pp 55-62.

23. British Standards Institution. BS 5497: Part 1: 1987 (ISO 5725-1986). Precision of test methods: Part 1. *Guide for the determination of repeatability and reproducibility for a standard test method by inter-laboratory tests.*

A CEMENT MAKER'S VIEW OF CEMENTS AND THEIR PERFORMANCE

P LIVESEY
Chief Chemist
Castle Cement Ltd, UK

Abstract
Cement is produced on a massive scale, geared to efficiency and consistency of one main product. Other specialist cements are available based on the standard clinker, possibly with additional constituents, or including special clinkers. Minor differences between source works can influence the suitability of a cement for specific applications. Cement makers are carrying out standard testing to demonstrate compliance with the product standard and also undertake a range of non-standard tests to investigate and monitor special characteristics. Information is available to the user on request covering such characteristics as mineralogy, performance in concrete relative to standard mortar, heat of hydration, and reactivity with secondary materials and admixtures. Procedures exist for early warnings of significant changes in cement composition or performance.
Keywords: Admixtures, cement, concrete, early warnings, heat of hydration, minor additional constituents, secondary materials, special properties.

1.   Introduction

Cement production is a capital intensive business. To establish a new works having an annual capacity of 1 million tonnes, modest by modern standards, would involve the investment of perhaps £200 millions depending on the location and raw materials. By comparison cement is a low-cost material selling on a unit weight basis for less than many basic household products e.g. potatoes at three or four times the price of cement or sugar at twelve times the price. In order to meet this expectation the cement producer has to maximise efficiency producing on a continuous and massive scale, hence the million tonne plant. Production on this scale requires large stocks of materials at all of the intermediate production stages and brings the added advantage of reduced variability of product. Increasingly there is a demand for special cements

Euro-Cements: Impact of ENV 197 on Concrete Construction. Edited by R.K. Dhir and M.R. Jones. Published in 1994 by E & FN Spon, 2–6 Boundary Row, London SE1 8HN. ISBN: 0 419 19980 2.

or ordinary cements with added benefits for the specialist user. Some of these specialist cements can be produced with minimal disruption of the main process but others will require special raw materials or processing and this will be reflected in their cost. On the other hand ordinary cements are required to be exceptionally versatile in their daily application fulfilling roles ranging from hand-moulded decorative items to the active ingredient in high strength concrete for multi-storey buildings; from retarded mortars to fast-track road construction for heavy duty use within twenty-four hours; and to be reactive to secondary binders but not to siliceous aggregate.

2.   Current and future availability of cement types

The modern cement works has, at its heart, the kiln in which the raw materials are burnt to form an intermediate product known as clinker. This is normally of a chemistry suitable for production of CEM I cement, previously referred to in the UK as "Ordinary Portland Cement". Production of special clinkers, such as that required for Sulfate-resisting cement to BS 4027, tends to be concentrated at one or two locations within each cement group and shipped around the UK as demanded. The large volume of production requires that the bulk of raw materials are available locally. Minor constituents can be brought in to make fine adjustments but the characteristic chemistry, within the overall requirements imposed by the cement standard, will be specific to a particular works. These slight differences in characteristics between cements will be considered again when we discuss cement performance in more detail.

With the basic clinker as the main ingredient certain options are available to the cement maker to produce cements with different characteristics. The fineness of the grind will affect particularly the rate of reaction and it is possible to produce slower cements with a coarser grind and rapid hardening cements with a finer grind. Fineness can also affect the water demand of a cement and this can be used to advantage when producing coarser cements for applications which include a dewatering requirement. Secondary materials can be introduced to modify or supplement the reaction of the basic clinker. The most common is the addition of limestone and air-entraining agent to produce a Masonry Cement to BS 5224 although because of the need to avoid contamination requiring a separate grinding facility production tends to be limited to one or two works in each Group.

Composite cements based on the standard clinker can be produced incorporating ground granulated blastfurnace slag or pulverised-fuel ash to produce cements to BS 146 and BS 4246 or to BS 6588 and BS 6610. The local availability of the secondary material tends to be the deciding factor in the production of these cements as the economics of the market are very keen and opportunity for the cement maker to recover additional costs is limited. Although factory production can give a high degreee of control over the quality of the composite it does reduce the degree of versatility available to the concrete producer relative to the separate site addition of secondary materials.

Limited amounts of traditional special purpose cements are available in the UK. Generally only Oilwell cement to the American Petroleum Institute specification is produced in the UK whilst other cements such as White Portland Cement to BS 12 and High Alumina (or Calcium Aluminate as it is coming to be known) Cement to BS 915 are only produced in limited locations in Europe and are imported. Other former traditional UK cements such as Low Heat Portland Cement to BS 1370 and Super Sulphated Cement to BS 4248 are no longer produced here and are limited in availability world-wide.

The introduction of the European pre-Standard for Common cements, ENV 197-1, and the revision of British Standards to align them has opened up a number of possibilities for UK cements. In particular it has introduced a new cement type, Portland limestone cement BS 7583, in which up to 20% of limestone is permitted. This cement has been the subject of an exhaustive research programme reported at the Building Research Establishment seminar in 1989 [1]. Although this type of cement has not yet been produced in commercial quantities in the UK it holds considerable possibilities for economic and environmental benefits. ENV 197-1 has been instrumental in introducing into British Standards the possibility of using up to 5% minor additional constituent in Portland cements to BS 12. The most common constituent used in those countries which previously had this option is limestone and this has been added to some UK cements to improve their workability or to fine tune their strength properties to ensure compliance with the appropriate strength class. Where minor additional constituents are added their presence is reported to those customers requesting such information.

British Standards also now permit the incorporation of up to 1% additives to improve the manufacture or properties of the cement. This option has already been exploited in the introduction into the UK of new multi-purpose cements having air-entraining properties in mortars to improve plastic properties and in concrete to improve frost resistance. The special nature of these cements is clearly indicated on the packaging and the technical literature. The option also permits the use of a wider range of grinding aids during cement production which brings benefits in terms of economy of production.

The use of such additions and additives enables the performance of cements to be tailored for specific purposes. Their effect on general properties has to be taken into account by the cement maker and the various means for assessing these will be considered later.

3.   Cement properties and their relevance to users

Cement from any works has to meet the requirements of the standard for chemical and physical properties. Within this constraint the local combination of properties, especially chemistry, fineness and particle size distribution, can have a significant effect on the performance in specific applications.

The various aspects of a cement which affect its performance for a particular end use are, to say the least, complex. Cements are required to perform such a variety of purposes which can often be contradictory. Cement is required to be chemically reactive with the aluminium when producing aerated products; to be chemically resistant in concretes for dairies and breweries; to be suitable for use in lightweight, fire-resistant cladding and to make high-density, radiation shielding concrete; to be compatible with air stability in foam concrete and to be able to release air when producing micro-defect free cement components; to resist bleed in normal concrete and permit water release in de-watering production systems.

Whilst a cement standard can lay down a specification and test methods for general properties it is impossible to be so specific as to ensure that the cement will be suitable for all of these diverse requirements. Indeed the contradictory nature of some of these would preclude that. In most instances users have become aware of which cements suit their purpose through trial and error. The cement maker must be aware of those aspects of the cement which have a bearing on the successful use in these situations. In addition to applying the standard tests to demonstrate compliance with the product specification various non-standard testing will be carried out on a sufficiently regular basis to monitor continuing special performance. In these cases consistency of the special performance is more important to the specialist user than maximising results against any standard test.

The modern cement works applies state of the art methods of raw material surveying, quarrying strategies, blending and on-line analyses to ensure a consistent product. Nevertheless minor variations in chemistry or the burning process will result in variations in the reactivity of the clinker. The art of cement making is to balance the chemistry with the process and the particle characteristics in order to maintain consistency.

4.   Standard testing of cement

Finished cement is tested for all of the chemical and physical requirements of the standard. However, it is too late at that stage to find that there is a compliance problem and the important testing is carried out at the intermediate stages in the production process. In particular the correct chemistry has to be established at an early stage and this has the advantage that should there be any significant change it can be identified in sufficient time to alert users - the early warning procedures will be discussed later. It means that extensive information is available on the chemistry of main oxides of silicon, calcium, aluminium, iron and magnesium together with alkali metal (sodium and potassium) oxides, sulfur trioxide, chloride, free lime, insoluble residue and loss on ignition. This information is available to users on request. The relevance of some of these may seem vague but to the cement chemist they are invaluable for controlling the reactivity and freshness of the cement.

It is only after the final milling stage that the testing of physical properties can commence and that the indications from the chemistry can be verified. Test reports will provide information on these tests for fineness, setting time and compressive strength of mortar prisms. Whilst the fineness is known to have a bearing on the reactivity and water demand of the cement this effect is comparative and will principally depend upon the characteristics of the clinker. Fineness is therefore not subject to specification as it is principally a means for ensuring that other properties such as setting and strength are met. The relevance of mortar prism strength to the prediction of strength in practical concrete is often queried. The precision of the mortar prism test is greater than that of the concrete test and as such is preferred for quality control during manufacture. Furthermore it is unusual for a cement with a consistent mortar strength to vary significantly in concrete strength. Also if the correlation between early and 28 day mortar strength remains constant then that of concrete should also be consistent. It does mean, however, that the comparative strength of concrete with two different cements cannot be determined directly from consideration of their relative mortar strengths. This has limitations for the concrete industry and is the subject of ongoing dialogue with cement makers.

The one standard test of physical property for which there is no good justification in modern cements is that for soundness. When cement kiln controls were less sophisticated there was a possiblity that cement unsound to the Le Chatelier expension test might be produced but this is no longer the case. Rather the varied use of cement and their increased reactivity over earlier years brings its own problems of unsoundness in a different form. When concretes are subjected to excessive high temperatures there is a possibility that the alumino-sulfate phases become unstable and if subsequently exposed to a moist environment can expand causing damage. The factors involved in this process are the subject of ongoing research and until this is resolved it is recommended that the temperature of concrete is limited to not more than 75°C during curing [2].

5.   Non-standard testing of cement

A wide variety of non-standard tests are available to the cement maker and the user to establish the characteristics of a cement in a specific circumstance. Some may be old established tests fallen into dis-use for general specification but which are relevant within a more narrow application. Many will be specific to certain instruments or equipment, difficult to calibrate, and possibly of poor precision and as such whilst providing some guidance are unsuited to a general specification. Others will be new, sometimes requiring highly specialised equipment, and may not be generally available or their full significance be understood.

Cement makers are increasingly undertaking additional testing of this type either to more closely understand the interaction with the standard properties of their cement or to provide the user with more relevant information. The extent of this testing will depend upon the uses of the cement, the circumstances of a particular works and the cement company.

5.1   Chemical methods

The bulk chemistry of cement is often used to calculate the theoretical mineralogy according to the Bogue formula [3]. In practice this can be very misleading as modern methods of X-ray diffraction analysis have demonstrated that the actual proportions of the cement minerals are quite different. The value of the Bogue calculation is limited to a comparative role demonstrating the consistency of the cement and the burning process or as a general type test. Even when the precise proportions of the minerals are known the story is only part told since the crystal size and amount of compounds in solid solution also affect the reactivity and this can only be determined by experienced optical electron microscopy. Research is continuing into the detail and application of this technique [4] which, because of its early stage of development and expense, remains more appropriate as an aid to the cement maker in optimising the process rather than as an indicator of cement performance.

Frequently it is necessary for the concrete producer or his customer to carry out hardened analysis of concrete to determine, amongst other things, cement content and type. Cement makers are able to advise on the analysis and to provide typical analyses for their cements for the time at which the concrete was placed. This enables analyses in accordance with the standard method to be carried out [5]. More advanced analyses have been carried out on occasion using scanning electron microscopy on trace unhydrated clinker particles in the concrete to determine the cement type, particularly for Sulfate-resisting Portland cement. On occasion, where possible source works have some characteristic differences in clinker, this technique has been able to indicate the source of the cement.

5.2   Physical methods

Although the water demand to produce a cement paste of standard consistence is a standard test the proposal that the result can be used as an indication of water demand in concrete [6] is a further extension. It is questionable whether there is a strong correlation between the two, particularly for minor variations in standard consistence, when related to slump changes of the order of 20mm and considering the effects of aggregates which will be dealt with later.

The change in the British Standards for cements from testing the strength of standard concrete cubes to that of mortar prisms has lead to a demand for continued information based on the strength and workability of standard concrete. Cement makers have continued to provide such information although a glance at Figure 2 will show how limited this information can be in relation to the more complex relationship between field aggregates, water and strength. It is doubtful whether such information merits the cost of continued testing. It should be possible to devise a more useful test to improve understanding of the relationship between mortar strength and performance in concrete. Cement makers and the concrete industry are continuing to look for more meaningful methods.

Particle size distribution of cement is regularly measured during production as a means to optimise the grinding process and particularly the mill separator. The information has been suggested [7] as a means of optimising concrete mix design.

Whilst it can be a useful tool in the design of concrete for the more demanding applications minor variations in sand gradings in normal concrete can be far more significant as shown in Figure 4. Care must also be taken if attempting to compare the information on particle size distribution between laboratories, or even between different makes of equipment within the same laboratory. There are no calibration methods suitable for this test at present and results can vary widely.

5.3   Heat of hydration

The CEN Technical Committee TC 51 have accepted two draft methods for determination of the heat of hydration of cement. These have been described in an earlier paper. The Semi-adiabatic method has proved to be a valuable means of providing the concrete engineer with meaningful information based on a common, calibrated format in which a continuous record of heat with time is available. This information can be used to predict the temperature rise of concrete since initial comparisons indicate that the thermal characteristics of the calorimeter approximate closely to those set out in the CIRIA Report [8] for 18mm plywood formwork on a section of $\leq$ 300mm. Further research is needed to more closely define this relationship.

Typical values for the heat of hydration, the time to reach peak temperature, the peak temperature and the total heat of hydration up to that time are shown in Table 1.

Table 1. Heat of hydration (kJ/kg) of typical UK cements

Time	CEM-I PC 42.5			CEM-I	CEM-I	CEM-II	CEM-III
(hrs)	(A)	(B)	(C)	SRPC	52.5	/B-V	/B
6	75	95	125	80	145	50	25
12	270	255	245	220	335	155	70
18	305	300	280	270	370	205	100
24	315	325	300	295	380	230	125
72	335	345	340	340	390	280	220
168	350	360	360	355	405	300	265

Peak temperature (tests at 20°C ambient)

Time to peak (hrs)	13.1	15.5	13.8	17.2	12.8	20.2	36.0
Peak temperature (°C)	58	56	52	52	65	45	36
Total heat to peak temperature time (kJ/kg)	280	285	260	265	340	220	280

This information can also be used to predict the temperature rise of equivalent grade concrete using different cements. In Figure 1 it can be seen that taking account of the differences in cement content to achieve the same 28-day concrete grade the heat evolution from CEM-II/B-V concrete is almost identical to that using a CEM-I cement.

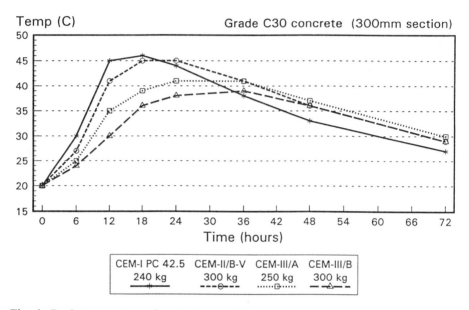

Fig. 1. Peak temperature of equivalent grade concretes

5.4   Performance in normal concrete

Cement makers are aware of the importance of consistent performance of cement in everyday concrete to ensure that the controls exercised by the concrete producer are valid. Cement laboratories in the UK are all carrying out a certain amount of regular testing of cements using field aggregates. In some cases routine test programmes have been set up monitoring the performance of cement in 'real' concrete so as to measure the degree of consistency and better understand the relationships between the standard cement tests and its characteristics as perceived by concrete producers. This enables the cement maker to adjust production control target values, within the constraints of the cement standard, to optimise the performance in use. From this testing and experience in service the cement maker is able to advise on the typical performance in concrete although, as illustrated in Figure 2, the characteristics of the local aggregates will have a large bearing on this.

Using commercial grade field aggregates for testing allows a greater degree of flexibility in mix design, cement content and water/cement ratio than would the use of standard aggregates, particularly the 10mm maximum size BS 4550 granite. However, the use of field aggregates in routine comparative testing has to be carefully controlled since they are subject to much wider variation in quality than are those aggregates carefully selected and certified for standardized concrete. Experience has

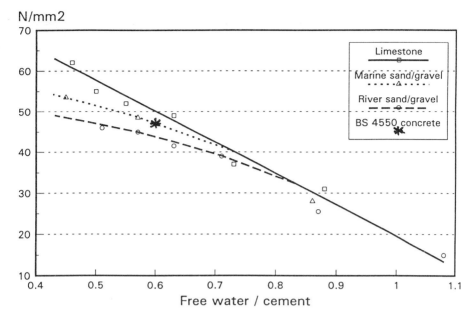

Fig.2. The effect of different aggregates on the performance of a CEM-I PC.

shown it to be necessary to set up a control to monitor and correct for changes in concrete arising between aggregate batches. Figure 3 illustrates the changes which have been monitored over a two year period for a standard concrete (315 kg/m³ cement and 50mm slump) using a single batch of reference cement. The major changes occurred with changes in batches of fine aggregate, coarse aggregate was not found to be as critical.

5.5   Cement reactivity with secondary materials
Routine testing is carried out to demonstrate the reactivity between specific sources of ground granulated blastfurnace slag or pulverised-fuel ash with specific sources of Portland cement. This is intended to demonstrate their equivalence in standard tests with composite cement standards and is undertaken by both the secondary material suppliers and cement makers. The cement makers co-operate in this by supplying composite monthly samples of their cements.

Cement makers also monitor the reactivity of their cements with these materials and with micro-silica to check the effects of secondary material variations and to be able to understand the effects of cement properties and the overall effect on such aspects as concrete grade, water demand and, as previously demonstrated, heat of hydration.

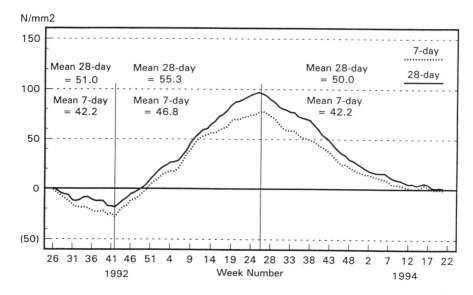

Fig.3. Cusum of control concrete with different batches of aggregates

There is a wide range of proprietory admixtures for concrete, mortars and renders so that it is not possible for the cement maker to monitor the performance of a particular cement with all of these. However, it is understood that these are becoming an important part of the UK construction industry and that their compatibility with cements can be critical for a given contract. Cement makers have long co-operated by supplying to the Cement Admixtures Association a reference cement for their product testing. Additionally cement makers monitor the performance of their cements against a range of admixture types so as to better understand the relationships with cement properties.

Taken overall the reactivity information forms the basis for evaluating the effects of any change in cement composition, e.g. the effect of introducing a filler, change in gypsum or grinding aid supply, or significant change in cement chemistry. By this means the cement maker is able to give meaningful advice to users.

5.6   Cement performance in non-routine concrete situations
Cement users often require guidance on the performance of cements in non-routine situations such as high/low temperatures; strengths at ages other than the standard

1, 3, 7 or 28 days and particularly projections to ages beyond 28 days. These will vary with cements and particularly cement types and reasonable guidance can usually be given based on the cement maker's own testing.

Equally some indication of performance in such specialised concrete situations as semi-dry mixes, high early strength concrete for fast-track applications and grout formulation for varying flow or open-time properties can usually be made available to assist in the intial mix design for further evaluation by the user.

6.   Advanced and early warning of changes in cement performance.

From the foregoing it is apparent that the cement maker will normally possess considerable information on the performance of his cements in a wide range of applications. Whenever a significant change in composition or chemistry is introduced the maker will evaluate the effects and give advanced notice of the change and it's anticipated effects.

When any significant change in performance arising from minor changes in the manufacturing process is observed the cement maker will provide as early a warning as possible of the change and its likely effects. Cement makers, through their in-process testing can often pick up such changes before the cement grinding stage and adjust the finished cement to compensate. Occasionally the changes are of a type which affects cement performance without affecting the standard test results. The non-standard testing described earlier will enable the cement makers to identify and possibly quantify the effect.

There is an agreed proceedure on early warnings between the Cement Industry and the Ready-Mix Industry so that whenever significant changes in water demand or strength are detected automatic warnings to all ready-mix users are triggered. Arrangements for including users in other industries have also been set up on an individual basis and these can be extended by consultation with your cement supplier. It is customary that even without such prior agreement, in the event of a significant change, the Cement Company Technical Manager would normally notify all those customers considered to be at risk.

7.   References

1   BRE Publication BR 245 (1993) Performance of limestone-filled cements. Building Research Establishment, Garston, UK.

2   Lawrence, C.D., Dalziel, J.A., and Hobbs, D.W. (1990) Sulphate attack arising from delayed ettringite formation. BCA Interim Technical Note 12. British Cement Association, Crowthorne, UK.

3   ASTM C-150 (1993) Standard Specification for Portland Cement, Clause 6 Chemical Composition. ASTM Book of Standards, Volume 04.01 Cement; Lime; Gypsum. Philadelphia, USA.

4   Harrison, A.M., (1993) Quantification of analytical data relating to cement clinker. Proceedings of the Fourth Euroseminar on Microscopy Applied to Building Materials. Swedish National Testing and Research Institute. SP Report 1993:15 Boras, Sweden.

5   Methods for analysis of hardened concrete (1988). BS 1881 : Part 124 : 1988 British Standards Institution, London, UK.

6   Dewar, J.D., and Anderson, R. (1987) Manual of Ready-Mixed Concrete. Blackie, London, UK. pp 30-1 .

7   Dewar, J.D. (1986) The particle structure of fresh concrete. Sir Frederick Lea Memorial Lecture, Institute of Concrete Technology 14th Annual Convention. Institute of Concrete Technology, Beaconsfield, UK.

8   Harrison, T.A. (1981) Early-age thermal crack control in concrete. CIRIA Report 91. CIRIA, London, UK.

A CONCRETE PRODUCER'S VIEW OF FUTURE CEMENT STANDARDS

T A HARRISON
Technical Director
British Ready Mixed Concrete Association, UK

Abstract

The future European cement standard, EN197, will not be significantly different from existing UK cement standards except that the range of cements will be wider. There are, however, potential differences that are likely to disadvantage the UK, such as the loss of the low early strength class.

Aspects of prEN197-1 are reviewed from the perspective of a concrete producer. In many cases the specifier is better advised to specify direct requirements from the concrete instead of specifying the cement type and class. There is no need to specify cement strength sub-class and the need to specify the cement strength class is mainly in prescribed mixes. Whilst there is a case for specifying the permitted cement types, concrete producers would prefer to have a list linked to mix limitations and exposure class in an informative annex to the European concrete standard.

The vital information for concrete producers relates to consistency and pre-warning of sudden significant changes of properties such as cement strength. This information exchange is best agreed between the cement supplier and the concrete producer and for it to remain outside the standards.

Keywords: Cement, combinations, concrete, specification, standards.

1 Introduction

A cement standard has a number of functions. Firstly it must ensure that the cements are fit for their intended use. The standard must also provide the means by which, if required, a cement can be uniquely selected and also a means by which information needed by users can be obtained. Cement is not used on its own. Its main use is as a constituent material for concretes, mortars and grouts. It is these products that have to perform and therefore how cement is used is the dominant factor, e.g. a sulfate resisting cement will not give a sulfate resisting concrete if it is used in an incorrect

Euro-Cements: Impact of ENV 197 on Concrete Construction. Edited by R.K. Dhir and M.R. Jones. Published in 1994 by E & FN Spon, 2–6 Boundary Row, London SE1 8HN. ISBN: 0 419 19980 2.

concrete mix; a high alkali cement will not lead to damaging ASR if the concrete is designed appropriately. Therefore, in general, cement standards are best written to provide information on the levels of relevant factors and to provide rules for controlling variability. As explained later, the ready-mixed concrete producers prefer that some of the rules for controlling variability should remain outside the standard.

ENV197-1:Common cements[1], contains 25 types of cement and 6 strength classes. This gives, in theory, 150 cements, but in reality the number will be less as not all the types of cement can be produced at all strength classes. Nevertheless, the number of choices of cement will be large and the task of specification difficult. Do you specify just the type(s) of cement, or the type(s) and class(es) of cement, or the type(s), class(es) and sub-class(es) of cement? Alternatively, is it necessary to specify the cement, or could the choice be left to the concrete producer? Concrete producers believe that the complexity of choice is due to the way in which cements have been classified and, in performance terms, differences between the cement types are often small or non-existent. The British standard for concrete, BS5328[2], provides robust guidance on durability and with the exception of sulfate attack, it should not be necessary to specify the cement type.

Concrete plants do not have sufficient silos to hold a wide range of cements and it is unlikely that a producer will empty a silo and fill it with a different cement unless the order is very large or the price high. All UK concrete plants can supply concretes containing CEM I and most can supply a range of equivalent combinations to cements based on either ground-granulated blastfurnace slag (ggbs)[3] or pulverized-fuel ash (pfa) conforming to BS3892:Part1[4]

2 Equivalent combinations

Most UK concrete producers have developed a system whereby they have a silo of a high strength Portland cement (CEM I) and a silo of either ggbs to BS6699 or pfa to BS3892:Part 1. This gives the producer the flexibility to supply either CEM I concretes or concretes containing equivalent combinations to the range of cements containing slag or fly ash.

Table 1.Options in 'cement' types from plants stocking ggbs or pfa

Plant stocking ggbs	Plant stocking pfa
CEM I	CEM I
CEM II/A-S	CEM II/A-V
CEM II/B-S	CEM II/B-V
CEM III/A	CEM IV/A
CEM III/B	CEM IV/B
CEM III/C	
(24% of the types listed in ENV197-1)	(20% of the types listed in ENV197-1)

This is a very good system and is in advance of the rest of the world. Its advantages include minimising the number of silos needed, flexibility, the ability to cover a wider range of cement types (but still less that 25% of those listed in ENV197-1), good stock rotation and it helps to keep concrete competitive with other materials. The UK does not wish to move away from this system.

The alternative nominal k-value system of using additions has attractions as it requires no testing to establish equivalence, and if concrete strength controls the mix design there will be no mix design advantage in using the more complex UK equivalence procedure. However, the k-value system does not embody the concept of equivalent combinations and therefore, if a CEM II-V cement is specified, the producer cannot supply a combination of CEM I plus fly ash using the k-value approach and claim an equivalent combination. Given the technically suspect nature of the nominal k-values system, and the commercial pressures, it is unlikely that the nominal k-value system will ever form a basis for claiming an equivalent combination. Developments are likely to be in one or both of the following directions:

1 The equivalence procedure will be applicable to any addition that is standardised. For example, the University of Dundee has a project which is examining whether the equivalence procedure can be applied to BS EN450 fly ash[5] and not restricted to BS3892:Part 1 pfa[4]. As the equivalence procedure is simply a routine for showing that the powder combination has the properties and the proportions of a permitted cement, its principle cannot be faulted. Any grounds for concern have to be focused on the adequacy of the cement standard and concrete specification.

2. Concrete is specified by performance, i.e. structural strength and, as appropriate, durability performance. In Technical Committee CEN TC104/SC1, the exposure classes being proposed for prEN206 relate to specific forms of deterioration, namely carbonation induced corrosion, chloride induced corrosion, sea water attack, other chemical attack and freeze/thaw. By splitting exposure classes in this way, it makes it much easier to develop performance tests and criteria. For example, the Tuutti 2-phase model of corrosion, Figure 1, can be used as a basis for calculating the criteria for carbonation induced corrosion.

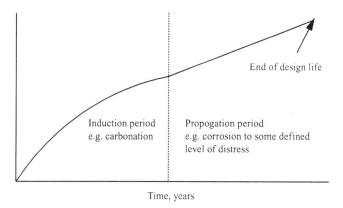

Figure 1. Tuutti 2-phase model of corrosion

If the failure criteria for corrosion is taken as corrosion induced cracks of 0.1 to 0.2mm, i.e. about 100µm of corrosion, the propagation period becomes 100 divided by the characteristic corrosion rate (CR). The time to carbonate to the minimum cover then becomes

Time to carbonate to the minimum cover = Notional design life - (100/CR)

This approach reduces carbonation induced corrosion to carbonation performance that can be predicted from a real time or accelerated test. Such a system is not yet in operation but is being developed. Considerable work is needed to develop this approach to specification and it is likely to be several years before the system has developed sufficiently to be included in a standard. When this is achieved concrete will not be specified by mix limitations, and the equivalence procedure will become redundant.

3 Control of concrete production

The following comments apply to plants that are members of the Quality Scheme for Ready Mixed Concrete (QSRMC). The control of concrete has several elements:

mix design;
contract review and mix selection;
control of constituent materials;
control of production.

The first element requires a mix design exercise to establish the relationship between cube strength, workability, free water and cement/addition content for a 'family' of mixes. The water/cement ratio is calculated from the free water and cement (combination) content. Every two years these main relationships are verified by a repeat of the mix design exercise. Between times the relationships are modified on the basis of production control data.

When a concrete specification is received, its requirements are assessed and a mix is selected by interpolation that satisfies all of the specified requirements. For example, a simple specification of C30 would result in the selection of a mix with a target mean strength of $(30+margin)N/mm^2$. However, if a designated mix, RC30 were to be specified, the cement contents needed to satisfy a target mean strength of $(30+margin)N/mm^2$, a maximum water/cement (combination) ratio of 0.65 and a minimum cement (combination) content of $275kg/m^3$ would be determined and the mix selected would be the one with the highest cement (combination) content.

The QSRMC regulations require that routine checks are made on the plant's functioning, particularly weigh scales, and on the constituent materials used in concrete production to ensure that they have not changed significantly. Concrete is batched at the same mix proportions until a significant change is detected and then the proportions are adjusted appropriately. The routine checks on constituent materials provided information that may trigger a change in mix proportions, e.g. changes in aggregate grading. However, there are other changes that will only be detected when the concrete is tested for strength.

Producers test concrete strength at a rate that will detect changes in constituent materials. Higher rates of testing lead to auto-correlation and provide no significant benefit. Batches from the range of production are randomly selected for strength testing. For control purposes, the actual cube strengths are adjusted to the equivalent value of the control mix. For example, if the plant's control system is based on a C30 concrete and a C40 concrete sample gave a strength of 49N/mm^2, this would be reduced by 10, to 39N/mm^2, before being entered onto the control chart.

One of the methods for detecting significant changes in concrete strength is the Cusum technique[6][7]. This is where the differences between the actual cube strengths (after adjustment to the equivalent values of the control mix) and the target mean strength are added cumulatively and plotted onto a graph, Figure 2. If the Cusum remains horizontal, no real change in strength has occurred; if it progressively rises above the horizontal, the actual concrete strengths are higher than predicted; if it falls progressively below the horizontal, the actual concrete strengths are lower than predicted. Statistical techniques are used to determine when a change in strength is a real reflection of a change in constituent materials and is significant. At this stage corrective action is taken, normally by adjusting the cement content.

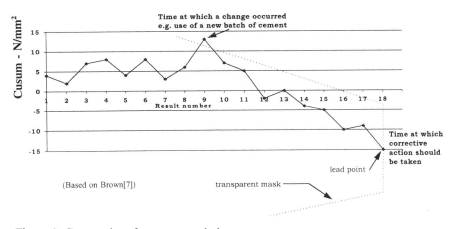

Figure 2. Cusum plot of mean strength data

The ideal design for a Cusum is one that gives a quick response to real shifts in the quality of the constituent materials and a very rapid response to a sudden change in material quality. To speed the response of a Cusum, most producers base the control on 7-day strength and run a continuous check on the relationship between 7 and 28 day strengths. It should be obvious that a Cusum cannot detect a sudden significant change in under 7 days and it may take twice that time before a real change has been established. During this period a large volume of concrete may have been dispatched.

The key to the control of concrete lies in the control of the variability of the constituent materials. The absolute value of, say, cement strength, is less important than the need for it not to vary significantly from this value. As illustrated above, a slow gradual change in, cement strength, would be detected by the Cusum control chart and progressive adjustments would be made to the cement content. Our most difficult control problem is where there is a sudden significant drop in, cement strength. With current UK CEM I-42.5, such a sudden drop in strength would not lead to it falling outside its class as the mean strength is typically in the range 57 to 58N/mm^2; the mean strength could drop by 10N/mm^2 and the cement would still remain within the 42.5 class. However, changes which are substantially less than this would lead to major problems with strength conformity of concrete.

Most cements are tested at 2 days and there are other quality control indicators which show a change of product. The cement is often placed into silos before discharge and there is often some delay before the cement is dispatched. The cement producer, therefore, has knowledge of a change in product as a much earlier stage than the concrete producer. This information is vital to the concrete producer and the ready-mixed concrete producers have an informal arrangement with the cement industry whereby they will be informed when the cement strength changes outside agreed limits.

The requirement for cement not to change suddenly by more than fixed limits is not part of the British standards for cement nor ENV197-1. As this is so vital to concrete producers, it may appear wrong for it not to be included in the cement standards. For pragmatic and commercial reasons, however, concrete producers do not want this requirement to be part of the standard. The current system of being informed of sudden changes in strength works reasonably well. If there is a sudden drop in cement strength, cement contents are increased and a commercial settlement negotiated. However, if the same limits that are currently used were put into the cement standard, the consequences of the same loss of strength could be far more severe, perhaps even leading to loss of certification. As the consequence of such a change could be much more severe to cement producers, the values that could be agreed in a standard would almost certainly be higher than those currently being used. If it was necessary to operate at these higher values, the concrete margin may have to be increased, with a consequent increase in concrete costs. If we can continue operating informally with our present limits, having wider limits in the cement standard serves no useful purpose. The present system suits both the cement industry and the concrete producers.

4 Concrete producer's comments on aspects of ENV197-1

4.1 Main constituents
The wide range of constituent materials reflects practices in different countries. Provided specifiers do not think that they are all needed or will be available, this range does not give us grounds for concern

4.2 Minor additional constituents
In the UK, limestone filler is generally used as the minor constituent for CEM I cements. There has been at least one case in the UK where the change to using a minor constituent coincided with problems of low strength concrete that could not be attributed to changes in the cement strength nor other concreting materials. Whilst it is not proven that the change to using a minor additional constituent was the prime cause of the sudden change in concrete strength, it reinforces the fears that producers hold that there can be changes to cement within the standard that have a significant impact

on concrete performance, but are not reflected in the information we are normally supplied with. The UK cement and concrete producers are working together to establish if there are real grounds for concern and, if so, how they can be solved.

4.3 Additives
This clause gives the cement producer immense power to alter the characteristics of cement. For example, we now have cements in the UK than contain powdered air entraining agents. Currently these cements are only available in the bagged market and for their designated end uses they have advantages over traditional cements.

Because of this clause, the cement producer can now add, as he sees fit, water reducers, retarders, accelerators, etc. These could have significant effects on the admixtures added by the concrete producer. They could reduce the effectiveness of the concrete producer's water reducer and could have significant effects on air entraining agents, making them ineffective.

Concrete producers are not attempting to have this clause removed from the standard or its scope limited. However, we expect the cement industry to keep us fully informed of any changes they are making to their products and the effects they will have on concrete performance. Developments will be monitored closely. By working together in a positive way we can ensure that any changes are beneficial and the reliability of concrete maintained.

The ready-mixed concrete producers also support the cement producers in resisting having to add additives to cement to prevent chromium dermatitis. This sounds irresponsible but it is not. There are a number of risks in handling fresh concrete. Alkali burns is the most significant followed by various forms or dermatitis. Concrete and cement producers warn purchasers of the risks of using fresh concrete and of the need to use protective clothing. For example, this advice is often on concrete delivery tickets. The use of protective clothing is effective against all the risks of using fresh concrete, including chromium dermatitis, and therefore there is no need to use additives

4.4 Strength class
Table 2 gives strength information on the three cement strength classes. There is a small overlap of mean strengths between classes. When cements fall into this range, they tend to be classified by the producer as being in the lower strength class as this reduces the risk of non-conformity.. CEM I cements tend to be at the top of the 42.5 class or into the 52.5 class whilst CEM II/B-V cements tend to be at the bottom of the 42.5 or into the 32.5 class.

Table 2. Cement strength classes

Strength class	Standard strength N/mm^2	Limit value for single test N/mm^2	Practical range of mean strengths N/mm^2
32.5	32.5 - 52.5	30	37 - 48
42.5	42.5 - 62.5	40	47 - 58
52.5	$\geq$52.5	50	$\geq$57

European standards embrace the concept of classes for all characteristics. Whilst this concept and classification is often useful, there are times when it serves no useful purpose. For the specification of a prescribed mix, the cement strength class may be a useful means of defining needs. However, prior to having cement strength classes in the UK, we found ways of specifying cement for prescribed mixes because in a competitive market cement strengths vary little between different sources; and that is still true with cement produced to the new standards. All bulk CEM I-42.5 cements have mean strengths in a narrow band at the top of the range.

As explained in section 3, with designed concretes the strength class of a cement is less important than a low variability of strength. It should be made clear that this is a technical statement related to production control and that cement strength will be important when the commercial decisions are made on what cement to purchase.

We do not believe that it is necessary to specify the strength class when a designed concrete mix is specified. If the producer elects to use a low strength cement, he will have to use more of it to achieve the specified concrete strength. On the other hand, if he elects to use a very high strength cement, he will still have to use sufficient to satisfy the specified maximum water/cement ratio and the minimum cement contents.

The British standard for concrete, BS5328[2] has adopted this philosophy and 'strength class' gets down-rated into the optional item 'any special requirements for the specification of the cement'.

4.5 Strength sub-class
Sub-classes for strength only have a lower limit and therefore, for example, any 42.5R cement would also qualify as a 42.5. Dual classification is considered to be bad standard writing, but the UK has failed to persuade TC51 to change. There may be some rare situations where the specifier of a prescribed mix may wish to specify a high early strength cement. However, if the early strength of concrete is important to him he would be better advised to specify a designed concrete with an early concrete strength criterion. The producer will then decide if he will achieve the early strength by using a high early strength cement, admixtures or a higher grade of concrete.

The difficulties for specifiers occur when they do not wish to have a high early strength cement. For example, they may wish to indirectly achieve a lower rate of heat evolution from the cement. Because an 'R' cement also qualifies as the normal cement, they cannot use the cement standard to achieve this objective. The alternative would be to put a direct requirement on the concrete, such as an adiabatic temperature rise, but to be fair to the concrete producer the cement type and class should not then be specified nor should the minimum cement content. The water/cement ratio will ensure enough cement for durability and the BS ENV206[8] water penetration test (or the prEN206 deemed to satisfy minimum fines content) will ensure enough fine material to fill the voids between the aggregates.

Sub-class specification also creates problems for concrete producers. What do we do when, say, 42.5 cement is specified? Can we supply a 42.5R without consultation, as it complies with the requirements for a 42.5? Do we simply get two certificates from the cement producer and show him the appropriate one? Perhaps this is another good reason why cement strength class and sub-class should not be specified as you cannot, in ENV197-1[1], specify one without the other. British standards are much better as you have the choice of specifying the type of cement, the strength class and the sub-class by using the letters L, N or R. If the sub-class is not specified, any of the sub-class options permitted in the standard for that type of cement may be used.

As cement strength sub-classes are likely to remain in prEN197-1, the UK has attempted to have the 'L' class (low early strength) introduced and the use of 'N' when normal early strength gain is required. The 'L' class is important to the UK as some of our combinations of CEM I and ggbs will be too strong at 28 days if they are made to comply with the early strength requirement, or too weak at 2 days when they satisfy the 28 day strength requirements. So far the UK has not been successful in introducing these changes. However, a draft for the low heat cement standard has not yet been produced and, when it is, there is the anticipation that a low early strength will have to be introduced. At this stage it may be easier for the UK to introduce it into prEN197-1.

5 Performance orientated cement standard

Within the European Technical Committee TC51:Cements and limes, a performance orientated version of prEN197-1 has been drafted. This has attempted to expand performance requirements into areas such as carbonation and freeze/thaw. This early draft has been rejected by the UK mirror committee and, if the approach is to stand any chance of success, a clear philosophy needs to be developed. The fundamental problem is that carbonation and freeze/thaw resistance are properties of concrete, not cement. Performance cannot be transferred to cement unless it is based on a reference concrete. This reference concrete could be based on the mix limitations given in prEN206, but the current view is that agreement on standardised mix limitations is unlikely. Work on developing a carbonation test has indicated that this may not be sufficient and it may be necessary in a standardised cement test to define, for example, the sources of aggregates.

This approach to drafting a cement standard would address a question posed by the committee revising BS ENV206[8] which was, "Can all ENV197-1 cements be used in a fixed mix limitation specification to achieve the intended performance?" At the time there was the hope that the durability table would be retained and that new boxes would be added that listed the permitted cement types. The possibility that some cements would not be on the list worried cement producers and they were not keen on these developments. Fortunately for them, agreement on mix limitations for prEN206 is unlikely and, without this basis, carbonation and freeze/thaw performance tests for cements has no sensible technical basis.

It is therefore the author's view that useful carbonation and freeze/thaw tests for cement will not be developed and that the performance orientated version of prEN197-1 will not be taken to the standardisation stage.

From a concrete producer's viewpoint, this expected outcome is a disappointment. Lists of suitable cements within the standardised durability requirements would make it unnecessary, except in rare circumstances, for cement type to be specified and the producer would have the freedom to use any of the permitted types.

6 Concluding comment

The market for cement is unlikely to change significantly when the UK adopt EN197-1. Producers of concrete will continue to use what is available and gives cost effective solutions. As currently practised, ready-mixed concrete producers will require additional information related to variability and change of product that is outside standardisation.

Many of the requirements that are specified in EN197-1 (and other standards) are not relevant to concrete producers and, in our view, not relevant to most concrete specifications.

7 References

1 British Standards Institution.. *Cement - composition, specifications and conformity criteria. Part 1 : Common cements.* BS ENV197-1. To be published in 1994

2 British Standards Institution. *Concrete. Part 1 : Guide to specifying concrete. Part 2 : Methods for specifying concrete. Part 3 : Specification for the procedures to be used in producing and transporting concrete. Part 4 : Specification for the procedures to be used in sampling, testing and assessing compliance of concrete. BS5328:Part 1:1991, Part 3:1991, Part 3:1990, Part 4:1990.*

3 .British Standards Institution. *Specification for ground granulated blastfurnace slag for use with Portland cement.* BS6699:1992

4 British Standards Institution. *Pulverized-fuel ash. Part 1 : Specification for pulverized-fuel ash for use in concrete.* BS3892:Part 1:1993

5 British Standards Institution. *Fly ash for concrete - definitions, requirements and quality control.* BS EN450, To be published in 1994

6 Dewar, J.D. and Anderson, R. *Manual of ready-mixed concrete.* Second edition, 1992. Chapman & Hall

7 Brown, B.V. *Monitoring concrete by the Cusum system.* Concrete Society Digest No.6, Concrete Society, London. 1984, 8.

8 British Standards Institution. *Concrete - performance, production, placing and compliance criteria.* BS DD ENV206:1992

SUBJECT INDEX

This index has been compiled from the keywords assigned to the papers, edited and extended as appropriate. The page references are to the first page of the relevant paper.

RILEM Technical Recommendations for the Testing and Use of Construction Materials

RILEM (The International Union of Testing and Research Laboratories for Materials and Structures), France

This book is a compilation of 170 Technical Recommendations prepared by RILEM Technical Committees since 1975, bringing together in a single volume a wealth of Technical Recommendations previously only available in a specialist journal. They give authoritative procedures for testing and use of many construction materials. The book will be an important source of reference for engineers and scientists involved in development of construction materials and for testing organisations carrying out both routine and specialised tsest programmes on materials and structures.

Contents: Introduction. Concretes and cements - materials and technology. Concrete and cement - experimental and theoretical studies. Special concrete. Other inorganic materials. Hydrocarbons and synthetics. Timber. Structures and masonry. Durability and maintenance. Index.

April 1994 297x210 500 pages, 200 line illustrations, 5 halftone illustrations
Hardback 0-419-18810-X £125.00

E & F N Spon
An imprint of Chapman & Hall

Conservation of Stone and Other Materials

Edited by **M-J Thiel**, Unesco, Paris

RILEM Proceedings 21

This book forms the Proceedings of the International RILEM/UNESCO Congress in Paris, June 1993, organized with the cooperation of ICCROM, EUREKA/EUROCARE, ICOM, ICOMOS and The Getty Conservation Institute. It contains a wealth of new information from international researchers and practitioners on current approaches to conservation of stone and other construction materials in historic building structures.

Contents: **Volume 1: Causes of Disorders and Diagnosis**. Pollution and chemical effects. Physical effects. Biological effects. Petrography. **Volume 2: Prevention and Treatments**. The role of structure. Prevention and treatments. Author index. Subject index.

June 1993: 234x156: 944 pages, 340 line illus, 215 halftone illus
Hardback: 0-419-18410-4: £95.00

E & F N Spon

An imprint of Chapman & Hall

For further information on other RILEM titles and to order please contact:
The Promotion Dept., **E & F N Spon**, 2-6 Boundary Row, London SE1 8HN
Tel 071 865 0066   Fax 071 522 9623